Understanding Stepfamilies: Their Structure and Dynamics

Craig A. Everett, PhD
Editor

The Haworth Press, Inc.
New York • London

Understanding Stepfamilies: Their Structure and Dynamics has also been published as *Journal of Divorce & Remarriage*, Volume 24, Numbers 1/2 1995.

The Haworth Press, Inc., 10 Alice Street, Binghamton, NY 13904-1580 USA

Paperback edition published in 1997.

Cover design by Stephanie Torta.

Library of Congress Cataloging-in-Publication Data

Understanding stepfamilies: their structure and dynamics / Craig A. Everett, editor.
p. cm.
"Has also been published as Journal of divorce & remarriage, volume 24, numbers 1/2, 1995"–T.p. verso.
Includes bibliographical references and index.
ISBN 0-7890-0225-6 (alk. paper)
1. Stepfamilies. 2. Stepfamilies–Psychological aspects. 3. Family psychotherapy. I. Everett, Craig A.
HQ759.92.U543 1996
306.874–dc20 95-52580
CIP

Understanding Stepfamilies: Their Structure and Dynamics

∞ ALL HAWORTH BOOKS AND JOURNALS
ARE PRINTED ON CERTIFIED
ACID-FREE PAPER

INDEXING & ABSTRACTING

Contributions to this publication are selectively indexed or abstracted in print, electronic, online, or CD-ROM version(s) of the reference tools and information services listed below. This list is current as of the copyright date of this publication. See the end of this section for additional notes.

- ***Abstracts of Research in Pastoral Care & Counseling***, Loyola College, 7135 Minstrel Way, Suite 101, Columbia, MD 21045
- ***Applied Social Sciences Index & Abstracts (ASSIA) (Online: ASSI via Data-Star) (CD-Rom: ASSIA Plus),*** Bowker-Saur Limited, Maypole House, Maypole Road, East Grinstead, West Sussex RH19 1HH, England
- ***CNPIEC Reference Guide: Chinese National Directory of Foreign Periodicals,*** P.O. Box 88, Beijing, People's Republic of China
- ***Current Contents . . . . see: Institute for Scientific Information***
- ***Expanded Academic Index***, Information Access Company, 362 Lakeside Drive, Forest City, CA 94404
- ***Family Life Educator "Abstracts Section,"*** ETR Associates, P.O. Box 1830, Santa Cruz, CA 95061-1830
- ***Guide to Social Science & Religion in Periodical Literature***, National Periodical Library, P.O. Box 3278, Clearwater, FL 34630
- ***Index to Periodical Articles Related to Law***, University of Texas, 727 East 26th Street, Austin TX 78705
- ***Institute for Scientific Information, 3501 Market Street, Philadelphia, Pennsylvania 19104. Coverage in:***
  - a) Social Science Citation Index (SSCI): print, online, CD-ROM
  - b) Research Alerts (current awareness service)
  - c) Social SciSearch (magnetic tape)
  - d) Current Contents/Social & Behavioral Sciences (weekly current awareness service)
- ***INTERNET ACCESS (& additional networks) Bulletin Board for Libraries ("BUBL"), coverage of information resources on INTERNET, JANET, and other networks.***
  - JANET X.29: UK.AC.BATH.BUBL or 00006012101300
  - TELNET: BUBL.BATH.AC.UK or 138.38.32.45 login 'bubl'
  - Gopher: BUBL.BATH.AC.UK (138.32.32.45). Port 7070
  - World Wide Web: http: / / www.bubl.bath.ac.uk./BUBL/ home.html
  - NISSWAIS telnetniss.ac. uk (for the NISS gateway)

  The Andersonian Library, Curran Building, 101 St. James Road, Glasgow G4 ONS, Scotland

(continued)

- ***Inventory of Marriage and Family Literature (online and CD/ROM),*** Peters Technology Transfer, 306 East Baltimore Pike, 2nd Floor, Media, PA 19063
- ***Mental Health Abstracts (online through DIALOG)***, IFI/Plenum Data Company, 3202 Kirkwood Highway, Wilmington, DE 19808
- ***PASCAL International Bibliography T205: Sciences de l'information Documentation***, INIST/CNRS-Service Gestion des Documents Primaires, 2, allee du Parc de Brabois, F-54514 Vandoeuvre-les-Nancy, Cedex, France
- ***Periodical Abstracts, Research II*** (broad coverage indexing & abstracting database from University Microfilms International (UMI), 300 North Zeeb Road, P.O. Box 1346, Ann Arbor, MI 48106-1346), UMI Data Courier, P.O. Box 32770, Louisville, KY 40232-2770
- ***Periodical Abstracts Select*** (abstracting & indexing service covering most frequently requested journals in general reference, plus journals requested in libraries serving undergraduate programs, available from University Microfilms International (UMI), 300 North Zeeb Road, P.O. Box 1346, Ann Arbor, MI 48106-1346), UMI Data Courier, Attn: Library Services, Box 34660, Louisville, KY 40232
- ***Psychological Abstracts (PsycINFO)***, American Psychological Association, P.O. Box 91600, Washington, DC 20090-1600
- ***Published International Literature On Traumatic Stress (The PILOTS Database),*** National Center for Post-Traumatic Stress Disorder (116D), VA Medical Center, White River Junction, VT 05009
- ***Sage Family Studies Abstracts (SFSA)***, Sage Publications, Inc., 2455 Teller Road, Newbury Park, CA 91320
- ***Social Planning/Policy & Development Abstracts (SOPODA)***, Sociological Abstracts, Inc., P.O. Box 22206, San Diego, CA 92192-0206
- ***Social Science Citation Index. . . . see: Institute for Scientific Information***
- ***Social Work Abstracts***, National Association of Social Workers, 750 First Street NW, 8th Floor, Washington, DC 20002
- ***Sociological Abstracts (SA)***, Sociological Abstracts, Inc., P.O. Box 22206, San Diego, CA 92192-0206
- ***Studies on Women Abstracts***, Carfax Publishing Company, P.O. Box 25, Abingdon, Oxfordshire OX14 3UE, United Kingdom
- ***Violence and Abuse Abstracts: A Review of Current Literature on Interpersonal Violence (VAA),*** Sage Publications, Inc., 2455 Teller Road, Newbury Park, CA 91320

(continued)

SPECIAL BIBLIOGRAPHIC NOTES

related to special journal issues (separates) and indexing/abstracting

- ❑ indexing/abstracting services in this list will also cover material in any "separate" that is co-published simultaneously with Haworth's special thematic journal issue or DocuSerial. Indexing/abstracting usually covers material at the article/chapter level.
- ❑ monographic co-editions are intended for either non-subscribers or libraries which intend to purchase a second copy for their circulating collections.
- ❑ monographic co-editions are reported to all jobbers/wholesalers/approval plans. The source journal is listed as the "series" to assist the prevention of duplicate purchasing in the same manner utilized for books-in-series.
- ❑ to facilitate user/access services all indexing/abstracting services are encouraged to utilize the co-indexing entry note indicated at the bottom of the first page of each article/chapter/contribution.
- ❑ this is intended to assist a library user of any reference tool (whether print, electronic, online, or CD-ROM) to locate the monographic version if the library has purchased this version but not a subscription to the source journal.
- ❑ individual articles/chapters in any Haworth publication are also available through the Haworth Document Delivery Services (HDDS).

Understanding Stepfamilies: Their Structure and Dynamics

CONTENTS

ABOUT THE EDITOR

Craig A. Everett, PhD, is a marriage and family therapist in private practice in Tucson, Arizona, and Director of the Arizona Institute of Family Therapy. In addition to his 20 years of experience in clinical practice, he was formerly President of the American Association for Marriage and Family Therapy. Dr. Everett's previous positions include Director of Family Therapy Training and Associate Professor at both Florida State University and Auburn University. He has been the Editor of the *Journal of Divorce & Remarriage* (formerly the *Journal of Divorce*) since 1983 and is an editorial board member of six professional journals.

Introduction

This volume examines, in perhaps more optimistic and hopeful ways, the dynamics and resources available within the complex variables of a stepfamily system. It has always been my belief as a clinician that if we can understand the underlying structural patterns and dynamics of a dysfunctional family, we can be much more successful in gaining positive outcomes in treatment. The contributors to this volume offer unique theoretical approaches to understanding stepfamily typologies and behaviors, specific clinical models for assessment and intervention, as well as more empirically-based findings regarding parent-child interactions.

In 1993 I edited *The Stepfamily Puzzle: Intergenerational Influences*, published as a book and also Vol. 19, No. 3/4 of *Journal of Divorce & Remarriage*, and indicated then that it had taken me over 2 years to assemble a suitable collection of manuscripts. This volume acknowledges that more professionals, both clinicians and researchers, are developing contributions in the stepfamily field. I am particularly pleased that 5 of the 11 manuscripts included here represent international contributions from Canada, Israel and The Netherlands.

In the 1993 volume, I also indicated the relative failure of most works in achieving an integration of the many variables present in understanding the stepfamily system. While clear integration is still somewhat elusive, the works here offer a large step in that direction.

Craig A. Everett, PhD
Tucson, AZ

[Haworth co-indexing entry note]: "Introduction." Everett, Craig A. Co-published simultaneously in *Journal of Divorce & Remarriage* (The Haworth Press, Inc.) Vol. 24, No. 1/2, 1995, p. 1; and: *Understanding Stepfamilies: Their Structure and Dynamics* (ed: Craig A. Everett) The Haworth Press, Inc., 1995, p. 1. Single or multiple copies of this article are available from The Haworth Document Delivery Service [1-800-342-9678, 9:00 a.m. - 5:00 p.m. (EST)].

Incomplete Institution or Culture Shock: Institutional and Processual Models of Stepfamily Instability

David Jacobson

SUMMARY. This paper reviews and evaluates two models commonly used to explain divorce rates for remarried couples. One of them, the model of the incomplete institution, is conceptually flawed and empirically unwarranted. The other, a processual model that focuses on the merging of mini-cultures, is more powerful, although it, too, has limitations. A strategy for strengthening the processual model is indicated. *[Article copies available from The Haworth Document Delivery Service: 1-800-342-9678.]*

INTRODUCTION

The instability of remarriages that occur after divorce is problematic for both participants and observers. Various studies indicate that whereas approximately half of first marriages are likely to terminate in divorce, even more remarriages are likely to end that way (cf. Cherlin, 1992). The higher divorce rate for remarriages is remarkable, given that they typically involve partners who are older, more experienced, and presumably more

---

David Jacobson, PhD, is Associate Professor of Anthropology, Department of Anthropology, Brandeis University, Waltham, MA 02254.

The author wishes to express his appreciation to Robert Hunt, Lois Jacobson, and Robert Manners for their assistance in the preparation of this paper.

[Haworth co-indexing entry note]: "Incomplete Institution or Culture Shock: Institutional and Processual Models of Stepfamily Instability." Jacobson, David. Co-published simultaneously in *Journal of Divorce & Remarriage* (The Haworth Press, Inc.) Vol. 24, No. 1/2, 1995, pp. 3-18; and: *Understanding Stepfamilies: Their Structure and Dynamics* (ed: Craig A. Everett) The Haworth Press, Inc., 1995, pp. 3-18. Single or multiple copies of this article are available from The Haworth Document Delivery Service [1-800-342-9678, 9:00 a.m. - 5:00 p.m. (EST)].

mature (Cherlin, 1978:638; Cherlin, 1992:28), characteristics usually associated with marital stability.

Two models (or variants of them) are commonly used to explain this pattern of remarriage divorce. One, an "institutional" model, emphasizes a deficiency in the cultural concepts and normative rules that might regulate remarriage and, more specifically, stepfamily households. The other, a "processual" model, focuses on the difficulties of merging people with different expectations into one household. Although widely cited, the institutional model is seriously flawed. The processual model is more powerful, although it, too, has shortcomings. This paper analyzes both models and indicates ways in which the processual model can be strengthened.

THE INSTITUTIONAL MODEL OF STEPFAMILY INSTABILITY

Although remarriage divorces include couples with and without children, stepfamily households–those which include a couple, one or both of whom have been married before, and a child or children from a previous union–are particularly vulnerable to dissolution (Becker et al., 1977; Cherlin, 1978; Clingempeel and Brand, 1985; White and Booth, 1985; Benson van der Ohe, 1987). The institutional model seeks to explain this instability. It focuses on an alleged absence of or ambiguity in social norms regarding stepfamily functioning.

Bohannan (1970) was one of the first to advance this type of explanation. He argued that remarriages and the stepfamilies they create are culturally unstructured. That is, according to Bohannan, the rules for relationships created by remarriage are "poorly charted" in American culture which "provides no norms to tell us . . . what ought to be done about them or toward them" (1970:118, 119). He noted, for example, that there is potentially a problem of sexual relations between stepsiblings who are not related and who are not covered by incest prohibitions. This concern with a lack of codified and uncodified rules pertaining to stepfamily relationships is also central to more recent reiterations of the sort of argument Bohannan proposed.

Cherlin (1978, 1981, 1992) has elaborated upon the theme of cultural deficiencies in his model of remarriage as an "incomplete institution." For Cherlin (1978:634, 636), an "institution" is an organization of "social roles" and the normative "guidelines" or "social norms" that specify the behavior expected of role occupants and which "contribute to the unity and stability of families." His argument, in short, is that remarriage is particularly fragile because of a lack of social norms that regulate behavior in such relationships. That is, the elements of "law," "custom," and "social norms," and the "social roles" implied by them, that constitute an institution and that regulate behavior are absent or inadequate in the case of stepfamilies based on remarriage after divorce (1978:634, 646; cf. Cherlin, 1981:89, 1992:84ff). Cherlin uses examples from language and law to support his argument.

With respect to language, Cherlin argues that when there are no terms for a role then there will be little acceptance of it. In remarriages after divorce, he suggests, this lack occurs in terms of address and in terms of reference. Thus, he notes that "there is no term a child living with his mother can use to describe his relation to the woman his father remarried after he divorced the child's mother" (1978:644), and that "[i]n some situations, no term exists for a child to use in addressing a stepparent" (1978:643). Cherlin concludes that these "linguistic inadequacies correspond to the absence of widely accepted definitions for many of the roles and relationships in families of remarriage," adding that, "[t]he absence of proper terms is both a symptom and a cause of some of the problems of remarried life" (1978:644).

In the legal domain, Cherlin argues that the absence of laws pertaining to certain aspects of stepfamily relationships both reflects and generates their anomalous status and threatens the unity of the family (cf. Beer, 1992:158). First, he refers to an absence of legal provisions for "balancing the financial obligations of husbands to their spouses and children from current and previous marriages" (1978:644). Then, he notes that "[l]egal regulations concerning incest and consanguineal marriage are also inadequate for families of remarriages" (1978:644). He refers, as an example, to the absence of restrictions pertaining to sexual relationships among the members of a stepfamily, e.g., between stepparents and stepchildren and between stepsiblings. This deficiency, Cherlin concluded, led to a lack of "adequate security and protection for children in households of remarriage" (1978:644).

Assessing the Institutional Model

Although the institutional model has been widely cited, as Furstenberg and Spanier note (1984:180; cf. Ahrons and Rodgers, 1987; Dahl et al., 1987; Pasley, 1987; Papernow, 1988; Keshet, 1990; Beer, 1992), it is limited in several ways. First, it assumes that American social norms about family and household relationships are uniform, an empirically unjustified supposition. Second, it is unnecessarily complicated analytically, presupposing one explanation of instability for first marriages and a different one for remarriages, when it is possible, and simpler, to utilize a single model (e.g., the processual model) for both cases. Third, even with regard to the hypothesis of cultural inadequacy, the institutional model is factually unwarranted.

For example, Cherlin's argument about language deficiencies falls short for three reasons. First, obviously, there are terms a child can use to describe his or her relationship with the person a parent marries after divorce (and also after the death of a spouse). The term of reference for both father's wife and mother's husband, is "stepparent," and those for one or the other are, respectively, "stepmother" or "stepfather." Second, there are several ways for a child to address stepparents, normative alternatives that are similar to those for addressing other relatives by marriage. For example, in the case of parents-in-law, a person can address the parents of his or her spouse by parental terms (e.g., Mother, Father, Mom, Dad, etc.), by first names (e.g., Mary, John), by surnames (e.g., Mrs. Smith, Mr. Smith, Mrs. S, Mr. S, etc.), or by what Schneider refers to as a "zero form of address" or "no-naming" (1968:84; cf. Duvall, 1954:7). The term a person selects will vary with the social or emotional closeness or distance (experienced or desired) between speaker and parent-in-law. In the case of children and stepparents, parental terms, first names, and no-naming seem to be the primary alternatives for addressing stepparents (cf. Dahl et al., 1987:43; Keshet, 1988:36; Cherlin, 1992:84).

The third reason that Cherlin's argument is suspect is related to the fact that there are alternative terms of address for relatives by marriage and that people vary in the ways in which they apply these terms. That is, not only do terms "justify the enactment" of roles, as Cherlin notes (1978:643), but behavior also justifies the use of role terms. The attribution of fictive kinship exemplifies this principle, as when kinship terms are applied to non-kin who act as kin and are expected to act and/or to mark social or emotional closeness (cf. Liebow, 1967; Schneider, 1968; Stack, 1974; Scheffler, 1976).

In short, rather than an absence of terms, there is in American culture a number of terms available for stepfamily members, although, as with kinship terms and norms in general, they are characterized by great variation in form and by the freedom permitted in their use (cf. Schneider, 1968; Spanier and Furstenberg, 1987:429; Furstenberg, 1990:397).

Cherlin's argument about the absence of legal constraints in structuring stepfamily relationships is also unwarranted by the evidence. In the case of a man's "balancing financial obligations" to former and current spouses, to children from first and subsequent marriages, and to children and stepchildren, there are laws relevant to such situations. A man's responsibilities to his ex-spouse and to his current spouse are covered by law, in the former by divorce agreements and/or court orders and in the latter by legal precedents defining the rights and duties of marital partners. Moreover, his responsibilities to his children are also covered by law, regardless of the different marriages that produced them. In the case of a man's obligations to his children and to his stepchildren, most states have specific laws on the matter: stepparents have no financial obligations to their stepchildren and stepchildren have no claims on their stepparents' assets (cf. Ramsey, 1986; Fine and Fine, 1992).

Furthermore, there are several laws that apply to the sexual behavior of the members of stepfamilies. For example, in Massachusetts, sexual relations between stepparents and stepchildren are barred by laws against incest and adultery, and sexual relations between unmarried stepsiblings are barred by laws against fornication (see *Massachusetts General Laws Annotated,* 1987, v. 33, Ch. 207, Sect. 1 and 2; 1990, v. 44A, Ch. 272, Sect. 14, 17, and 18).

Thus, the data do not support Cherlin's hypothesis that stepfamilies are unstable because of an absence of regulations, evident in kinship language and family law. There is, however, an alternative model that better explains the instability of stepfamily households.

THE PROCESSUAL MODEL OF STEPFAMILY INSTABILITY: CULTURE SHOCK OR THE DIFFICULTIES OF MERGING DOMESTIC CULTURES

An alternative to the model of institutional deficiency is one that focuses on the processes of integrating people with different "mini-cultures," since remarriages typically create households within which members have different conceptions, expectations, and standards of behavior. Such differences may generate a form of "culture shock" (see Visher and Visher, 1979:24-32; 1982:107-108). The processual model describes the obstacles to merging into a unified domestic unit people with different cultures as well as ways of overcoming them.

It should be emphasized that the locus of the alternative model is the *household,* rather than either the marital relationship or the family (or families) associated with it. Because in the ideal-typical case of American culture, marriage is expected to entail the formation of a new household (cf. Schneider, 1968; Bohannan, 1971), they are often intertwined (and confused). Although the terms marriage (or marital couple), family (or stepfamily), and household may be used interchangeably in this discussion, the analytical focus of the alternative model is on the ways in which people who live together develop a common understanding that facilitates their interaction.

Although this processual model addresses the problematics of remarriages and stepfamily households, it also applies to first marriage households. That it explains similar processes in different types of households is, of course, a primary source of its power (and appeal) as an analytical paradigm. Thus, before discussing the relevance of the processual model for understanding stepfamily households, it is instructive to examine its application to first marriages and the households based upon them.

Berger and his associates (1964, 1966) have played a central role in analyzing the relationship between the problematics of merging domestic mini-cultures and the question of marital stability. Berger and Kellner contrast marriage as an "institution" (1964:1) with the "social processes affecting the individuals in any specific marriage, although," as they note, "of course, the larger framework of these processes will have to be understood" (1964:2). Similarly, Berger and Luckmann distinguish between an "institution" and the "processes" by which it is established (1966:53-4). That is, they acknowledge that institutions "control human conduct by setting up predefined patterns of conduct" (1966:55), yet, in their view, the "processes of habitualization," based on frequently repeated behavior (1966:53), "precede any institutionalization" (1966:54). Berger and Kellner give analytical priority to the processes by which behavior becomes institutionalized rather than to the normative rules that constitute an institution.

Ironically, Cherlin, in his formulation of his incomplete institution hypothesis, alludes to Berger and Luckmann's discussion of "habitualized action" and "social norms" (1978:636), although he does not develop the significance of the difference between these analytical concepts. Cherlin does not distinguish, as do Berger and Luckmann (and Berger and Kellner), between the expectations and standards of evaluation that are developed within and are specific to particular marriages and families (i.e., habitualized action) and those that are general to society (i.e., social norms). Thus, he doesn't address the processes by which every couple (married or not, first or subsequent marriage, with or without children) develops its own shared understanding (or, in other terms, its own world, worldview, or culture), within the wider context of institutionalized guidelines.

In the processual model, marriage is seen as a relationship in which individuals construct a shared understanding of the world in terms of which they make sense of themselves, their actions, and those of others. According to Berger and Kellner, this shared understanding constitutes a marital (and familial) "sub-world" (1964:9, 20), a worldview based on common "fundamental definitions of reality" (1964:4, 11, 13). Berger and Kellner refer to this process as "nomos-building" (1964:1).

Constructing a marital world is a problematic process. As Berger and Kellner suggest (1964:5), marriage brings together "two strangers," in the sense that partners bring to their union different understandings of the world, based on their different experiences, familial and otherwise. This is not to say that there are no general understandings, concepts, or norms that the couple share. However, these general notions have to be interpreted and given specific meanings by the couple. "This," Berger and Kellner note, "will require a dramatic change in their definitions of reality and of themselves" (1964:10). The dramatic changes that the marriage entails constitute a "nomic rupture" that is repaired through the process of a nomic "transformation," by which "two individual definitions of reality" are matched and merged into a "common overall definition" (Berger and Kellner, 1964:11, 13). The transition from the "standard instructions" of the "larger society" to the shared understandings of the "little world" of the marriage requires "considerable effort" on the part of the marriage partners (Berger and Kellner, 1964:9). In this sense, all marriages, first or subsequent, are likely to be "precarious," at least in their beginnings (Berger and Kellner, 1964:10).

In addition to the efforts undertaken by the couple themselves, the model posits that the children they bring into it also play a significant role in stabilizing their marital world. Although the marital world of a couple is constructed in their interactions and conversations with one another, it is strengthened in and by the process of their socializing children. As Berger and Kellner note, the "marital conversation" through which common definitions of reality are developed "is now in the process of becoming a family symposium" (1964:17), a process that gives greater weight and stability to the worldview being constructed by the couple. In conveying their shared understandings to their children, the couple reinforces their own sense of and investment in the cultural constructs and normative guidelines that constitute their marital world and domestic culture.

Although Berger and his collaborators have played a significant role in constructing this alternative model, other researchers have also contributed to it, albeit using different theoretical frameworks and different analytical terms. For example, Parkes' analysis (1971; cf. Cowan, 1991) of "psycho-social transitions" is in many ways akin to the study of nomic "transformations." He argues that an individual's behavior is shaped by the concepts and beliefs that constitute his or her "assumptive world," which "includes everything we know or think we know . . . our interpretation of the past and our expectations for the future, our plans and our prejudices" (1971:103). In this respect, Parkes' assumptive world resembles the socially constructed marital world and worldview of Berger and his colleagues. In Parkes' model, changing a worldview is a stressful experience, which entails a process by which old ideas are given up and new ones are taken on. This involves a "painful reviewing of redundant assumptions and restructuring of the assumptive world" (1971:105). This process is painful because people are emotionally invested in their assumptive worlds and because these conceptual structures provide a measure of significance, without which life seems meaningless.

Although Parkes notes that each person's assumptive world is particular to himself or herself (1971:105), it is apparent that for him, as for Berger and Kellner, marriage entails a matching and merging of a couple's assumptive worlds. This is evident in his comments on the sources of marital instability. Parkes notes that of the conditions that "seem particularly likely to predispose to marital breakdown, one is a major discrepancy between the assumptive worlds of husband and wife," adding that in "such circumstances it is seen as less painful to abandon the marriage than for both partners to change their assumptive worlds. . . . " (1971:107).

Goldner (1982) presents another variation on the theme of the processes and problems involved in building a shared assumptive world or, in her terms, a "family culture." She, too, suggests that families can be seen as separate sub-worlds, in the sense that first marriage families operate like "tiny insulated cultures" (1982:192). Moreover, the development of a family culture involves processes similar to those characterized by Berger and Kellner as habitualization and institutionalization. Thus, Goldner writes, a first marriage family develops its own "social norms" (1982:192), guidelines that regulate domestic daily life and family interactions, on the basis of repetitive interactions that are, essentially, "transactional ruts" (1982:193). It is in terms of such a family culture that its members perceive and experience the world and understand themselves and others. As Goldner puts it, the rules of a family culture "shape the most elemental human experiences of mind, self, body, and relations to others, and provide the stability and continuity necessary for the integrity of the family system" (1982:192; cf. Mattessich and Hill, 1987:441).

Although the idea of constructing a marital world and the problems it entails was initially developed with reference to first marriages (cf. Berger and Kellner, 1964:18-19), the model also applies to remarriages and the stepfamilies they create. Furstenberg (1979), for example, drew on the work of Berger and Kellner in raising questions about the ways in which a remarried couple builds a common worldview. He argues that a couple in a remarriage, like one entering a first marriage, must develop a shared worldview, but the process is likely to be more complicated "for they must simultaneously develop this 'construction of reality' at the same time that they rework the one on which their previous marriage was based" (1979:16). Moreover, Furstenberg observes, the "experience of the second marriage can be similar to the experience of a psychological conversion accompanying an abrupt change in religious or political beliefs . . . [in that it] may involve a radical revision of self-conception, substantial revision of conjugal roles, and a sharp departure from the private worldview that emerged during the course of the first marriage" (1979:16). This formulation of the nomic rupture and transformation experienced in a remarriage recalls Parkes' account of the characteristics of a psychosocial transition.

Subsequently, Furstenberg and his associates have elaborated upon his earlier observation. For example, Furstenberg and Spanier have noted that "All marriages, as Berger and Kellner (1964) remind us, involve a building of a common *nomos,* or worldview, which sustains the couple's dealings with one another. In the process of remarriage, individuals must both revise and disassemble the micro-culture of their first marriage and create a new belief system" (1984:54; see also Spanier and Furstenberg, 1987:425 and Furstenberg and Cherlin, 1991:83-84). In this process of cognitive and emotional reorganization, Furstenberg and Spanier note that remarried individuals often cast ex-spouses in a "negative light" (1984:64). While this sort of comparison and evaluation may serve, as Furstenberg and Spanier suggest, to strengthen "solidarity in the new relationship" (1984:65), it also enables the speaker to maintain his or her view of self and of marriage. A similar pattern of comparing new marriages favorably to old ones was also observed by Burgoyne and Clark in their study of stepfamilies (1984:92). As Parkes notes, ex-spouses are more likely "to denigrate the other and to blame him [or her] for the breakdown of the marriage. This is necessary to enable the divorcee to maintain his [or her] own sense of mastery of his [or her] assumptive world. If the fault lies elsewhere a less radical change is necessary" (1971:107).

Although the process of building a common worldview in a remarriage is described as dependent upon disassembling those constructed in first marriages, it is typically the case that the worldview that has to be relinquished is one developed *between* marriages. That is, the worldview to be changed may be that of the single-person or single-parent household. For children entering a stepfamily situation, it is typically the latter.

Others have reached similar conclusions. Goldner, for example, sees the merging of family cultures in the case of remarriage as problematic and typically characterized by stress and resistance (cf. Espinoza and

Newman, 1979; Visher and Visher, 1979, 1990; Keshet, 1987, 1988, 1990; Papernow, 1988; McGoldrick and Carter, 1989). It is, in Goldner's terms, "an inherently disorganizing experience that involves the total transformation of the individuals' intimate world" (1982:193). All definitions of the situation are subject to review and revision, including "the seemingly trivial details of daily life" (Goldner, 1982:194; cf. Keshet, 1987:72-76). This view has been summarized by the Vishers in their observation that "All stepfamilies share the basic task of accomplishing a satisfactory transition from previous family cultures to a stepfamily culture" (1990:4).

The processual model especially illuminates the instability of remarriages that contain children from prior marriages. For example, it explains why children often balk at the efforts of their parent and stepparent to construct a marital world. As the new couple engages in the work of developing their world, they tend to exclude others from it, part of the process of defining its boundaries and establishing a sense of togetherness. In the case of first marriage, this typically involves the exclusion and reassessment of friends, as Berger and Kellner noted (1964:11-12). But in the case of remarriage and stepfamily formation, it also involves children, who typically experience it as rejection, and who, correspondingly, resist such exclusionary tendencies.

Moreover, children in stepfamilies play a different role than do children in first marriages in the process of constructing a marital world and a family culture. Unlike the case of first marriages, where socializing children is supposed to "thicken" and "harden" the worldview of their parents (Berger and Kellner, 1964:14; cf. Berger and Luckmann, 1966:59), children from previous marriages often are obstacles to this process, since they are anchors to a former, and different, social reality. Furthermore, by virtue of their efforts to revise and reassemble it, adults are aware that the marital world they construct is manufactured and changeable. Children, however, do not see it as a merely constructed world and therefore resist its modification. That is, the worldview or culture which children first learn is not seen as simply the "*ad hoc* conceptions" of their parents, but constitutes their assumptive world and is experienced as objective reality, fixed and unalterable (Berger and Luckmann, 1966:58-9). It is their world and the only one they know. This suggests why the process of building a common world in a remarriage with children is so precarious.

Given that the socialization of children into one family culture becomes an impediment to their acceptance of another, it follows that the age of children is likely to influence the stability of remarriages. That is, it would seem that the younger the children are (and the less hardened their beliefs) when exposed to divorce and remarriage, the more likely they will be able and willing to adopt those changes. Evidence from research on children of divorce supports this hypothesis. For example, it appears that children under the age of nine more readily accept a stepparent than do those who are older (Hetherington, Cox, and Cox, 1981; cf. Wallerstein and Kelly, 1980:288-289; Wallerstein and Blakeslee, 1989:207-08).

Other evidence comes from research on household reorganization after divorce and remarriage. For example, Burgoyne and Clark report (1984:161) that ". . . the younger the children are when parents divorce and remarry, the easier it is for their new family group to rebuild an ordinary, unremarkable domestic life together." Based on their interviews, Burgoyne and Clark suggest that the process of stepfamily integration was easiest when children were less than five years old (1984:152).

Moreover, they found that the age of children at the beginning of co-residence influenced the development of unity between stepparents and stepchildren. For example, stepparents said that they felt closer to the youngest of their stepchildren, having spent more time and a greater part of the latter's formative years with them. Burgoyne and Clark report that one stepparent stated, when asked whether there was much difference in his relationships with his stepchildren: "There is, yes, I think it's mainly due to the fact that I've been with some of them for a greater proportion of their lives . . . I'm closest, definitely closest, to the youngest girl. . . . It tails off, definitely does tail off towards the eldest" (1984:151).

This pattern also pertains to the relationships between stepgrandparents and stepgrandchildren. Cherlin and Furstenberg (1986) found that the age of a child when he or she first became a part of a stepfamily household and whether or not he or she lived there full-time influenced the relationship between the child and his or her stepparent's parents. That is, the younger children are when they become part of a stepfamily household, the more likely their stepparent's parents were to interact with them as if they were biological grandchildren.

The work of developmental psychologists further illuminates the experiences of children in stepfamily households and thereby reinforces the processual model. For example, Watson and his colleagues (Watson and Amgott-Kwan, 1984; Watson and Fischer, in press) claim that children younger than seven are unable to understand "role intersection," that is, the idea that a person can occupy two or more roles simultaneously (e.g., that a woman can be both a mother to her child and a wife to her husband). And Piaget (1928) found that children at about that age believe that "family" includes all those who live with them, regardless of (culturally defined) marital or kinship relationships, and, conversely, that the lack of co-residence precludes being counted as family (cf. Pederson and Gilby, 1986).

These findings suggest why younger children would have an easier time, and older children a more difficult time, in adjusting to stepfamily life. If a child does not understand that roles can be uncoupled, it is unlikely that he or she will comprehend that the termination of a spousal relationship does not also mean the abdication of a parental role. Moreover, if a parent moves out of the child's home, the status of that person as a family member would be problematic for a child. Conversely, it would be reasonable for a child younger than seven or eight to accept a co-resident stepparent as a parent (or at least, as a kind of parent) and as a family member when he or she is married to the custodial parent and lives with the child. Although there are few studies that systematically examine this issue, Bernstein (1988) suggests that children under the age of about seven in fact define co-resident stepparents as parents and consider them as family.

Strengthening the Processual Model

The processual model accounts for the stresses of stepfamily formation, but it does not explain why that stress should result in divorce. This limitation is overcome by supplementing the processual model with one that focuses on the ways in which beliefs about marriage have changed. For example, in studies that address divorce rates in first marriages, some researchers emphasize non-normative circumstances that constrain and/or facilitate divorce, including the increasing participation of women in employment outside the home, with its implications of changes in domestic roles and activities and in gender relationships (Furstenberg and Spanier, 1984; Furstenberg, 1990; Furstenberg and Cherlin, 1991; Skolnick, 1991; Cherlin, 1992). Cherlin (1992:31ff) characterizes this as a "cohort" type of explanation, in contrast to "period" explanations, which focus on the attitudes and values which underlie the choices people make from among alternative courses of action.

Although circumstances and conditions define possible courses of action, they do not necessarily lead to one or another choice. Rather, people choose between alternatives in terms of their concepts, norms, and values. Thus, several researchers focus on the role of beliefs about individualism and emotional gratification as factors undermining marital stability (Furstenberg and Spanier, 1984; Dizard and Gadlin, 1990; Furstenberg and Cherlin, 1991; Skolnick, 1991). For example, in describing the emergence of these values as the primary principles of evaluating marriage, Furstenberg argues that the "standard shifted from one which required couples to remain married even if they were not in love to one which virtually demanded divorce unless they remained in love" (1990:380; cf. Cherlin, 1992:130).

In short, the processual model may be strengthened by linking it to more general arguments about the role of beliefs about individualism and personal gratification in undermining marital stability. Both lines of reasoning are necessary: the problems posed in the process of building a stepfamily household explain why a marriage, or a family, may be judged to be unsatisfactory, and the pursuit of personal gratification explains why individuals may choose to end unsatisfactory marriages.

CONCLUSIONS

Analyzing the instability of remarriages and stepfamily households in terms of the processes underlying the integration of different "mini-cultures" constitutes an important alternative to a model that characterizes remarriage as an incomplete institution. It makes sense of the problems experienced by the members of stepfamily households, and it explains the differential rates of divorce between remarried couples with resident children from previous unions and those without such offspring. Moreover, it facilitates comparative study of the similarities and differences between first marriages and those that may follow. It also does not depend upon the supposition that there is only one ideal-type of marriage, family, and/or household in American culture (i.e., neolocal marriage and nuclear family households). Thus, even where (or when) stepfamilies are (or come to be) viewed as a normal variant of American domestic life, the alternative model will still be necessary to explain the processes and problems of merging individuals who were raised in different families and households and who have different worldviews. Even Cherlin supports this conclusion. In reflecting on his model of cultural deficiency, Cherlin notes (1992: 89-90) that he had speculated that, as stepfamilies became more common, new "standards of conduct" would be generated that would redress the incomplete institution. He adds, however, that this did not happen because general awareness of the problems of stepfamily formation or the development of social norms regarding stepfamily relationships "could not substitute for the lengthy period of adjustment to the break-up of a family [or of a single-parent household] or to the presence of a new stepparent." This, of course, is precisely what the processual model predicts.

REFERENCES

Ahrons, C. R. and Rogers, R. H. (1987). *Divorced Families: A Multidisciplinary Developmental View.* New York: W.W. Norton and Co.

Becker, G. S., Landes, E. M., and Michael, R. T. (1977). An economic analysis of marital instability. *Journal of Political Economy, 85,* 6, 1141-1187.

Beer, W. R. (1992). *American Stepfamilies.* New Brunswick, NJ: Transaction Books.

Benson-von der Ohe, E. (1987). *First and Second Marriages.* New York: Praeger.

Berger, P. L. and Kellner, H. (1964). Marriage and the construction of reality. *Diogenes, 46,* 1-24.

Berger P. L. and Luckmann, T. (1966). *The Social Construction of Reality: A Treatise in the Sociology of Knowledge.* New York: Doubleday and Company.

Bernstein, A. C. (1988). Unraveling the tangles: Children's understanding of stepfamily kinship. In W. R. Beer (Ed.), *Relative Strangers: Studies of Stepfamily Processes* (pp. 83-111). Totowa, NJ: Rowman and Littlefield.

Bohannan, P. (1970). Divorce chains, households of remarriage, and multiple divorcers. In P. Bohannan (Ed.), *Divorce and After* (pp. 113-123). New York: Doubleday and Co.

Bohannan, P. (1971). Dyad dominance and household maintenance. In F. L. K. Hsu (Ed.), *Kinship and Culture* (pp. 42-65.) Chicago: Aldine Publishing Company.

Burgoyne, J. and Clark, D. (1984). *Making a Go of It: A Study of Stepfamilies in Sheffield.* London: Routledge and Kegan Paul.

Cherlin, A. J. (1978). Remarriage as an Incomplete Institution. *American Journal of Sociology, 84,* 3, 634-650.

Cherlin, A. J. (1981). *Marriage, Divorce, and Remarriage.* Cambridge: Harvard University Press.

Cherlin, A. J. (1992). *Marriage, Divorce, and Remarriage (Revised and Enlarged Edition).* Cambridge: Harvard University Press.

Cherlin, A. J. and Furstenberg, F. F., Jr. (1986). *The New American Grandparent.* New York: Basic Books.

Clingempeel, W. G. and Brand, E. (1985). Quasi-kin relationships, structural complexity, and marital quality in stepfamilies: A replication, extension, and clinical implications. *Family Relations, 34,* 401-409.

Cowan, P. A. (1991). Individual and family life transitions: A proposal for a new definition. In P. A. Cowan and M. Hetherington (Eds.), *Family Transitions* (pp. 3-30). Hillsdale, NJ: L. Erlbaum Associates.

Dahl, A. S., Cowgill, K. M., and Asmundsson, R. (1987). Life in remarriage families. *Social Work, 32,* 1, 40-44.

Dizard, J. E. and Gadlin, H. (1990). *The Minimal Family.* Amherst: University of Massachusetts Press.

Duvall, E. M. (1954). *In-laws: Pro and Con: An Original Study of Inter-Personal Relations.* New York: Association Press.

Espinoza, R. and Newman, Y. (1979). *Stepparenting.* Rockville, MD: DHEW Publication No. (ADM) 78-579.

Fine, M. A. and Fine, D. R. (1992). Recent changes in laws affecting stepfamilies: Suggestions for legal reform. *Family Relations, 41*, 334-340.

Furstenberg, F. F., Jr. (1979). Recycling the family: Perspectives for a neglected family form. *Marriage and Family Review, 2*, 3, 12-21.

Furstenberg, F. F., Jr. (1990). Divorce and the American family. *Annual Review of Sociology, 16*, 379-403.

Furstenberg, F. F., Jr. and Cherlin, A. J. (1991). *Divided Families: What Happens to Children When Parents Part.* Cambridge: Harvard University Press.

Furstenberg, F. F., Jr. and Spanier, G. B. (1984). *Recycling the Family: Remarriage After Divorce.* Beverly Hills: Sage.

Goldner, V. (1982). Remarriage family: Structure, system, future. In J. C. Hansen and L. Messinger (Eds.), *Therapy with Remarriage Families* (pp. 189-206). Rockville, MD: Aspen Systems Corp.

Hetherington, E.M., Cox, M. and Cox, R. (1981). The aftermath of divorce. In E. M. Etherington and R. D. Parke (Eds.), *Contemporary Readings in Child Psychology (2nd edition)* (pp. 99-109). New York: McGraw-Hill.

Keshet, J. K. (1987). *Love and Power in the Stepfamily.* New York: McGraw-Hill.

Keshet, J. K. (1988). The remarried couple: Stresses and successes. In W. R. Beer (Ed.), *Relative Strangers: Studies of Stepfamily Processes* (pp. 29-53). Totowa, NJ: Rowman and Littlefield.

Keshet, J. K. (1990). Cognitive remodeling of the family: How remarried people view stepfamilies. *American Journal of Orthopsychiatry, 60*, 2, 196-203.

Liebow, E. (1967). *Tally's Corner.* Boston: Little Brown.

Massachusetts General Laws Annotated (1987). St. Paul, MN: West Publishing Co.

Massachusetts General Laws Annotated (1990). St. Paul, MN: West Publishing Co.

Mattessich, P. and Hill, R. (1987). Life cycle and family development. In M. B. Sussman and S. Steinmetz (Eds.), *Handbook of Marriage and the Family* (pp. 437-469). New York: Plenum.

McGoldrick, M. and Carter, B. (1989). Forming a remarried family. In B. Carter and M. McGoldrick (Eds.), *The Changing Family Life Cycle (2nd edition)* (pp. 399-429). Boston: Allyn and Bacon.

Papernow, P. L. (1988). Stepparent role development: From outsider to intimate. In W. R. Beer (Ed.), *Relative Strangers: Studies of Stepfamily Processes* (pp. 54-82). Totowa, NJ: Rowman and Littlefield.

Parkes, C. M. (1971). Psycho-social transitions: A field for study. *Social Science and Medicine, 5*, 101-115.

Pasley, K. (1987). Family boundary ambiguity: Perceptions of adult stepfamily members. In K. Pasley and M. Ihinger-Tallman (Eds.), *Remarriage and Stepparenting: Current Research and Theory* (pp. 206-224). New York: Guilford Press.

Pederson, D. R. and Gilby, R. L. (1986). Children's concepts of the family. In R. D. Ashmore and D. Brodzinsky (Eds.), *Thinking About the Family* (pp. 181-204.) Hillsdale, NJ: L. Erlbaum Associates.

Piaget, J. (1928). *Judgement and Reasoning in the Child.* New York: Harcourt, Brace and Co.

Ramsey, S. H. (1986). Stepparent support of stepchildren: The changing legal context and the need for empirical policy research. *Family Relations, 35,* 363-369.

Scheffler, H. C. (1976). The 'meaning' of kinship in American culture: Another view. In K. H. Basso and H. A. Selby (Eds.), *Meaning in Anthropology* (pp. 57-91). Albuquerque: University of New Mexico Press.

Schneider, D. M. (1968). *American Kinship: A Cultural Account.* Englewood Cliffs, NJ: Prentice-Hall.

Skolnick, A. (1991). *Embattled Paradise: The American Family in an Age of Uncertainty.* New York: Basic Books.

Spanier, G. B. and Furstenberg, F. F., Jr. (1987). Remarriage and reconstituted families. In M. B. Sussman and S. K. Steinmetz (Eds.), *Handbook of Marriage and the Family* (pp. 419-434). New York: Plenum.

Stack, C. (1974). *All Our Kin: Strategies for Survival in a Black Community.* New York: Harper and Row.

Visher, E. B. and Visher, M. J. (1979). *Stepfamilies: A Guide to Working with Stepparents and Stepchildren.* New York: Brunner/Mazel.

Visher, E. B. and Visher, M. J. (1982). Stepfamilies in the 1980s. In J. C. Hansen and L. Messinger (Eds.), *Therapy with Remarriage Families* (pp. 107-119). Rockville, MD: Aspen System Corporation.

Visher, E. B. and Visher, M. J. (1990). Dynamics of successful stepfamilies. *Journal of Divorce & Remarriage, 14,* 1, 3-12.

Wallerstein, J. S. and Kelly, J. B. (1980). *Surviving the Break-up: How Children and Parents Cope with Divorce.* New York: Basic Books.

Wallerstein, J. S. and Blakeslee, S. (1989). *Second Chances: Men, Women, and Children a Decade After Divorce.* New York: Ticknor and Fields.

Watson, M. W. and Amgott-Kwan, T. (1984). Development of family-role concepts in school-age children. *Developmental Psychology, 20,* 5, 953-959.

Watson, M. W. and Fischer, K. W. (in press). Structural changes in children's understanding of family roles and divorce. In R. R. Cocking and A. Renninger (Eds.), *The Development and Meaning of Psychological Distance* (pp. 123-140). Hillsdale, NJ: L. Erlbaum Associates.

White, L. K. and Booth, A. (1985). The quality and stability of remarriages: The role of stepchildren. *American Sociological Review, 50,* 689-698.

The Clarity and Content of the Stepparent Role: A Review of the Literature

Mark A. Fine

SUMMARY. The manner in which the role of the stepparent is defined and implemented has been identified as an important determinant of how well family members adjust to living in stepfamilies. This article reviews the literature on the role of the stepparent, focusing primarily on two independent aspects of this role: its clarity and its content. After information is presented on these two aspects of the stepparent role, the limited research on how the clarity and content of the stepparent role relate to the adjustment of stepfamily members is reviewed. Finally, some implications for professionals who work with stepfamilies are provided. *[Article copies available from The Haworth Document Delivery Service: 1-800-342-9678.]*

One of the crucial issues facing stepfamilies is how the role of the stepparent is defined and implemented. The clinical and conceptual literature on stepfamilies has suggested that the adjustment of individuals, the couple, and the entire stepfamily system is dependent on how issues pertaining to the role of the stepparent are negotiated and resolved (Crosbie-Burnett, 1989; Visher & Visher, 1988). The purpose of this article is to review the literature pertaining to the stepparent role. To accomplish this end, I first provide background information on the importance and nature

---

Mark A. Fine, PhD, is Professor, Department of Human Development and Family Services, University of Missouri, 31 Stanley, Columbia, MO 65211.

[Haworth co-indexing entry note]: "The Clarity and Content of the Stepparent Role: A Review of the Literature." Fine, Mark A. Co-published simultaneously in *Journal of Divorce & Remarriage* (The Haworth Press, Inc.) Vol. 24, No. 1/2, 1995, pp. 19-34; and: *Understanding Stepfamilies: Their Structure and Dynamics* (ed: Craig A. Everett) The Haworth Press, Inc., 1995, pp. 19-34. Single or multiple copies of this article are available from The Haworth Document Delivery Service [1-800-342-9678, 9:00 a.m. - 5:00 p.m. (EST)].

of parenting roles. Second, literature pertaining to the clarity of the stepparent role is presented, followed by information on the content of the stepparent role. Third, the available literature on the adjustment correlates of the clarity and content of the stepparent role is reviewed. Finally, some implications for professionals who work with stepfamilies are provided.

THE IMPORTANCE AND NATURE OF PARENTING ROLES

According to Rodgers and White (1993), a social role is defined as "all the norms attached to a given social position" (p. 234). Social norms are beliefs that prescribe (i.e., allow or encourage) certain behaviors that are considered to be desirable (e.g., helping others) and proscribe (i.e., do not allow or discourage) others that are not considered to be desirable (e.g., harming others) (Burr, Day, & Bahr, 1993). Because a parenting role is one type of social role, a parenting role can be defined as a set of beliefs pertaining to how parents should behave toward their children.

Based on a typology of cognitions proposed by Baucom, Epstein, Sayers, and Sher (1989), two aspects of the parenting role can be identified: assumptions and standards. Assumptions are cognitions concerning how frequently typical parents engage in parenting behaviors, and standards are cognitions regarding how frequently parents should engage in parenting behaviors. Standards more closely represent what most individuals mean by roles than do assumptions. However, one's assumptions about how parents typically behave may influence one's standards about how parents should behave. Thus, in several of the studies reviewed following, both standards and assumptions were examined.

Two domains of parenting–control and warmth–have been identified as critical determinants of children's development (Amato, 1990; Lamborn, Mounts, Steinberg, & Dornbusch, 1991; Maccoby & Martin, 1983; Steinberg, Dornbusch, & Brown, 1992). Control refers to the degree to which parents set and enforce limits and monitor their children's activities. Warmth refers to the extent to which parents support, spend time with, and communicate with their children. Empirical evidence (Steinberg, Elmen, & Mounts 1989) has consistently shown that the more parents exhibit both control and warmth, the more positive is children's and adolescents' adjustment (although parental control may have curvilinear effects on children's and adolescents' adjustment [Kurdek, Fine, & Sinclair, in press; Kurdek & Fine, 1994]). Given the importance of both control and warmth parenting behaviors in children's development, several of the investigations reviewed below examined the role of the stepparent in each domain.

An important conceptual distinction needs to be drawn between the clarity of a parenting role and the content of that role. These two aspects of a parenting role are independent. For example, consider a stepmother who is very clear that she should actively discipline her stepchild, and a stepfather, in another stepfamily, who is clear that he should allow the mother to be the child's primary disciplinarian. In this example, both the stepmother and stepfather are clear about their parenting role (i.e., they have little role ambiguity), but the content of their perceived role differs (actively disciplining vs. not actively disciplining, but supporting the active discipline of the biological parent).

As another example, consider two stepparents who both believe that they should refrain from actively disciplining their stepchildren. Although these two stepparents have the same perceptions of the content of the stepparent role, one is very clear and confident that that role is the one that she should adopt, whereas the other is not so sure (i.e., is somewhat ambiguous). In this instance, the content of the parenting role is similar for both parents, but the extent of role ambiguity differs. With the distinction between the clarity and content of the stepparent role in mind, the next two sections provide information about each of these aspects of the stepparent role.

THE CLARITY OF THE STEPPARENT ROLE

Over 15 years ago, Cherlin (1978) noted that the role of the stepparent is less than optimally clear. He argued that remarriage is an "incomplete institution," because there are few societal norms that inform remarried parents about how they are expected to behave toward their stepchildren. Since then, several conceptual and clinical writers have argued that the stepparent role is less clear than is the role of the biological parent (Crosbie-Burnett, 1989; Visher & Visher, 1978) and that this lack of clarity–which is also called role ambiguity–negatively affects stepfamily members.

There are several possible ways that the role of the stepparent can be conceptualized. With respect to discipline, a stepparent (or other stepfamily members) might believe that he or she should: (a) actively discipline stepchildren, (b) support the discipline of the biological parent, but not establish household rules, or (c) not engage in any discipline at all. With respect to the provision of warmth, a stepparent (or other family members) might believe that he or she should: (a) act very friendly toward the stepchild or (b) be detached from the stepchild. That these different ways of conceptualizing the role of the stepparent appear to have some plausibility illustrates the lack of clarity of the stepparent role.

A further distinction needs to be drawn between a lack of social consensus concerning the role of the stepparent and an individual's perception of role ambiguity. When different individuals have different conceptualizations of the stepparent role, there is a lack of social consensus, but not necessarily role ambiguity. For example, although the stepparent, biological parent, and (step)child in a stepfamily may have very different conceptualizations of the stepparent role, each may have a very clear notion of the appropriate role for the stepparent. The few studies that have been conducted in this area have generally assessed the extent of social consensus rather than the individual's experience of role ambiguity.

Social consensus on the stepparent role. With respect to the extent of social consensus on the role of the stepparent, limited empirical findings support the contention that this consensus is lacking. Schwebel, Fine, and Renner (1991) asked college students to rate how likely it was that a parental figure *would* engage in a designated parental behavior relevant to a case scenario (which assessed assumptions of how parents typically behave) and to what extent the parental figure *should* engage in the parental behavior (which assessed standards of how parents should behave). To determine the extent of social consensus (the extent to which people agree about parental roles) on the role of the stepparent, the variabilities in ratings of biological parents and stepparents were compared. Results indicated that there was generally greater variability in ratings of what stepparents would do and should do than there was in ratings of what biological parents would and should do, although this varied somewhat by the gender of the rater. Consistent with Cherlin's (1978) hypothesis, these findings support the notion that there is less consensus in how stepparents do and should act than there is in reference to biological parents.

In Marsiglio's (1992) study of stepfathers from the National Survey of Families and Households, there was a great deal of variability in the extent to which stepfathers agreed with seven statements (e.g., "stepparents don't have the full responsibility of a parent," "it is just as easy to discipline your stepchildren as it is your own children," and "a stepparent is more like a friend than a parent to stepchildren"). For example, on the item "a stepparent is more like a friend than a parent to stepchildren," 33%, 18%, 16%, 29%, and 4% of the stepfathers responded *definitely false, somewhat false, neither true nor false, somewhat true,* and *definitely true.* The extent of variability on this, and the other items, indicates that there is little consensus among stepfathers about their role.

Via a mailed questionnaire, Fine and Kurdek (1994) asked both spouses in 115 stepmother/father and 100 mother/stepfather families (recruited form the Stepfamily Association of America) to complete measures of parenting cognitions related to their control and warmth parenting behaviors directed toward a 5-15 year-old target child living in the home. The parenting cognitions involved perceptions of how often they engaged in parenting behaviors, assumptions of how often the typical parent in their position [i.e., stepmother, father, stepfather, mother] engaged in parenting behaviors, and standards of how often a parent in their position should engage in parenting behaviors. The spouses' satisfaction with parenting was also assessed.

On the warmth parenting dimension, there was significantly greater variability in stepparents' ratings of how much they should show warmth (i.e., standards) than in biological parents' ratings of how much they should show warmth. Consistent with findings from Marsiglio (1992), this suggests that there is less consensus among stepparents in how they should behave than exists among biological parents. No such differences were found on the control dimension.

Although the studies reviewed above suggest that there is a lack of social consensus on the role of the stepparent, two studies have found that spouses in stepfamilies tend to agree on the parenting role of the stepparent. Bray, Berger, and Boethel (1994) found that parents and stepparents in stepfather families tended to agree on appropriate childrearing arrangements (i.e., the relative extent to which each spouse was responsible for childrearing). Similarly, Ganong and Coleman (1994), in their 4-year longitudinal study of stepfamilies with adolescent stepchildren, found that stepparents and parents of adolescents tended to agree on how much responsibility the stepparent had in raising the stepchild. These studies raise the possibility that, at least within stepfamilies, some consensus may be emerging on the appropriate role for the stepparent (Bray et al., 1994).

Role ambiguity. In the one known study of adults that assessed stepparent role ambiguity and not the extent of a social consensus on the stepparent role, Kurdek and Fine (1991) asked 27 mothers and 27 stepfathers from stepfather families to complete a 10-item measure of the extent of the ambiguity of the stepfather's role. There were no differences between mothers and stepfathers in the extent of the ambiguity of the stepfather's role, although the means of approximately 3.2 per item on a 1-7 scale (with higher scores reflecting higher levels of ambiguity) indicated the presence of some ambiguity.

One known empirical study has examined the clarity of children's perceptions of the stepparent role. Fine, Kurdek, and Hennigen (1992) studied 81 7th and 8th grade children in stepfamilies. Each child completed a 3-item measure of the ambiguity of the roles of each of the parents that they lived with (i.e., "It was difficult for me to decide what I'd like to call my [step]father," "I am hardly ever sure what to expect from my [step]father," and "I have hardly any examples in real life to show me what a good (step)father is like"). Children rating stepfathers reported more role ambiguity than did those rating biological fathers. Children rating stepmothers reported more role ambiguity than did those rating biological mothers.

In sum, despite the persuasiveness of the clinical and theoretical arguments that the role of the stepparent is ambiguous for all stepfamily members, there is only limited empirical support for this proposition. The studies that have been conducted generally support the notion that there is a lack of social consensus in how stepparents should behave. However, even fewer studies have been conducted that have shown that parents, stepparents, and children in stepfamilies experience ambiguity with respect to the stepparent role.

Variables to Consider in Understanding the Clarity of the Stepparent Role

A number of variables may be related to the extent to which the role of the stepparent is ambiguous. First, the gender of the stepparent may relate to the extent of stepparent role ambiguity. There has been speculation that the role of the stepmother is more ambiguous than is that of the stepfather (Ihinger-Tallman, 1988). Given the relative infrequency of stepmothers living with their stepchildren (18% of all stepfamilies: Coleman & Ganong, 1990), it can be argued that stepmothers have fewer socially-accepted role prescriptions than stepfathers (Ihinger-Tallman, 1988), which may, in turn, lead to greater role ambiguity.

An additional reason why the role of the stepmother may be more ambiguous than the role of the stepfather concerns different expectations for men and women in families. As discussed as follows, women are typically expected to be actively involved in caring for children (Thompson & Walker, 1989). When the woman is a stepmother, the societal expectation that she should play an active role in childrearing may conflict with the expectation that a stepmother should not be actively involved with her stepchildren (see below). These conflicting expectations, which stepfathers do not experience to as great an extent because men are not expected to be active in childrearing, may exacerbate role ambiguity for stepmothers.

Second, the role of the stepparent may be more ambiguous when the nonresidential parent is highly involved with his or child, particularly when the nonresidential parent is the mother (Visher & Visher, 1988). When there is an active nonresidential parent, the stepparent, residential biological parent, and the child may feel that there is little need for the stepparent to assume an active parenting role. Without a perceived need for the stepparent to be active, stepfamily members may be especially unclear about how the stepparent should relate to his or her stepchild.

Third, the residential status of the stepparent may influence the extent of stepparent role ambiguity. Nonresidential stepmothers (i.e., those not living with their [step]children) have reported more stress than have residential stepmothers (i.e., living with their [step]children) (Ambert, 1986), perhaps because their limited amount of contact with their stepchildren does not allow them an opportunity to develop clearer roles. Thus, role ambiguity may be greater for nonresidential stepparents than for residential ones.

Fourth, there has also been speculation that role ambiguity is greater in "complex" stepfamilies than in "simple" stepfamilies (Fine & Schwebel, 1991; Visher & Visher, 1988). In complex stepfamilies, each spouse brings children with him or her into the remarried families, whereas in simple stepfamilies only one spouse does so. The heightened role ambiguity in complex stepfamilies is thought to arise because each spouse in a complex stepfamily is both a biological parent (to his or her children) and a stepparent (to the children of his or her spouse). Particularly if the spouse believes that one should behave differently towards one's biological children and one's stepchildren, simultaneously enacting the roles of biological parent and stepparent may exacerbate confusion and ambiguity.

Fifth, the length of time that the stepfamily has been together may be related to the extent of role ambiguity. Two competing forces are at work in this regard. On the one hand, one would expect that family members in stepfamilies that have been together for longer periods of time, compared to those who have not been together as long, would have less stepparent role ambiguity because the increased length of time would provide an opportunity for some consensus to develop among family members on the appropriate role for the stepparent (Visher & Visher, 1988). On the other hand, it is conceivable that the appropriate role for the stepparent changes as the stepfamily develops and enters new developmental stages. Because of these possible changes, there may be a waxing and waning of the extent of role clarity, with increasing role clarity within particular developmental stages and decreasing clarity at the outset of a new stage.

Finally, and related to the developmental stage of the stepfamily, the age of stepchild may be associated with the extent of stepparent role ambiguity. Although there has been little speculation on how the age of the stepchild may relate to stepparent role ambiguity, it is plausible that younger stepchildren experience less role ambiguity than older children because they have had less time (since the divorce of their parents) to become accustomed to a family without the stepparent. Further, because their cognitive capabilities are greater, one would expect that older children would have a greater potential to experience role ambiguity than younger children.

THE CONTENT OF THE STEPPARENT ROLE

Researchers who have addressed the content of the stepparent role have generally found that the stepparent role is a less active one than is the role of the biological parent. Three lines of empirical findings support this claim. First, with respect to beliefs, stepparents report that they should exhibit fewer warmth and control parenting behaviors toward stepchildren than biological parents report that they should exhibit toward their children (Fine & Kurdek, 1994). Giles-Sims (1984) found that spouses in stepfamilies expected stepparents to be less involved in childrearing duties than biological parents, although over half of the respondents reported that they expected stepparents and biological parents to share childrearing duties equally. Further, in Schwebel, Fine, and Renner (1991) described above, college students perceived that both biological parents and adoptive parents were more likely to engage in the designated parental behaviors and should engage in the behaviors to a greater extent than stepparents.

Second, with respect to reported parenting behaviors, Fine, Voydanoff, and Donnelly (1993) found that stepfathers reported engaging in fewer positive and negative responses to their children than biological fathers in stepfamilies and that mothers in stepmother families exhibited fewer negative responses toward their children than did biological mothers in stepfamilies. Giles-Sims (1984) found that stepparents reported being less involved in making decisions regarding stepchildren than were biological parents. Ganong and Coleman (1994) found that biological parents assumed primary responsibility for disciplining children, although stepparents were reported to be actively involved in childrearing and became increasingly involved over the course of the four years of their study.

Finally, with respect to behaviors that stepparents have been observed to engage in, stepfathers are more likely to show a disengaged parenting style, characterized by low levels of involement, control over stepchildren's behavior, parental monitoring, and discipline (Hetherington & Clingempeel, 1992; Hetherington, 1993).

Because stepparents believe that they should behave and do behave less actively toward children than biological parents, these findings suggest that stepparents perceive their parenting role as distinct from that of biological parents. However, findings inconsistent with this notion have been reported by Marsiglio (1992), who found that a substantial number of stepfathers reported that they should act like fathers to their stepchildren. In an analysis of the National Survey of Families and Households, Marsiglio found that 52% of stepfathers (who also had their own biological children living in the home) disagreed at least somewhat with the idea that "it is harder to love stepchildren than your own children," 68% disagreed at least somewhat with the notion that "stepparents don't have the full responsibility of a parent," and 58% agreed at least somewhat with the statement that "it is just as easy to discipline your stepchildren as it is your own children." These data indicate that a majority of stepfathers agreed at least somewhat that they should adopt a "father-like" role.

A factor that may help explain why Marsiglio's (1992) findings differ from the general trend is social desirability responding. In Marsiglio's study, the items pit a stepparent's experience against that of a biological parent's. Because members of our culture consider biological parents to be the norm (Ganong, Coleman, & Mapes, 1990), it is possible that there is a built-in tendency for stepparents to perceive that they *should* respond that their experiences parallel those of biological parents. Thus, stepfathers' responses may reflect what they believe that they should say, rather than (or in addition to) what they actually believe.

Very few studies have assessed how members of stepfamilies view the general content of the stepparent role (i.e., the specific label that they use to describe the role). In their longitudinal study of adolescents in stepfamilies, Ganong and Coleman (1994) found that only 47% of the stepparents identified themselves as stepparents at Time 1, but that 86% indicated that they thought of themselves as stepparents at Time 2. This may suggest an increased awareness and acceptance of one's role as a stepparent over time.

Ganong and Coleman (1994) also found that adolescent stepchildren perceived that fewer stepparents assumed the role of *primary* disciplinarian at Time 2 than did so at Time 1 and that the parents increasingly shared discipline over time. Despite the insights provided by these findings, we have much to learn about how members of stepfamilies view the specific role of the stepparent (i.e., as an active disciplinarian, a friend, a supportive adult, someone who supports the discipline of the biological parent, or some other role conception) and how this view changes over time.

In sum, several lines of research have converged to suggest that the role of the stepparent is more distant and less active than is the role of the biological parent. We need to know more about how members of stepfamilies conceptualize the specific content of the stepparent role.

Variables to Consider in Understanding the Content of the Stepparent Role

As was the case with the clarity of the stepparent role, several variables may be related to the content of the stepparent role, although most of the supportive evidence has come from the conceptual and clinical literatures. First, there has been speculation that the role of the stepmother is constructed to be more active than is the role of the stepfather (Ihinger-Tallman, 1988). According to this claim, women are expected to and expect themselves to be heavily invested in and to take primary responsibility for the well-being of children (Leslie, Anderson, & Branson, 1991; Thompson & Walker, 1989). By contrast, because the traditional role of men is to provide for the family, men may be relatively uninvolved in childrearing (Harris & Morgan, 1991; Thompson & Walker, 1989). Thus, when they assume the role of stepparent, stepmothers believe that they should be more involved and are more involved with their stepchildren than are stepfathers.

Second, although supportive empirical evidence is scant, one would expect that the content of the stepparent role would change over the lifespan of the stepfamily. For example, one might expect that stepparents would become increasingly active as disciplinarians of their stepchildren over time. However, such changes need to be considered within the context of the age of the stepchild. For example, although one might expect stepparents to assume a greater disciplinary role over time, this trend may be affected when stepchildren reach adolescence. Given adolescents' press for autonomy (Montemayor, 1983), stepparents (and biological parents as well) may attempt to provide adolescent stepchildren with more frequent opportunities to make their own decisions. Further, young stepchildren may be more willing to accept active discipline from a stepparent than are adolescent stepchildren (Ganong & Coleman, 1994). These factors may lead stepparents to discipline their stepchildren less actively when they reach adolescence than when they were younger.

Third, the content of the stepparent role may differ in different types of stepfamilies. Very little has been written about how the content of the stepparent role may differ in simple and complex stepfamilies. One factor that may affect how the stepparent role is conceptualized is that spouses in complex stepfamilies are simultaneously biological parents and stepparents. It is conceivable that, because they believe in an ethic of equity, these spouses may feel pressured to treat their biological children and their stepchildren similarly, which may result in the stepparent role being defined and implemented in a manner similar to the role of the biological parent. By contrast, stepparents in simple stepfamilies do not have this particular pressure to behave like biological parents. Thus, if these arguments are valid, stepparents in complex stepfamilies may be more active in parenting (in a manner similar to biological parents) than are stepparents in simple stepfamilies. Similarly, stepparents who have "mutual" children (i.e., children born to the remarried couple) also are simultaneously biological parents and stepparents. Thus, these stepparents may also feel pressures to treat their children and stepchildren similarly.

Fourth, stepfamily members' conceptualization of the content of the stepparent role may relate to the extent to which the nonresidential parent is actively involved with his or her child. One would expect that there would be an inverse relation between the nonresidential parent's level of involvement and the extent to which the stepparent disciplines and shows warmth to the stepchild. In particular, when the nonresidential parent is actively involved with his or her child, the stepparent, residential biological parent, and the child may feel that the stepparent does not need to assume an active parenting role.

Finally, the gender of the stepchild may be related to how the role of the stepparent is conceptualized. Ganong and Coleman (1994) found that stepparents seemed to discipline their stepsons less actively as they reached adolescence, but did not decrease their disciplinary activity level for their stepdaughters. This finding suggests that the disciplinary role of the stepparent may be conceptualized (at least by stepparents) as being more active for stepdaughters than it is for stepsons.

THE RELATIONS BETWEEN THE CLARITY AND CONTENT OF THE STEPPARENT ROLE AND ADJUSTMENT

There is limited evidence that both the extent to which the stepparent role is clear and the content of the stepparent role are related to the adjustment of members of stepfamilies. With respect to the clarity of the stepparent role, there is evidence that greater stepparent role ambiguity is associated with poorer adjustment. Kurdek and Fine (1991), in their study of spouses in stepfather families, found that high levels of stepparent role ambiguity were related to mothers' reports of low family/marital/personal life satisfaction and stepfathers' reports of low parenting satisfaction. Similarly, Fine, Kurdek, and Hennigen (1992) found that adolescents living with stepmothers reported high self-competence to the extent that they perceived the stepmother's role as clear.

In terms of the content of the stepparent role, children's adjustment appears to be promoted when stepparents, at least initially, do not take an active role in discipline (Bray & Burger, 1993; Hetherington, 1993; Hetherington & Clingempeel, 1992). In addition, there is evidence that the marital adjustment of stepfathers may be positively related to the extent to which the mother believes that the stepfather should not assume a parental role with the children (Bray et al., 1994). Thus, the adjustment of stepfamily members may be faciliated when the stepparent role is conceptualized as less active than the role of the biological parent.

However, inconsistent with this claim, Marsiglio (1992) found that more "father-like" perceptions were positively related to the perceived quality of the stepfather-stepchild relationship. Although this relation may indicate that perceiving the role of the stepparent as similar to the role of the biological parent is related to positive adjustment, it is also possible that a social desirability response set was responsible for this positive association. As noted earlier, it is possible that there is an incentive for stepparents to perceive that they *should* respond that their experiences parallel those of biological parents and that they *should* report positive relations with their stepchildren.

The adjustment correlates of parenting behaviors may depend on the specific domain examined. Fine, Voydanoff, and Donnelly (1993), in their study of stepfamilies in the National Survey of Families and Households data set, found that parental perceptions of positive child outcomes were positively related to perceptions of the frequency of parental warmth. The relations between parental control and child outcomes were more complex and varied for different dimensions of child well-being and in different types of stepfamilies. Similarly, Fine and Kurdek (1994), in their study of both spouses in stepfamilies, found that parents and stepparents who perceived themselves as engaging in control and warmth parenting behaviors as often as they should and as often as typical parents do were more satisfied with their parenting experiences than were other parents. However, this effect was greater on the warmth parenting domain than on the control domain. Fine and Kurdek posited that warmth may be perceived by parents as a uniformly desirable parental behavior, whereas control may be perceived in a more complex way. In particular, moderate levels of control may be perceived as more conducive to children's development than low or high levels. Thus, when one evaluates one's performance negatively on the warmth parenting dimension, parenting satisfaction may diminish because warmth is perceived as an ideal way to behave towards children.

IMPLICATIONS FOR PROFESSIONALS WHO WORK WITH STEPFAMILIES

As should be clear from this literature review, research into how the stepparent role is conceptualized, how it is enacted, and how it affects stepfamily members is still in its early stages. As a result, professionals who work with stepfamilies should be cautious in basing their clinical and educational work on these empirical findings. Nevertheless, the literature that is available does allow for some suggestions for professionals who work with members of stepfamilies.

There is a sufficient amount of clinical and anecdotal evidence to suggest that the manner in which issues pertaining to the role of the stepparent are resolved may have important consequences for stepfamilies. In particular, in many stepfamilies, it is likely that there will be some ambiguity regarding how the stepparent should behave toward his or her stepchild(ren) and there may be disagreements among stepfamily members regarding desirable stepparent behavior. As a result, practitioners (either family life educators or therapists) working with spouses who are either contemplating entering a stepfamily or who are already in a stepfamily should encourage these spouses to discuss their views of the appropriate role for the stepparent. These discussions would hopefully help each spouse develop a clearer notion of the appropriate role for the stepparent, engender greater consensus between spouses on this role, and perhaps enhance the extent to which the roles of the biological parent and stepparent complement each other. The practitioner can help set a positive tone for these discussions by sharing a point made by Visher and Visher (1988): ambiguity provides freedom because it allows the couple to define the stepparent role in many different ways.

Visher and Visher (1988) propose that the development of a strong couple relationship in stepfamilies should take place before it is clinically prudent to work on the stepparent-stepchild relationship. Because of this recommendation, it may be best if the initial discussions about the stepparent role involve only the two spouses. However, because the (step)child is a critical player in the stepfamily system, he or she could be given the opportunity, at a level appropriate with his or her developmental level, to participate in some of the later discussion sessions. Depending on the child's developmental level and the spouses' values, the child may or may not be given the chance to have a say in determining how the role of the stepparent is defined. At the very least, the child can be informed of what the spouses have decided and given a chance to ask questions.

In terms of the specific nature of the stepparent role, practitioners are advised to consider Visher and Visher's (1988) point that there may be several appropriate ways to define the role of the stepparent. Further, there has not been enough research on the adjustment correlates of different conceptualizations of the stepparent role to give parents definitive guidance. However, with these caveats in mind, the literature seems to converge on the interpretation that, particularly with older (i.e., adolescent) stepchildren, it may be beneficial if the stepparent at least initially does not assume an active role in disciplining stepchildren (Bray & Burger, 1993; Hetherington, 1993). Coupled with clinical evidence that the development of positive stepparent-stepchild relations emerges slowly over time (Papernow, 1993; Visher & Visher, 1988), prospective and current members of stepfamilies might be encouraged to allow the stepparent-stepchild relationship to develop gradually. If stepfamily members hold the realistic expectation that step-relationships take time to develop, they may be less likely to suffer the negative consequences of believing the myth that the stepparent-stepchild relationship can be instantly cohesive (Visher & Visher, 1988).

Thus, perhaps the best guidance that professionals can provide spouses in stepfamilies at the present time is to try a parenting model in which the biological parent assumes primary responsibility for disciplining the child; the stepparent supports the discipline of the biological parent, but does not independently establish household rules; and the stepparent allows cohesiveness in the stepparent-stepchild relationship to develop at its natural course at a pace comfortable for the stepchild. Once again, this guidance must be qualified by informing spouses in stepfamilies that this model is unlikely to be successful in all stepfamilies, that a number of alternative models may be effective in specific stepfamilies, and that the model may need to be modified according to such variables as the age and gender of the stepchild, the gender of the stepparent, and the level of involvement of the nonresidential parent.

REFERENCES

Amato, P. R. (1990). Dimensions of the family environment as perceived by children: A multidimensional scaling analysis. *Journal of Marriage and the Family, 52,* 613-620.

Ambert, A. (1986). Being a stepparent: Live-in and visiting stepchildren. *Journal of Marriage and the Family, 48,* 795-804.

Baucom, D., Epstein, N., Sayers, S., & Sher, T. (1989). The role of cognitions in marital relationships: Definitional, methodological, and conceptual issues. *Journal of Consulting and Clinical Psychology, 57,* 31-38.

Bray, J. H., & Berger, S. H. (1993). Developmental issues in stepfamilies research project: Family relationships and parent-child interactions. *Journal of Family Psychology, 7,* 76-90.

Bray, J. H., Berger, S. H., & Boethel, C. L. (1994). Role integration and marital adjustment in stepfather families. In K. Pasley & M. Ihinger-Tallman (Eds.), *Stepparenting: Issues in theory, research, and practice* (pp. 69-86). Westport, CT: Greenwood.

Burr, W. R., Day, R. D., & Bahr, K. S. (1993). *Family science*. Pacific Grove, CA: Brooks/Cole.

Cherlin, A. (1978). Remarriage as an incomplete institution. *American Journal of Sociology, 84*, 634-650.

Coleman, M., & Ganong, L. H. (1990). Remarriage and stepfamily research in the 1980s: Increased interest in an old family form. *Journal of Marriage and the Family, 52*, 925-940.

Crosbie-Burnett, M. (1989). Application of family stress theory to remarriage: A model for assessing and helping stepfamilies. *Family Relations, 38*, 323-331.

Fine, M. A., & Kurdek, L. A. (1994). Parenting cognitions in stepfamilies: Differences between parents and stepparents and relations to parenting satisfaction. *Journal of Social and Personal Relationships, 11*, 95-112.

Fine, M. A., Kurdek, L. A, & Hennigen, L. (1992). Perceived self-competence and its relations to stepfamily myths and (step)parent role ambiguity in adolescents from stepfather and stepmother families. *Journal of Family Psychology, 6*, 69-76.

Fine, M. A., & Schwebel, A. I. (1991). Stepparent stress: A cognitive perspective. *Journal of Divorce & Remarriage, 17*, 1-15.

Fine, M. A., Voydanoff, P., & Donnelly, B. W. (1993). Relations between parental control and warmth and child well-being in stepfamilies. *Journal of Family Psychology, 7*, 222-232.

Ganong, L. H., Coleman, M., & Mapes, D. (1990). A meta-analytic review of family structure stereotypes. *Journal of Marriage and the Family, 52*, 287-297.

Ganong, L. H., & Coleman, M. (1994). Adolescent stepchild-stepparent relationships: Changes over time. In K. Pasley & M. Ihinger-Tallman (Eds.), *Stepparenting: Issues in theory, research, and practice* (pp. 87-104). Westport, CT: Greenwood.

Giles-Sims, J. (1984). The stepparent role: Expectations, behavior, and sanctions. *Journal of Family Issues, 5*, 116-130.

Harris, K. M., & Morgan, S. P. (1991). Fathers, sons, and daughters: Differential paternal involvement in parenting. *Journal of Marriage and the Family, 53*, 531-544.

Hetherington, E. M. (1993). An overview of the Virginia Longitudinal Study of Divorce and Remarriage with a focus on early adolescence. *Journal of Family Psychology, 7*, 39-56.

Hetherington, E. M., & Clingempeel, W. G. (1992). Coping with marital transitions: A family systems perspective. *Monographs of the Society for Research in Child Development*, 57(2-3, Serial No. 227).

Ihinger-Tallman, M. (1988). Research on stepfamilies. *Annual Review of Sociology, 14*, 25-48.

Kurdek, L. A., & Fine, M. A. (1991). Cognitive correlates of adjustment for mothers and stepfathers in stepfather families. *Journal of Marriage and the Family, 53*, 565-572.

Kurdek, L. A., & Fine, M. A. (in press). Family acceptance and family control as predictors of adjustment problems in young adolescents: Linear, curvilinear, or interactive effects? *Child Development.*

Kurdek, L. A., Fine, M. A., & Sinclair, R. J. (in press). Social competence in sixth graders: Parenting transitions, family climate, and peer norm effects. *Child Development.*

Lamborn, S. D., Mounts, N. S., Steinberg, L., & Dornbusch, S. M. (1991). Patterns of competence and adjustment among adolescents from authoritative, authoritarian, indulgent, and neglectful families. *Child Development, 62,* 1049-1065.

Leslie, L. A., Anderson, E. A., & Branson, M. P. (1991). Responsibility for children: The role of gender and employment. *Journal of Family Issues, 12,* 197-210.

Maccoby, E. M., & Martin, J. (1983). Socialization in the context of the family: Parent-child interaction. In E. M. Hetherington (Ed.), P. H. Mussen (Series Ed.), *Handbook of child psychology: Vol. 4. Socialization, personality and social development.* New York: Wiley.

Marsiglio, W. (1992). Stepfathers with minor children living at home: Parenting perceptions and relationship quality. *Journal of Family Issues, 13,* 195-214.

Montemayor, R. (1983). Parents and adolescents in conflict. *Journal of Early Adolescence, 3,* 83-103.

Papernow, P. L. (1993). *Becoming a stepfamily: Patterns of development in remarried families.* San Francisco: Jossey-Bass.

Rodgers, R. H., & White, J. M. (1993). Family development theory. In P. G. Boss, W. J. Doherty, R. LaRossa, W. R. Schumm, & S. K. Steinmetz (Eds.), *Sourcebook of family theories and methods: A conceptual approach* (pp. 225-254). New York: Plenum.

Schwebel, A. I., Fine, M. A., & Renner, M. A. (1991). An empirical investigation of perceptions of the stepparent role. *Journal of Family Issues, 12,* 43-57.

Steinberg, L., Dornbusch, S. M., & Brown, B. B. (1992). Ethnic differences in adolescent achievement: An ecological perspective. *American Psychologist, 47,* 723-729.

Steinberg, L., Elmen, J. D., & Mounts, N. S. (1989). Authoritative parenting, psychosocial maturity, and academic success among adolescents. *Child Development, 60,* 1424-1436.

Thompson, L., & Walker, A. J. (1989). Women and men in marriage, work, and parenthood. *Journal of Marriage and the Family, 51,* 845-871.

Visher, E., & Visher, J. S. (1988). *Old loyalties, new ties.* New York: Brunner/Mazel.

Three Types of Stepfamilies

Roni Berger

SUMMARY. A multi-dimensional typology of non-clinical stepfamilies was developed on the basis of in-depth interviews with a non-sample group of remarried couples. Competitive Learning Analysis of the data yielded three types of stepfamilies, based on three psychosocial and four sociodemographic features: Integrated families, Invented families and Imported families. Profiles of these types are portrayed and demonstrated. No difference in levels of functioning and satisfaction was found. Theoretical and practical implications of the typology are discussed. *[Article copies available from The Haworth Document Delivery Service: 1-800-342-9678.]*

Stepfamilies are created by a remarriage into which one or both spouses bring at least one child from a previous marriage. A growing proportion of families in the Western World are stepfamilies, due to the rising frequency of divorce and remarriage. Currently every other marriage in the U.S. ends in a divorce, followed by remarriage of most divorced people (Booth & Edwards, 1992). Thirty two percent of the population and at least one of every 4-5 children are estimated to live in stepfamilies, most of them stepfather stepfamilies (Marsiglio, 1992).

Stepfamilies have multiplied to the point that some writers refer to them as the future traditional American family. Consequently, more knowledge about their unique features is of utmost importance.

In the last two decades, we have witnessed a growing number of stepfamily studies (Sager et al., 1983; Visher & Visher, 1988). Many of these

---

Roni Berger, PhD, is on the faculty of Adelphi University School of Social Work, Garden City, NY 11530.

[Haworth co-indexing entry note]: "Three Types of Stepfamilies." Berger, Roni. Co-published simultaneously in *Journal of Divorce & Remarriage* (The Haworth Press, Inc.) Vol. 24, No. 1/2, 1995, pp. 35-49; and: *Understanding Stepfamilies: Their Structure and Dynamics* (ed: Craig A. Everett) The Haworth Press, Inc., 1995, pp. 35-49. Single or multiple copies of this article are available from The Haworth Document Delivery Service [1-800-342-9678, 9:00 a.m. - 5:00 p.m. (EST)].

studies used clinical populations and focused on pathological or demographic aspects of stepfamilies. Few studies of non-clinical stepfamilies were carried out (Carter & McGoldrick, 1990). Some generalizations about stepfamilies, mostly descriptions of structural and dynamic features and major areas of conflict, are well-established; other findings are controversial and unclear. One possible source for such incongruencies may result from viewing stepfamilies as one undifferentiated group of families.

Typologies of stepfamilies are scarce, in spite of the recognition of their diversity. The few attempts to develop guidelines for differential thinking about stepfamilies are based on one dimension, and mostly demographic, like comparing stepfamilies after divorce with stepfamilies following death, stepfamilies with young children versus stepfamilies with adolescents, stepfamilies with and without a common child. One exception is the typology suggested by Gross (1986), based on the way adolescents in stepfamilies perceive their family.

Families in general, let alone stepfamilies, are complicated multi-faceted systems that need to be classified on the basis of more than one dimension (Olson et al., 1979). The current research suggests a multi-dimensional, empirically based typology of stepfamilies. The dimensions in the typology are based on dynamic features of family functioning rather than sociodemographic factors. They include: family past orientation, family acceptance/rejection of difference from intact families, and focal sub-system.

Past orientation. How families monitor references to pre-remarriage patterns, relationships, memories and items, as reflected in family rules about how much space is allowed for past-related matters, who is allowed to refer to them, under what circumstances and in what manner (Wolpert-Lur & Bross, 1982; Sager et al., 1983; Sluzki, 1983; Hodder, 1985; Kaslow, 1986, 1988; Bradt & Bradt, 1988; Lin, 1990).

Acceptance/rejection of difference. The self-perception of the family: How similar or different from other types of families the family perceives itself, especially in relation to nuclear families, who are still perceived as the "normative," "correct" type of family. The concept was first coined by Kirk (1964, 1981) based on his work with adoptive families. Stepfamilies, like adoptive families, have a family configuration that is different from the traditional nuclear intact family. As such, they have unique structural and dynamic characteristics. Acceptance/rejection of difference reflects the attitude of the family towards these characteristics. In order to be functional the family needs to accept and come to peace with its being different (Kaslow, 1986; Carter & McGoldrick, 1990; Hartin, 1990).

Focal sub-system. The dominant sub-system that has priority in situations of conflicting interests. Stepfamilies have a complicated structure that may include the following sub-systems: the remarried couple, parent-child, stepparent-stepchild (or children) and sibling-subsystems (natural, half- and step- siblings). Certain life situations may pose a need to set priorities between the marital and the parental subsystems. These situations occur in every family but are potentially more loaded in stepfamilies (Goetting, 1983). The focal sub-system reflects which sub-system has priority in the stepfamily.

METHOD

Subjects. A non-sample group of sixty-three non-clinical stepfamily couples participated in joint in-depth interviews. Couples were middle class, urban, educated, mostly non-religious and at least two years into the remarriage. Couples included divorced and subsequently remarried women, who brought at least one minor child from a previous marriage into the current family. A total of 41.2% of the husbands were never married before, 44.3% were divorced with children who lived with their mothers or on their own, 4.8% were divorced without children, 9.7% were widowed or divorced with living-in children. The age of subjects ranged from 29 to 54 for men (X = 40.5, SD = 5.9) and from 27 to 48 for women (X = 37.8, SD = 4.9). Wives had 1-3 children from previous marriage (X = 1.4, SD = .67), ages 4-27 (X = 14.3, SD = 4.8) and husbands had 1-4 children from previous marriage (X = 2, SD = 1.15) ages 7-30 (X = 16.2, SD = 4.9). Duration of current marriage was 2-13 years (X = 5.5, SD = 3.49). A total of 68.3% (n = 43) of the families had 1-3 children in the current marriage (X = 1.08, SD = .83) ages 1-13 (X = 4.9, SD = 2.93). A total of 60.3% of the families relocated after remarriage, while 39.7% went on living in a previous place of one of the spouses.

As the informants were the remarried couple while children were not interviewed, the findings of this study are limited to the perspective of the adults in the family.

Measures. Five variables were measured in each family: past orientation, acceptance/rejection of difference, focal sub-system, satisfaction and functioning. Measures included two self-report closed questionnaires and a semi-structured joint interview. The individual questionnaires are a Past Orientation Scale and a Scale of Satisfaction. The Past Orientation Scale was developed for the current study. The questionnaire includes 14 statements that describe how family members relate to past-connected matters. Subjects rate each statement on a 5-point scale, indicating to what degree the statement describes the situation in their own family. A sample item: "In our family, family members talk about the first marriage/s (1) never (2) seldom (3) sometimes (4) often (5) always." Reliability of the scale, computed on the basis of the subjects described above, was = .885. A family score on each item was calculated based on the average of both spouses (Lavee, NcCubbin & Olson, 1987; Draper & Marcos, 1990).

The Scale of Satisfaction was developed by Olson et al. (1982) as one of the FACES 2 questionnaires and has been validated in many studies. The questionnaire includes 14 statements that describe different aspects of family life, such as role allocation, rules, boundaries and the like. Subjects rate on a 5-point scale how satisfied they are with each aspect. Sample item: "How satisfied are you with the frequency of arguments between parents in your family? (1) very unsatisfied, (2) unsatisfied, (3) partly satisfied and partly unsatisfied, (4) satisfied, (5) very satisfied." In the current study one question was added about the level of satisfaction with life in the family in general. Reliability of the questionnaire is = .92 and test-re-test reliability after 5 weeks = .75.

The semi-structured interview yielded sociodemographic data about the families as well as information about their acceptance/rejection of difference (= .57), additional data about past orientation (= .71) and data about focal sub-system.

Level of functioning was measured by a Likert-type questionnaire that included eight questions about health, functioning in school (children) and in work (adults) of family members. Sample item: "Did any of the children have difficulties in school in the last year? ____ no one ____ yes, a few. Who? ______________ What type of difficulties? ______________ _____ yes, many. Who? ______________________ What type of difficulties? __________________________." Items were factor analyzed in order to test construct validity. Family score in functioning was calculated based on the number of problem areas, the number of family members who had problems and the severity of problems.

Data analysis. Neural net analysis of competitive learning was performed in order to identify profiles of stepfamilies. This technique enables a researcher to explore parallel distribution processing and to indicate associations between qualitative variables in small groups of subjects, identify characteristics that change simultaneously, establish "packages of features" (profiles) and evaluate the relative weight of each variable in differentiating between the clusters (Rumelhart & Zipser, 1985). This analysis yields empirically based (as opposed to apriori determined) categories, into which subjects are clustered.

FINDINGS

The analysis indicated that stepfamilies are not made in one mold. A multi-dimensional typology of stepfamilies emerged and three types of stepfamilies were identified. These types differ from each other in demographic as well as in dynamic features, but no type of stepfamily was found to be associated with a higher level of satisfaction or of functioning.

Profiles of stepfamily types in this study are based on seven variables: past orientation, acceptance/rejection of difference, focal sub-system, number of husband's children from a previous marriage, number of wife's children from a previous marriage, number of children from current remarriage and range of ages of children from all marriages. The three types of stepfamilies are described and illustrated as follows.

Integrated families. These types of families are reconstituted in the sense that they combine old and new perspectives. They score above average on past orientation as well as on acceptance of difference and are clearly couple-focused. In these families, both spouses have been married and had children in previous marriages, typically more than one child each. Their children are adolescents (wife) or young adults (husband), who are on their way to leave the family. In these families both partners feel that they are beyond most of the child-raising phase of their life. The partners came into the remarriage for the sake of the spouse relationship, which is their primary interest. Since they are interested in creating a new couple rather than a new family, they tend not to bear children in the remarriage and they expect their children, relatives and friends to adjust to their remarriage. A total of 39.7% (N = 25) of the families in the study were "Integrated."

The E. family is an example of an Integrated stepfamily (Figure 1). This family lives in the apartment that belonged to the wife and her first husband. The husband's daughters visit every week and occasionally give messages that they wish to come and live with the remarried family. The family scored above average on Past Orientation Scale and acceptance/rejection of difference.

The woman carries two last names of her two husbands and introduces herself by them. Her children from the previous marriage are registered in school under the name of their natural father and the couple is surprised by even being asked about it: "Is there any other possibility?" Both spouses discuss difficulties caused by the two names situation in dealing with the school system, health insurance companies and social agencies. Children refer to their stepparents by their given names and introduce them as "Mom's husband," and "Dad's wife." Both spouses introduce the children of the spouse from a previous marriage as "My husband's (wife's) child." They see

FIGURE 1. The E. Family

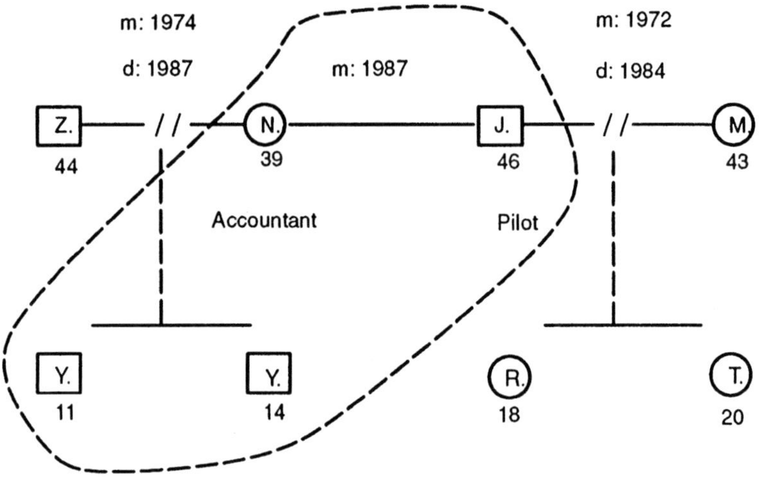

stepfamilies as totally different from intact families with more tensions even when ex-spouses co-parent well. The main difference in their opinion is that stepfamilies experienced a major crisis that affects their whole being. Both spouses function as parents, but each of them is the main parental figure for his/her children: "I can't decide for the children of my spouse without consulting him/her." The husband feels very guilty towards his daughters. The marital relationship is clearly the focus of this family: "Our bond comes first. This is the basis of this family. Everything starts and ends there. The rest is peripheral. We invest our most in our marriage and this is the secret of our success. This is the only way to make it as a stepfamily."

Invented families. This type of family creates a new present-oriented family-focused unit, into which the past is absorbed, as if nothing existed before. The focus of the remarried family is on family building and child raising. It is perceived by its members as "the Real family." They score below average on past orientation and on acceptance of difference and their focal sub-system is parental. The context of past-connected relationships, events and memories is erased and they are related to as if they occurred in the current family, which is perceived as the "real" family. In the majority of these families, the husband had never married or was in a short, childless first marriage and the wife has usually one child from a previous marriage. In these families, both spouses remarried in a relatively early phase of their life cycle, when the wife is in the early stages of raising her only child, and creating a new family together is a major goal for them. As the partners in these families are interested in building a new family unit and in raising children together, most of them have at least one child in the current marriage, thus creating a wide range of children's ages. The husband is expected to fulfill a parental role in respect to the wife's children, who are absorbed into the new unit. Twenty seven percent (N = 17) of the families in the current study were Invented type of stepfamilies. The L. family demonstrates the portrait of an Invented family (Figure 2).

The L. family moved into their apartment after the remarriage. The wife split with her first husband shortly after her daughter's birth and got divorced when the girl was three, after a marriage that lasted six years. A few months later she met her current husband, whom she married two years later, when the girl was five. The family scores below average on past orientation and on acceptance of difference. The stepfather's last name is the only name that appears on the mail box, in all the official papers, including the stepdaughter's registration in school. The mother initiated it, "in order not to raise questions," when the girl first started school and now the daughter follows through: she presents herself by her stepfather's last name, calls him "Dad" both at home and in front of others and he refers to her as "my oldest daughter," attends parent-teacher meetings in her school and regards her in a way similar to his attitude towards his biological younger daughters. The husband thinks that "when a man marries a mother, he must accept the child as his own. Any other kind of attitude disrupts the

FIGURE 2. The L. Family

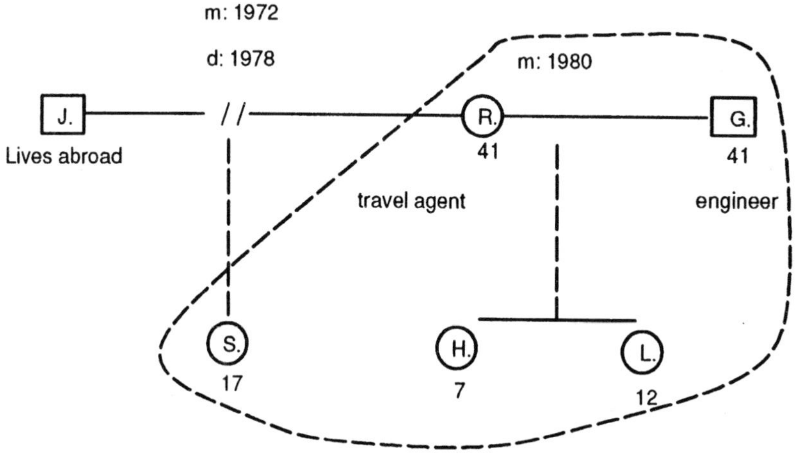

remarriage." The family never discusses past related issues and denies any comparison to the past: "what was is dead, as if it never existed." When the daughter from the wife's first marriage visits with her paternal grandmother, the two young girls go with her and refer to her as "grandma." Both spouses deny any difference between stepfamilies and intact families. Most of their friends, neighbors and colleagues do not know the wife is in a second marriage: "there is no reason for anybody to know. It's irrelevant and meaningless. There is nothing different about a remarried family. All children are treated equally with the same rights and chores. The oldest daughter sometimes feels she is deprived, but this is age-related and does not have anything to do with the family configuration." The couple minimizes the daughter's relationship with her natural father: "she is not really attached to him. She only takes advantage of him."

Imported families. These families function as if they are continuing the original family rather than creating a new family. Adults come together for the marital relationship and they are involved in raising each other's children as if they were born in the current marriage. The new family functions as a continuation of the previous marriage as if nothing had changed. They score below average in past orientation and in acceptance of difference, but less extremely than invented families. Their focal sub-system tends to be the spouse-relationship. The current family functions as a substitute of the original family, components of which are imported into the present, as if the unit remained the same, except some of the players have changed and the second husband accepts the role vacated by the first husband. Most families in this group do not have children in the remarriage and even though most husbands do not have their own children, they function as fathers to the wife's children, who become the children of the family. These families tend to have a small number of children (very often one child) within a limited age-range. A total of 33.3% (N = 21) of the families in the current study were imported. As this is a "mixed" portrait that includes components from both previous types and is similar to each of them in some aspects, it is more difficult to find a typical example. The F. family is an example of an Imported family (Figure 3).

The wife and her son moved into the husband's apartment. The husband was never married and relates to the son of his wife as his own: "Her child is now my child. He is our only son." The natural father spent time in jail because of financial crimes and is described as "irresponsible and unreliable," whereas the current husband "carries all the responsibilities of a husband and a father." Both spouses go to parent-teacher meetings and to events in school and both discipline the son. At the same time the husband

FIGURE 3. The F. Family

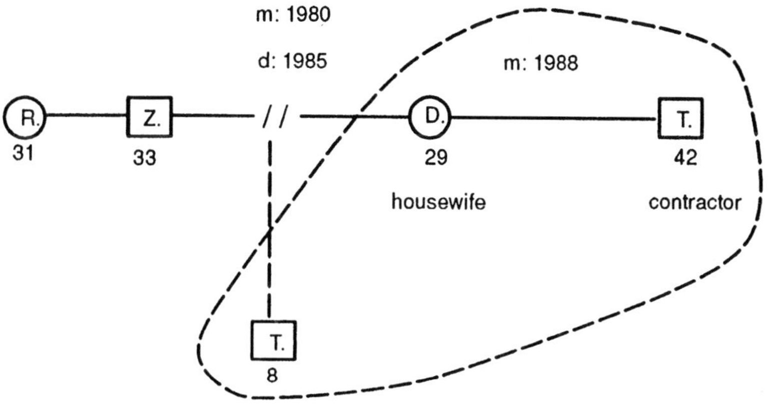

says, "I am more careful with him than I would have been with my natural child."

All family members, including the son from the wife's previous marriage, carry only the current last name everywhere, since "this is easier, makes things less complicated and prevents unnecessary questions." The only exception is that the child is registered in school in his natural father's last name, "because they would not allow us by law." The child himself introduces himself with both last names, refers to T. as his stepfather and calls him by his given name at home, and "Daddy" in public.

The family scores below average on past orientation and acceptance of difference. "The first marriage has been erased. The only things that remained are the child and the lesson learned."

The marital relationship is presented as the center of this family: "First is our marriage and then all the rest." Overtly, the husband is presented as the dominant figure, but at the same time he declares, "my wife always had a husband that was the sergeant major at home. I had no choice. I came into a pre-tailored role." The couple relationship is based on the model the wife "imported" from her previous marriage and the same basic roles are preserved in spite of the changes in casting.

Figure 4 presents the three types of families according to their profile.

Families in the three groups were compared by means of analysis of variance and proved to be similar in length of remarriage, education, perceived economic level, professions, ethnic origin, ages of spouses and living conditions. Analysis of variance was performed in order to study how families with different profiles compare in their degrees of satisfac-

FIGURE 4. Profiles of Stepfamilies

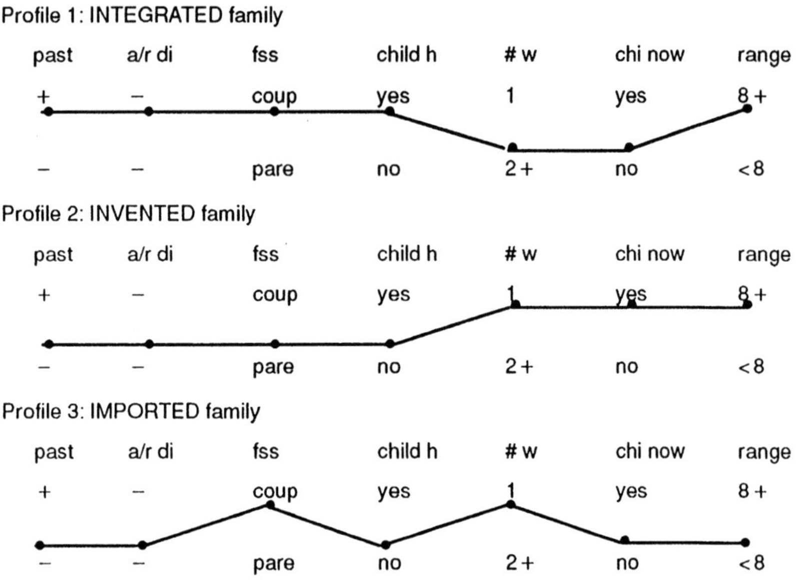

past = past orientation
a/r di = acceptance/rejection of difference: + high – low
fss = focal sub system: coup = marital, pare = parental
child h = husband's children from previous marriage
w = number of wife's children from previous marriage
chi now = children in current marriage
range = range of all children's ages

tion and functioning. Scores on the scale of satisfaction ranged from 38.5 to 69 (possible range: 15 to 75) and on functioning, 16 to 24 (possible range: 8 to 24). Variance analysis showed that families with different profiles do not differ from each other in degrees of satisfaction and functioning. Table 1 presents the distribution of the three groups in satisfaction and functioning.

Table 1 points to a possible difference between groups in satisfaction. The result seems to be almost statistically significant. One may wonder if in a larger group of subjects a significant difference will occur. In order to test this possibility Scheffe procedure was performed. Results indicated that no two groups are significantly different.

DISCUSSION

The findings of this study suggest several theoretical and practical implications. As the current sample is small and self-selected, the generalizability of the findings needs to be further validated in future research.

The major theoretical implication is suggesting that a differential perspective be adopted in future study of stepfamilies. Previous works focused on the study of differences between stepfamilies and intact families, emphasizing that it is important to understand and judge stepfamilies by criteria relevant to their unique features rather than in comparison to non-stepfamilies (Visher & Visher, 1988). This study takes the issue one step further and indicates that not only are stepfamilies different from intact families, but stepfamilies themselves may be of various types that differ from each other in major features. Most of the studies of stepfamilies dealt with them as one whole group, without systematic differentiation. In accordance with this view research questions tend to be general and refer to stepfamilies in general. For example: What is the dominant dyad in a remarried family after divorce? (Goetting, 1983); what are family process dynamics and coping behaviors which are associated with successful stepfamily life (Pill, 1990)? The current typology indicates that such a generalized approach neglects significant aspects of steplife.

Stepfamily theory and future research should focus on specific questions about specific types of stepfamilies. Furthermore, such research would explain some incongruencies and mixed findings in studies that approached stepfamilies as one homogenous group.

A differential, multi-dimensional and psychosocial empirically based typology of stepfamilies is strongly suggested. This is compatible with the

TABLE 1. Satisfaction and Functioning by Family Profile

	Hybrid Families (N = 25)	As If Families (N = 17)	Imported Families (N = 21)	Anova Results
Satisfaction*				
Mean	57.50	60.41	55.50	
SD	7.16	5.79	5.08	
				F = 2.985 p = .058
Satisfaction*				
Mean	20.76	21.00	21.48	
SD	2.24	2.50	2.16	
				F = .569 p = .57

*no two groups are significantly different at the .05 level

findings by Gross (1986), who in one of the few efforts to develop a typology of stepfamilies, asked 60 adolescents (aged 16 -18) from stepfamilies whom they considered to be members of their family. Based on their subjective perception, she developed a typology of four types of family structure: *Retention*–adolescents preserve the original family as the picture of their family; *Substitution*–adolescents considered the current family as their family with no reference to the past; *Reduction*–adolescents include only the living-in natural parent in their family perception; *Augmentation*–adolescents include all parent figures in their perception of the family. This typology is unidimensional and based on data from one family member–the adolescent. The typology in the current study is multi-dimensional, based on data from two informants and reflects adults' perspective. It yielded three "constructed types" of stepfamilies.

The importance of developing typologies as the basis for comparative analysis and for a comprehensive understanding of social phenomena has often been cited (e.g., Hughes, 1976). Since different types of stepfamilies were discovered, this study questions which of the common generalizations about stepfamilies are valid for each type of stepfamily. Most existing generalizations refer to "stepfamilies." The establishment of different types of stepfamilies raises the need to shape specific generalizations for different types of stepfamilies.

A second major implication of this study is, that contrary to common myth, stepfamilies are not necessarily unsatisfied or disfunctional. The mere fact that a family is remarried neither predicts nor explains low levels of satisfaction or of functioning. Furthermore, findings show that there are many ways to be a functioning and happy stepfamily, unlike the observation of Tolstoy that "All happy families are alike" (*Anna Karenina*).

The relative high degree/level of functioning and satisfaction of the research families is not surprising, considering a major inclusion criterion was non-clinical families. What is surprising is that the degree of satisfaction and functioning was found not to be associated with the profile of the family. It challenges the idea that there is one "correct" way to be a functional and satisfied stepfamily, namely, balanced between past and present orientation, between acceptance and rejection of difference, between marital dyad and parenthood.

This study is one step enroute to developing a differential understanding of stepfamilies. The full range of types of stepfamilies remains to be further studied from various members' perspectives. Additional issues that need to be addressed in future studies are "careers" of each type of stepfamily along the step life cycle as well as predictors for the specific type of stepfamily a given remarriage will become, as this study was done in one point of time and did not measure developmental issues, such as long-term effects of growing up in certain types of stepfamilies on child development. Applicability of the current findings, based on a self-selected group of subjects, to other groups of stepfamilies also remains to be addressed.

For practice there are two major implications. The first is the need to apply the principle of differential approach in treating stepfamilies. Programs, preventive and curative interventions and policy development must be based on understanding the unique needs and strengths of each type of stepfamily. For example, it is widely accepted that helping the remarried spouses develop a solid couple bond, validating the remarriage and having all other family members accept and integrate the ongoing existence of the couple are primary goals for intervention with remarried families. Findings of the current study raise the question if this is equally true for families of various types. Assessment of the type of the stepfamily is indicated prior to setting goals for intervention and to determining how to intervene. In order to enable clinicians to perform such an assessment, appropriate instruments are needed. Current surveys of existing assessment tools for families indicate the scarcity of such instruments (Ahrons & Rodgers, 1987; Touliatos et al., 1990). The findings of this study yield guidelines for the development of such instruments. They indicate that evaluation of a stepfamily should measure the number of children each spouse brings from the previous marriage, the existence of children in the remarriage, the duration of the current marriage, past orientation, acceptance/rejection of difference and focal subsystem. The scale that was developed in this research for the evaluation of past orientation proved to have a solid reliability. Its applicability to clinical usage needs to be tested in further studies. The scale for the evaluation of acceptance/rejection of difference needs to be elaborated, improved and tested again before its application to clinical usage. Measurement of the focal subsystem was the least developed in this study and appropriate instruments to evaluate this dimension need to be further developed.

The second implication for practice is the need of helping professionals to normalize different ways of dealing with the unique issues of stepfamilies and to adopt a broader perspective of what is normative for stepfamilies. Principles for counseling with stepfamilies need to be reconsidered. Findings in this study, in accordance with studies by Kurdek (1989) and Pill (1990), question the assumption that stepfamilies who do not accept their difference and do not leave space for past related issues in their present may be at risk and non-functional (Sager et al., 1983; Zucker-Anderson & White, 1986; Papernow, 1987; Bradt & Bradt, 1988; Carter &

McGoldrick, 1990). This may be true for certain types of stepfamilies, but not for others.

Consequently, in counseling with stepfamilies, workers need to recognize the existence of various functional types of stepfamilies, educate members of stepfamilies about this and validate various modes of coping, in order to help them feel relief and ease the burden of guilt many of them feel for not complying to one allegedly functional type of stepfamily. It is important to help people understand that they do not have to comply with one specific model and they may choose a way which is appropriate and tailored to their own needs and to what they feel works for them.

Both implications are still too general to be useful clinically in their current form and they should be used as a directive indication of a potentially fruitful direction for further exploration, rather than a fully-developed clinically applicable means.

REFERENCES

Ahrons, C.R. & Rodgers, H.R., (1987). *Divorced families*. N.Y.: Norton.

Booth, A. & Edwards, J.N., (1992). Starting over: Why remarriages are more unstable. *Family Issues,* 13(2), 123-141.

Bradt, J.O. & Bradt-Moynihan. C., (1988). Resources for remarried families. In M.A. Karpel (ed.), *Family resources*. N.Y.: Guilford.

Carter, B. & McGoldrick, M., (eds.), (1990). *The changing family life cycle*. Boston: Allyn & Bacon.

Draper, T.W. & Marcos, A.C., (1990). *Family variables*. Newbury Park: Sage.

Goetting, A., (1983). The relative strength of the husband-wife and parent-child dyads in remarriage: A test of the Hsu Model. *Journal of Comparative Family Studies,* 14(1), 117-129.

Gross, P., (1986). Defining post divorce remarriage families: A typology based on the subjective perceptions of children. *Journal of Divorce,* 10 (1-2), 205-217.

Hartin, N.W., (1990). Remarriage: Some issues for clients and therapists. *Australian & New Zealand Journal of Family Therapy,* 11(1), 36-42.

Hodder, E. (1985). The stepfamily: An introduction to its problems. *Journal of the Royal Society of Medicine,* 78, sup. 8.

Hughes, J.A., (1976). *Sociological analysis: Methods of discovery*. London: Nelson.

Kaslow, F.M., (1986). *Remarriage*. A workshop in the fifth International Congress of Family Therapy, Jerusalem.

Kaslow, F.M., (1988). Remarried couples: The architects of stepfamilies. *Family Therapy Collections,* 25, 33-47.

Kirk, D., (1964). *Shared fate*. N.Y.: Free Press.

Kirk, D., (1981). *Adoptive kinship*. Toronto: Butterworth.

Kurdek, L.A., (1989). Relationship quality for newly married husbands and wives: Marital history, stepchildren, and individual-difference predictors. *Journal of Marriage and the Family,* 51, November, 1053-1064.

Lavee, Y., McCubbin, H. & Olson, D., (1987). The double ABCX model of family stress and adaptation: An empirical test by analysis of structural latent variables. *Journal of Marriage and the Family,* 7, 811-825.

Lin, S.L., (1990). Changes in reproductive function among remarried women: The effects of spousal characteristics. *Sociological Perspectives,* 33(4), 501-516.

Marsiglio, W., (1992). Stepfathers with minor children living at home: Parenting perceptions and relationship quality. *Family Issues,* 13(2), 195-214.

Olson, D., Sprendlie, D. & Russel, C., (1979). Circumplex model of marital and family systems: Cohesion and adaptability dimensions, family type and clinical application. *Family Process,* 18, 3-28.

Olson, D. & Wilson, M., (1982). Family satisfaction. In D. Olson, H.I. McCubbin, A. Larsen, A. Muxen & M. Wilson (eds.), *Family inventories.* Minnesota: Family Social Science.

Papernow, L.P., (1987). Thickening the 'middle ground': Dilemmas and vulnerabilities of remarried couples. *Psychotherapy,* 24 (35), 130-139.

Pill, C.J., (1990). Stepfamilies: Redefining the family. *Family Relations,* 39, 186-193.

Rumelhart, D.E. & Zipser, D., (1985). Feature discovery by competitive learning. *Cognitive Science,* 9, 75-122.

Sager, C.J., Brown, H.S., Crohn, H.M. & Engel, T., (1983). *Treating remarried families.* N.Y.: Brunner/Mazel.

Sluzki, C.E., (1983). Process, structure and world view: Towards an integrated view of systemic models in family therapy. *Family Process,* 22, 469-476.

Touliatos, J., Perlutter, B.F. & Straus, M.A., (eds.), (1990). *Handbook of family measurement techniques.* Newbury Park: Sage.

Visher, E.B. & Visher, J.S., (1988). *Old loyalties, new ties.* N.Y.: Brunner/Mazel.

Wolpert-Lur, A. & Bross, A., (1982). The formation of the reconstituted family system: Processes, problems and treatment goals. In A. Bross & P. Papp, (eds.), *Family therapy.* N.Y.: Methuen.

Zucker-Anderson, J. & White, G.D., (1986). An empirical investigation of interaction and relationship patterns in functional and dysfunctional nuclear families and stepfamilies. *Family Process,* 25, 407-422.

Role Strain Prediction in Stepfamilies

Marie-Christine Saint-Jacques

SUMMARY. This article reports the existence of role strain prediction factors identified in stepfamilies. The data was collected from 162 individuals divided into 84 families reconstituted following a divorce. This sample applies to parents as well as stepparents. The principal results of this study revealed that the most important role strain prediction factor for the parents in a stepfamily is the competition between the children and the new spouse. As for the stepparents, a low level of consensus in relation to the parent's way of raising the children is the strongest prediction variable. Finally, the most significant prediction factor for individuals assuming a role of both parent and stepparent is a very high degree of consensus on the way in which the spouse, parent of the children, assumes his role of parent. *[Article copies available from The Haworth Document Delivery Service: 1-800-342-9678.]*

For the past twenty years, there has been a major change in the family life patterns. This change first showed itself in the increasing number of single-parent families and, recently, the appearance of stepfamilies. The dynamics and specific difficulties of this new family type gave rise to a series of essays

---

Marie-Christine Saint-Jacques is Research Associate at the Centre de Recherche sur les Services Communautaires, 2446, Pavillon De-Koninck, Cité Universitaire, Université Laval, Sainte-Foy, Québec, Canada, G1K 7P4, which funded the translation of this paper. The author is pursuing a PhD in Sciences Humaines Appliquées at Université de Montréal.

Marie-Christine Saint-Jacques completed this study for her master dissertation at Université Laval. Jacques Vachon, PhD, chaired this research.

[Haworth co-indexing entry note]: "Role Strain Prediction in Stepfamilies." Saint-Jacques, Marie-Christine. Co-published simultaneously in *Journal of Divorce & Remarriage* (The Haworth Press, Inc.) Vol. 24, No. 1/2, 1995, pp. 51-72; and: *Understanding Stepfamilies: Their Structure and Dynamics* (ed: Craig A. Everett) The Haworth Press, Inc., 1995, pp. 51-72. Single or multiple copies of this article are available from The Haworth Document Delivery Service [1-800-342-9678, 9:00 a.m. - 5:00 p.m. (EST)].

and scientific work on the subject (Hetherington & Arasteh, 1988; Hutchinson et al., 1989; Boisgelot, 1989; Pasley & Ihinger-Tallman, 1989; Glick, 1989; Whitsett & Land, 1992). But despite the increasing interest in the stepfamilies, they still remain a family structure that is not well-known. However, it appears from the research carried out up to now that this type of family leads to specific difficulties, for which causes remain obscure. Knaub et al. (1984) stress that the researchers have often tried to describe, define, and analyze the conflicts and problems inherent in a stepfamily's lifestyle. These authors add that there is: "One theme predominant in the stepfamily literature; those embarking on this family lifestyle should be prepared for problems" (p. 42). This stance, which is rather opposed to what is usually said when examining literature about nuclear families, reflects well enough the idea, frequently conveyed, that there is a sense of disquiet in stepfamilies.

It appears from the work carried out in this field that the establishment of a stepfamily is a stressful process (Goldstein, 1974) and it intensifies the conflicts and the strains while creating new ones (Duberman, 1973; Fine & Schwebel, 1991). The absence of norms and well-defined roles would also contribute to the complexity of a stepfamily's running and process adjustment (Cherlin, 1978; Wilson et al., 1975; Clingempeel et al., 1984-b; Furstenberg & Spanier, 1984-a). The fostering of unrealistic expectations from the family members is added to the absence of norms (Duberman, 1975; Cuerrier, 1982; Stollman, 1985; Germain, 1986).

So when it was noted that a stepfamily's lifestyle is characterized by an undoubted complexity which leads the members to be battling with difficulties in assuming their roles, the role strain matter was chosen to be explored. This variable seems to be quite relevant in the study of stepfamilies since it reflects a reality of life in this type of family: the difficulty of knowing how to behave when there are neither norms nor patterns. More precisely, this study focused on the family role strain within stepfamilies. This is a concept that has been rarely investigated in the field of family studies since the researchers, when studying the family role strain, mostly tried to measure the impact of variables on the role strain such as women breaking into the labour market (Anderson-Kulman, 1986) or men's involvement in domestic chores.

With this study, three objectives are to be reached: assessing the role strain degree which couples from stepfamilies go through, identifying factors that are related to it, and finally, managing to predict this strain. This article's aim is to present the three role strain prediction models that have been developed.

CONCEPTUAL FRAMEWORK

The notion of role strain allows the researchers to measure a dimension of the role phenomenon. It has been defined by Goode (1960), its initiator, as "the felt difficulty in fulfilling role obligations" (p. 483). However, this concept is distinguished from fear, anxiety or stress by virtue of which it is generated by the role assumed by a person (Biddle & Thomas, 1966). Role strain has also been modified because of its use in empirical research. This element has contributed to the development of operational definitions and the subdivision of that concept in variables which measure specific dimensions of role strain such as sex role strain (Snarey et al., 1986, Blackwell, 1984) and family role strain (Katz & Piotrkowski, 1983). In this study, that concept will refer to the difficulties in fulfilling family roles (Katz & Piotrkowski, 1983, p. 331).

The theoretical model of role strain provides a large number of concepts which allow its explanation (Goode, 1960; Burr et al., 1979; Pearlin, 1983). However, since it was not possible to retain all those concepts, only the most relevant ones for the study of stepfamilies have been kept. Thus, according to the point of view of several authors (Fast & Cain, 1966; Wilson et al., 1975; Clingempeel et al., 1984-a; Giles-Sims, 1987) who have pointed out that the role of a parent and, even more, the role of a stepparent in stepfamilies is characterized by the absence of norms and models which leads to some confusion about fulfilling one's role, the clarity of expectations and the consensus as regards the parent and the stepparent's expectations have been studied, since the absence of institutionalized norms has an impact on the clarity of a person's expectations. However, the clarity of these expectations is not sufficient; there must be a consensus about what they should be (Fast & Cain, 1966).

Moreover, another specific feature of the position of stepparent that is always due to the absence of norms and models is the role that the stepparent will decide or have to assume (Robert & Price, 1987). Thus, this idea refers to the concept of role prescription and is known as leading to role strain.

Now, under the consideration of the role of the parent in a stepfamily, it is noted that he occupies a central position, at least at the beginning of the marriage, since the parent is the one who links the new spouse to the children (Visher & Visher, 1979). Thus, a competition between the stepparent and the children for the love and attention of the parent can develop. Such a situation can lead to role conflict for the parent. Besides, that role conflict can carry strain since the roles already conflicting are as important (Pearlin, 1983).

A last element which characterizes the stepfamily is the complexity of that lifestyle, due to the large number of persons it involves and the fact of having to reunite two families with different lifestyles. Therefore, it would have been relevant to measure the overload of role for those persons because this concept can carry role strain (Van Meter & Agronow, 1982; Katz & Piotrkowski, 1983). However, since that subject could have been the object of a research in itself and in order to stay within the limits of feasability, only an indicator of the overload of role, that is the sharing of family duties by the couple, has been studied.

So, from observations made in the review of literature and the previous theoretical framework, five hypotheses have been formulated: (1) The more the parental and conjugal expectations between the stepparent and the parent are clearly perceived, the lower is the role strain degree; (2) The higher is the degree of parental consensus between the stepparent and the parent, the lower is the role strain degree; (3) The presence (versus the absence) of role prescription for the stepparent is associated with a higher degree of role strain; (4) The presence (versus the absence) of conflict for the parent is associated with a higher degree of role strain; (5) An equal division (versus unequal) of family duties between the spouses is associated with a lower degree of role strain. The first four hypotheses have been confirmed. However, the fifth hypothesis has been rejected. On that subject it appeared that it is not the division of the duties that affects role strain, but the satisfaction felt when faced with such a sharing. Thus, from these hypotheses and other control variables, the models of role strain prediction have been developed as follows.

METHODOLOGY

Subjects

The subjects are members of stepfamilies and, more specifically, biological parents and their spouses who are in the position of stepparent. The final sample is composed of 162 individuals divided into 84 different families. It includes as many men (81) as women (81) from 23 to 59 years of age. Most of them (80%) are presently common-law spouses and were separated (de facto or legal: 23%) or divorced (36%) when the remarriage took place. Moreover, 85% have a job (51% in professional and managing duties). This is reflected in the income level, since 63% of the respondents have a family income equal or superior to $50,000 per year.[1]

Data Collection

Considering the specific features of the population, it was not possible to use a probability sample method. So, in order to identify the stepfamilies likely to accept to participate in this study, the collaboration of an important School Commission was requested and obtained. It was then possible to contact the parents of 3,799 children attending twelve elementary schools. This first step allowed identifying 238 individuals divided up into 119 stepfamilies who accepted to take part in the study. Once the stepfamilies had been identified, the data collecting consisted in dispatching the research questionnaire to the parents who had agreed to take part in the study. Each spouse received his questionnaire, in a separate envelope addressed to each of them personally. It is important to mention that the instructions given to the respondents at the beginning of the questionnaire insisted on the importance of completing the questionnaire by themselves. This notice was intended to minimize the risks of contagion between the spouses. Furthermore, in order to check their respect for those instructions, 5% of the respondents have been called in order to collect their comments about the questionnaire. Those contacts allowed the researchers to assess, as precisely as possible, that the respondents conformed themselves well enough to the beginning instructions. All the couples who had not returned their questionnaires in time for the deadline received a phone call.

Instrument

The instrument of data collecting which was developed in this study was a self-rating questionnaire. It consisted of 35 closed, open or multiple-choice questions and was divided into three different parts. The first part was about general information on the family most of which were control variables. The second part was composed of questions measuring the role strain and the different independent variables. Finally, the last part of the questionnaire was composed of sociodemographic information. It is important to note that the two scales making up the instrument were submitted to a verification of their internal consistency. It appears from this analysis that the role strain scale obtained a Cronbach coefficient of 0.66 and the consensus scale obtained a Cronbach coefficient of 0.87.

Before it was administered to the subjects, the collecting instrument was validated by four experts and five individuals with the same features as this study's sample. The modifications brought to the pretest were essentially about the clarification of a few questions and the instructions given to the respondents.

Statistical Analysis

Once the questionnaires were returned, the collected data was coded for data processing. The content analysis of the open questions was made in order to create analysis categories that would be exhaustive, exclusive, homogeneous and relevant with the idea of giving an account of the obtained material. These categories have been coded for data processing. The data capture was done with the StatPac software, version 6.0 (Walonik, 1986), while the analyses have been carried out with the SAS/STAT software (1988). The coding, as well as keyboarding, were subjected to appropriate verifications. The data file appearing free from errors, the data analysis itself began.

The multivariate analysis allowed the researchers to reach the goal of the study which was to examine the combined effect of several independent and control variables on the family role strain. More specifically, a combination of variables had to be determined: some variables, which were put in interaction, allowed the researchers to reduce as precisely as possible the error in the dependent variable value prediction. To do so and considering the dependent variable's nature (which is numerical), the multiple regression analysis was used.

The independent and control variables which were to be included in the models were determined from correlation and contingency coefficients. Thus, every examined relation that demonstrated a force of association $\geq$ to .20 were first kept. It must also be noted that category variables that were to be included in the model have been changed to dummy variables. The stepwise method of multiple regression was used in order to determine which independent and control variables were to be kept in the model, that is, those that present the best prediction value. It must also be noted that the confidence line that was kept in the multiple regression is weaker than the one which is usually kept, since it is at $p. \leq .15$. It is the line that is commonly accepted in this type of analysis (SAS/STAT, 1988). Finally, several statistical tests have been applied in order to verify the appropriateness of the three models (studies of residuals, multicollinearity and studentized residuals). All these verifications enabled the researchers to conclude that the models are suitable.

RESULTS

Three models of role strain prediction were applied to the parents, the stepparents, and the individuals of this study. Table 1 shows all the variables submitted to the stepwise procedure.[2]

This procedure enabled the researchers to select some variables for the final models. Among the variables that were kept following this procedure, one variable was excluded all the same: the satisfaction as regards the sharing of tasks. Although this variable complies with the probability level fixed at p. ≤ .15, the fact that a large number of individuals had not answered this question resulted in the elimination of several respondents from the analysis.

Role Strain Prediction Model for the Parents

Table 2 shows the final step of the multiple regression model intending to predict family role strain for the parents. The variables are presented according to their order of importance. The first variable is the one which predicts the larger proportion of variance in role strain and so on.

TABLE 1. Variables Submitted to the Stepwise Procedure

Model 1 **Parent**	Model 2 **Stepparent**	Model 3 **Individual assuming the two roles**
Clarity of conjugal expectations	Clarity of conjugal expectations	All the variables presented in the two previous columns
Clarity of parental expectations	Clarity of expectations as regards the role of stepparent	
Conjugal consensus	Conjugal consensus	
Consensus on the role to be assumed by the stepparent	Consensus on the role to be assumed by the parent	
Consensus on the stepparent's way to raise the children	Consensus on the parent's way to raise the children	
Consensus on the spouse's way to raise the children of the present marriage	Clarity of the stepparent's authority role	
Scale of consensus as regards different family themes	Clarity of the stepparent's affective role	
Competition between the stepparent and the children (role conflict)	Scale of consensus as regards different family themes	
Satisfaction as regards the sharing of tasks	Motivation to assume a stepparent's role (prescription)	
Respondent's sex	Satisfaction as regards the sharing of tasks	
Type of stepfamily	Sex	
Number of children from 12 to 16 years of age	Type of stepfamily	
	Number of children from 12 to 16 years of age	

TABLE 2. Role Strain Prediction Model for the Parents

Rank	Variables	Beta (B) Coef.	(r^2p) Coef.	p.	C.I. 95%
1	Competition between the stepparent and the children	3.58	0.30	0.0001	(1.90, 5.26)
2	Very high level of consensus on the stepparent's way to raise the children	−2.05	0.06	0.0474	(−4.05, −0.01)
3	Presence of 2 children 12-16 years of age	3.28	0.06	0.0321	(0.29, 6.27)
4	Conjugal expectations frequently clear	−1.40	0.03	0.1276	(−3.22, 0.42)
N = 47 R^2 = .450 adj. R^2 = .398 significance level = 0.0001					

It is noted that the presence of competition between the stepparent and the children (role conflict) occupies the first place in the association with role strain after the other variables are known. There is a partial correlation R^2p. of .30. This means that the presence of competition allows a reduction of the error in a proportion of 30% in the role strain variance prediction when that factor is associated with all the other factors included in the model. Furthermore, the analysis of the Beta coefficient (3.58) shows that the presence of competition tends to increase role strain (because the Beta coefficient is positive).

Thus, parents who detect competition between their children and their spouse will get a higher score on the role strain scale than parents who do not (even though they are alike for all the other variables).

At the theoretical level, competition refers to role conflict. On that subject, it is interesting to recall the opinion of Pearlin (1983) who mentioned that the principal mean to counter role conflict is to establish priorities inside the different roles. Now, the family circle is where the separation of roles is most subtle. For instance, while it is possible to give greater place to one's family life than one's professional life, the situation gets more complicated when it is about establishing a priority between one's role of spouse and of parent.

Moreover, establishing priorities between family roles becomes even more real inside stepfamilies, when the "normal" cycle of family life is modified. The individuals become a couple at the same time as becoming parents. Thus, the adults must adjust themselves to married life, make the adaptation to that new lifestyle easier for the children, and develop a relation between the stepparent and the children. The stepparent might feel misplaced near his spouse and the children might be afraid of losing the parent's love and attention. All that might lead to competition between the stepparent and the children which has the effect of placing the parent in a position leading to role conflict. His only choice is trying to be fair with everyone and to reassure them as to the love he feels for them. Besides, this is what the respondents in the study said they did.

Still, those parents are subject to a great strain that was the most important prediction factor in the increase in role strain for those individuals. This result is very much like the ones that Anderson-Kulman (1986) obtained. Although his study was carried out in intact families, it appears that, this time, the presence of conflicts between the role of worker and mother was an important factor of role strain felt by those women.

The second variable included in this model is the presence of a very high consensus level (opposed to any other consensus level) about the stepparent's way to raise the children.[3] However, it is important to note that the impact of this variable, as well as the impact of the following ones, is proportionally less important since the value of the R^2p. is equal to .06. Thus, this variable allows for the reduction of 6% of the error of prediction in the role strain variance. Moreover, it results in a decrease in role strain since the Beta value is negative (B = -2.05).

Thus, on that point, the theoretical proposition formulated by Goode (1960) is confirmed. According to Pearlin (1983), role strain appears when one of the spouses considers that the other failed in fulfilling expectations as regards the role performance expected from him. Thus, in this case, the fact that the parent agrees totally with the stepparent's way to raise the children leads this parent to consider his spouse as answering to what is expected from him. Such a perception enables us to predict a decrease in role strain for the parent.

The results obtained in this study are very much like those of Van Meter and Agronow (1982). Their study had shown that the degree of agreement between the couple has an important impact on role strain. It is also possible to draw a parallel between these results and those obtained by Pasley et al. (1984) even if the notion of consensus that these authors have put forward is different from this study's. In their study on happy remarriages versus unhappy ones and the different styles of consensus, they observed that the majority of happily remarried couples had a convergent perception of the degree of agreement between them on several subjects.

Besides, these authors report that the marital consensus is usually considered as a basic dimension of marital relations. The results that were obtained here allow us to believe that a convergent perception not only has a positive impact on marital relation but also on role strain felt by an individual.

The third variable to appear is the presence of two children of 12 to 16 years of age. This variable has the same prediction value as the previous one (R^2p. = .06). However, it contributes to predicting an increase in role strain for the parents (B = 3.28). One may wonder why the presence of two children from this age category leads to an increase in role strain while the presence of three or more does not. This is explained by the fact that among the respondents of this study, only one family has more than two children from 12 to 16 years of age, which is certainly not sufficient to include this variable in the model.

A higher degree of difficulty in stepfamilies with teenagers has also been observed in other studies (Clingempeel et al., 1987; Hobart, 1988) which showed that a less positive relation tends to appear between the stepparent and the children when the children are teenagers. At that age, the development stage leads the youth to the search for affirmation and opposition and that makes relations even more difficult. Moreover, according to Hobart (1988), a teenager's "difficult" behaviour is naturally more accepted by a biological parent than by a stepparent. Thus, it is not surprising that the presence of teenagers in stepfamilies results in a raise of the role strain degree for these families.

Finally, it can be seen in Table 2 that when marital expectations are "very often clear," it slightly contributes to prediction of role strain. This contribution is said to be slight because the presence of this variable does not allow the researchers to reduce to more than 3% (R^2p. = .03) the error in the prediction of role strain variance. The presence of this variable tends to lead to a decrease in role strain (B = − 1.40). One must also be careful as regards this variable since, as the reader might have noticed, when the interval of confidence is viewed, it includes the zero interval (−3.22 to 0.42 degrees). It means that the examined relation could reverse, not leading to a decrease but to an increase in role strain. However, the relation might become null, which is more likely, that is, the dummy variable no longer has any effect on role strain. This type of situation occurs when the significance degree which is used is below .056. However, this variable has been kept since it increases noticeably the model value.

This result corresponds to the theoretical proposition of Goode (1960). It appears that the more an individual has a clear perception of what is expected from him in a role, the less he will feel strain. Moreover, it seems that for the persons solely assuming a role of parent, the clarity of expectations applied to the role of spouse is the most deciding factor.

However, one may ask why the marital level, and not the clarity of expectations related to a role of parent, is so important. On this subject, the work of Roberts and Price (1987) allows the researchers to think of a hypothesis. From the interviews carried out with mothers living in stepfamilies, it appears that these mothers view their actual family as being characterized by their own experience and the lack of experience of their spouse. It is then permitted to think that in a parental position, the parent may feel more confident since it is not a new role for him and the fact of not knowing what the spouse expects from him is more or less important. In contrast, the marital relation is all new. The parent might need to know more about what is expected from him in his spouse role since this aspect of the relation is the one which is all new.

This model might be considered as moderately effective since it allows us to reduce the error to 40% in the variance prediction observed in role strain felt by the parents in stepfamilies. Other variables which were not included in this study are thus responsible for the creation of role strain for the parents. Moreover, the study of residuals of this model including 47 subjects enables the researchers to say that it was very relevant since it was allowed to predict 40% of the variance of role strain for 46 respondents out of 47.

Role Strain Prediction Model for Stepparents

The second role strain prediction model which was developed includes individuals who play a role of stepparent and is composed of six variables. As it can be noted by the reader in Table 3, a low level of consensus on the parent's way to raise the children is the variable that provides the strongest variation of role strain for stepparents. This variable allows the researchers to reduce to 40% (R^2p. = 0.41) the error in the prediction of role strain degree felt by stepparents. It must be noted that only one person among all the respondents reported a very low consensus degree and that explains why a very low consensus degree on this theme does not appear in the model. On this theme, a low level of consensus tends to raise the level of role strain since the Beta value is positive (B = 3.94).

It is interesting to note that when the stepparent often disagrees with the parent as regards the ways to raise the children, the role strain for the stepparent will increase. The matter of children's education inside stepfamilies seems to be very important since the same element was brought up by the parents.

Second, the fact that the conjugal expectations are "very frequently clear" allows the researchers to reduce the error to 15% (R^2p. = .15) in the

TABLE 3. Role Strain Prediction Model for Stepparents

Rank	Variables	Beta (B) Coef.	(r^2p) Coef.	p.	C.I. 95%
1	A low level of consensus on the parent's way to raise the children	3.94	0.41	0.0108	(1.01, 6.86)
2	Conjugal expect. frequently clear	−3.42	0.15	0.0011	(−5.31, −1.53)
3	More or less frequent consensus as regards conjugal expectations	5.55	0.08	0.0005	(2.73, 8.37)
4	Presence of 2 children of 12-16 years of age	6.45	0.07	0.0011	(2.90, 10.0)
5	Conjugal expect. sometimes clear	6.79	0.07	0.0002	(3.63, 9.95)
6	Expect. as regards stepparent's role sometimes clear	−4.25	0.06	0.0050	(−7.07, −1.43)

N = 29 R^2 = .854 adj. R^2 = .815 significance level = 0.0001

variance prediction of role strain. This variable's presence tends to create a decrease in the strain score for the stepparent (B = −3.42).

Thus the questions of conjugal nature seem to be as important in the role strain prediction for stepparents. Because the fact that the conjugal expectations are "very frequently clear" predicts a decrease in role strain for the stepparents, while when they are "sometimes clear," there is an increase in strain for these individuals. Once again, Goode's theoretical model (1960) is confirmed.

A more or less frequent consensus as regards conjugal expectations (R^2p. = .08), the presence of two 12-16 year-old children and the fact that expectations are sometimes clear (R^2p. = .07) are respectively in 3rd, 4th and 5th position in the model. These variables all contribute to create an increase in role strain (B_3 = 5.55, B_4 = 6.45 and B_5 = 6.79).

Finally, the fact that expectations from the role of stepparent are sometimes clear slightly contributes to reduce the error of role strain prediction (R^2p. = .06). This variable tends to create a decrease in role strain (B = −4.25). A last factor of role strain prediction for these individuals is the fact that the expectations from their role of stepparent are "more or less" clear. Besides, it is important to note that this intermediate position contributes to predict a decrease in role strain.

The last result seems difficult to explain. Because it would have been more logical for such a position to predict an increase in role strain or at least not to predict anything. This result brings the necessity of carrying on with the understanding of role strain in stepfamilies. The hypothesis that a third factor that has not been studied here might have adjusted the observed relation could be brought up.

This model of family role strain prediction for stepparents is very effective because the examination of the adjusted R^2 value shows that this model allows the researchers to predict 82% of role strain variance for these individuals from the knowledge of other variables of the model. It is permitted to assert that there are few non-examined variables in this study that could contribute to the variation of role strain for these persons since hardly 18% of role strain variance could not be explained with this model.

Moreover, the examination of these residuals showed that the model has been appropriate to predict the role strain score for 28 stepparents out of 29 in a confidence interval of 95%.

Model of Role Strain Prediction for Respondents in a Role of Parent and Stepparent

The last developed regression model's goal was to predict family role strain for respondents assuming a double status, that is, being a parent and a stepparent. This model is composed of five variables (Table 4).

The variable which is the more closely associated with role strain variance is the presence of a "very frequent" consensus as regards the expectations of the role of parent because this variable allows the researchers to reduce the error of role strain prediction of 21% (R^2p. = .21). Thus, there is a decrease in the score on the role strain scale for the respondents who are both a parent and a stepparent and who detect a "very frequent" consensus as regards conjugal expectations (compared to those who do not have this perception).

The second variable to be included in the model is once again the consensus as regards expectations of the role of parent but, this time, to a different degree. The presence of a "frequent" consensus as regards expectations of the role of parent allows the researchers to reduce the error of prediction in role strain variance of 17% (R^2p. = .17). This variable also tends to make the dependent variable decrease (B = −2.23). Thus, it is permitted to conclude that a "frequent" and a "very frequent" consensus as regards the role of parent contributes to make the family role strain

TABLE 4. Model of Role Strain Prediction for Respondents Who Are a Parent and a Stepparent

Rank	Variables	Beta (B) Coef.	(r^2p) Coef.	p.	C.I. 95%
1	Very frequent consensus as regards expect. of the parent's role	−3.82	0.21	0.0001	(−5.56, −2.08)
2	Frequent consensus as regards expect. of the parent's role	2.23	0.17	0.0059	(−3.81, −0.67)
3	Low level of consensus on the stepparent's way to raise the children	3.18	0.06	0.0073	(0.89, 5.47)
4	Competition between the stepparent and the children	1.36	0.05	0.0429	(0.05, 2.69)
5	Stepparent's clear perception of his role of authority for the children	−1.54	0.04	0.0432	(−3.03, −0.05)
N = 60 R^2 = .529 adj. R^2 = .485 significance level = 0.0001					

decrease in contrast with other degrees of consensus which do not seem to reduce the error of prediction in the variance of the dependent variable.

In the third place of this model, there is the presence of a "low" consensus on the stepparent's way to raise the spouse's children (R^2p. = .06). The presence of this variable creates a raise of the role strain score (B = 3.18). The model could not include the variance explained by an even lower level of consensus since this situation could only apply to 3% of the respondents of this study. In contrast, higher degrees of consensus do not seem to affect the role strain variance for these persons since no dummy variable measuring these degrees has been included in the model.

It is important to keep in mind that the three factors of prediction which were previously introduced predict role strain for the persons playing a double role but that they reach them in their position of parent. In contrast, the two last factors of role strain prediction of this model reach the same persons, but in their position of stepparent.

Competition between the stepparent and the children predicts role strain for the persons playing a double role (R^2p. = .05) and tends, as in the first model, to increase role strain (B = 1.36).

The fact that the stepparent clearly perceives his role of authority as regards the spouse's children is the last variable to be included in the model (R^2p. = .04). This variable results in a decrease in role strain (B = − 1.54).

This result is not surprising since the notion of expectations clarity constantly came up in the different stages of analysis when the stepparent's role was taken up. As many authors mentioned (Ahrons & Wallisch, 1987; Whitsett & Land, 1992), the role of stepparent, more than any other, is characterized by the absence of definition and model, and it results in a confusion for the persons occupying this status. Moreover, a longitudinal study which was carried out by Guisinger et al. (1989) and notably revolving around the satisfaction of couples as regards their second marriage brought out that the ability of the couple to face the ambiguity of the roles of a remarried parent and the stepmother is an important factor of prediction of the satisfaction as regards the union. Thus, it seems that several of the factors that are associated with marital satisfaction are also associated with role strain.

In other respects, several authors (Goldstein, 1974; Duberman, 1975) stressed that one of the difficulties of the role of stepfather is linked to the fact that he usually does not hold all the prerogatives of the role of parent. More precisely, this position is characterized by the lack of authority to act as a "parent." Within the context of this study, the degree of authority held by the stepfather has not been measured as such. However, whatever the extent of this power, it appears that when one clearly perceives the limits of it, role strain is decreased. Finally, even if literature is almost solely about the matter of the stepparent's authority as regards the situation of stepfathers, it is believed that the same stakes are applied to the situation of stepmothers, especially since the responsibility of taking action with the children is even more assigned to women.

The ability of this regression model to reduce the error of prediction of role strain variance for the persons playing a role of parent and stepparent is 49%. As in the first model, it appears that other variables which are not present in this study contribute to predict role strain for these persons.

In other respects, the study of residuals showed that this model was appropriate to predict (still with a confidence interval of 95%) the variance of family role strain in 57 cases out of 60. Thus, it appears to be a fairly predictive model but a relevant one.

Although the number of persons included in a model affects its ability of prediction, the developed model for stepparents is still far from being the most effective.

Otherwise, one must not minimize too much the importance of the two other models because the ability to identify the most predictive factors of a phenomenon fits in with a relatively high level of knowledge. When the fact that, up to now, no study has tried to predict this strain for this population is taken into account, one must consider the results that were obtained in the three models as a basic description that seems interesting.[4] Moreover, it is necessary to apply these three models to a more important sample in order to examine the validity more closely.

Similarities and Differences of the Three Configurations of Factors of Family Role Strain Prediction

Although the three developed models are directed at individuals with different roles in the family, they all still live inside the same family structure and they share several roles. It explains some similarities that can be noted in the configuration of factors of role strain prediction for the three statuses. It is noted that a degree of consensus as regards the spouse's way to raise the children or assume his role of stepparent is a deciding factor for all the respondents of this study whatever their status. It is also noted that the clarity of conjugal expectations is important for role strain variance as much for parents as for stepparents but not for the persons assuming the two roles. It is the same as regards the impact of the presence of two teenagers in the family.

In other respects, the differences are seen when the degree of the clarity of expectations is examined. This factor seems to be more deciding in the situation of stepparent than in the parent's. This observation agrees with the consulted literature which brings out many times the specific stakes linked to the role of stepparent because of the absence of definitions and models that could guide the action of these persons. Moreover, the presence of competition between the spouse and the children is very deciding and also characteristic and specific to the persons who are a parent or a parent and stepparent.

Other differences also appear when one looks into the situation of persons who assume two roles. For these individuals, the dimension of the couple seems to be less deciding than the one linked to the role of parent or stepparent, because what seems to characterize more the situation of these persons is the notion of consensus on the way to play one's parent role or to raise the spouse's children. Finally, it must be noted that a specific factor of a stepparent also assuming a role of parent in his family was brought out, that is, the fact of clearly perceiving his role of authority as regards the spouse's children. On this subject, it seems that it is difficult for a person assuming two roles to develop distinct attitudes whether it concerns his own children or the spouse's. However that may be, the persons playing two roles seem to take advantage of the fact that this notion of "role of authority" as regards the spouse's children must be clarified.

CONCLUSION

Several results obtained in this study deserve to be emphasized. First, it appears that the notions of consensus and clarity of expectations are basic elements in role strain prediction in stepfamilies. Thus, although other factors seem to be associated with role strain when they are examined one by one, the variations they produce disappear in the multivariate analysis leaving space for clarity of conjugal and parental expectations as well as the degree of consensus as regards these matters.

This result is not surprising and leads to the principles which were developed by Messinger (1976) and Cherlin (1978) revolving around the absence of institutional norms for stepfamilies and stress and uncertainty created by the absence of clear roles and guidelines for these families. For Roberts and Price (1985), there is no doubt that "the higher divorce rate for remarried families is related to the difficulty of defining and maintaining roles" (p. 15). Thus, in order to reduce the stress attributable to the fact of living in a family structure for which society does not provide any model, it is of the highest importance, according to results which were obtained here, that the couple clarifies and agrees with one another as regards their own expectations. In other words, one might think that if it is impossible to rely on the social norms that ensure that behaviours and attitudes are obvious, the husband and wife must develop together what appears to them as being most desirable.

The second statement is that the children seem to occupy a central position in role strain prediction for the respondents because the matter of consensus as regards the education of the children was continually brought up. To this matter must be added that for the persons assuming a role of stepparent, the clarity of expectations' degree facing the role of authority with the children also proved to be an important factor of role strain prediction. Finally, the results of this study, as well as many others, brought out some specific stakes linked to the presence of teenagers in a stepfamily.

The children occupy an important position, but from the results of this study emerge the importance of the clarity of expectations' degree as far as conjugal relations are concerned. This factor appeared important for role strain prediction.

Finally, two elements more specific to the role assumed in the family are to be considered in role strain prediction. For the parent, it is the presence of competition between the children and the stepparent. For the stepparent, the clarity of the role of authority that he has to assume with the spouse's children appeared important. All these elements suggest different paths of research and intervention.

Prospective Research

The results which were obtained in this study bring up several questions which it would be relevant to answer in researches to come. These questions are alternately about the comprehension of this new family pattern, the analysis angle to favour and the intervention with those families. Those questions are the following :

1. What are the factors which affect the adaptation of stepfamilies to their new situation?
2. Does the study of this new form of family organization, in the light of the process of socialization according to sex, bring a relevant explanation to the greatest difficulties observed for the women in those families and to the specific difficulties observed according to sex?
3. What are the types of services that must be developed in order to help those families? Are some methods of intervention more efficient than others?

Implications for Practice

On a clinical point of view, it is noted that the motives of those families to consult is often linked to matters affecting the children. So, the children seem to be at the center of the difficulties brought up by stepfamilies. Moreover, couples usually consider that the conjugal dimension is not a problem. But it appears from this study that the matters of clarity and of conjugal and parental consensus are crucial and that they have nothing to do with the children. The results which were obtained show that when the expectations are clear and the spouses perceive a consensus as regards different family matters, they are less subject to strain. So it seems that even before looking into parent/stepparent/child relations, the practitioner will have to especially pay attention to the conjugal subsystem.

According to Visher and Visher (1989), one of the important features of successful stepfamilies is that they are run by a close and strong couple. If the couples who are seen in consultation are close, the role of the practitioner is to help them in solidifying this union. In the light of results obtained here, it appears that the practitioner will have to encourage these persons to examine their conjugal relation, to clarify their expectations and to come to a consensus that might be satisfying for everyone. There is no doubt that abilities of communication and problem resolving will be very useful tools.

Moreover, the matter of boundaries inside the family system must also hold the attention of the practitioner because it was noted that the presence of competition between the children and the new spouse is the most important factor of role strain prediction for the parents. Thus there is good reason to examine if the boundaries parting the children from the couple are clear, assuming that any ambiguity on that matter could lead to confusion and stress.

Similarly, it is important to provide these families with the chance to meet because the use of a group as a method of intervention appears to be more interesting, since it allows these families to come out of their isolation, to define themselves and to find solutions to their problems for which very few social norms have yet emerged. Ideally, that type of group could be used preventively in order to prepare the families for remarriage (Saint-Jacques et al., 1990). Finally, the practitioners should not be surprised that a larger number of difficulties are reported by stepfamilies when they involve teenagers. Marino and Fortier (1990) believe that the role of the practitioner on that point will be to help these families to decide between what is a specific feature of adolescence and what is due to the remarriage.

NOTES

1. Even if the family income reported here seems high, it is similar to the average income of the two cities our respondents are from. Thus, the average annual family income of Sainte-Foy residents is $43,585 and $63,284 in Sillery (Statistics Canada, 1987). It must also be noted that since most of the families of this study are dual-earner families, it raises the family income level.

2. All the category variables have been recodified in dummy variables. In fact, these are the two different possibilities of response for each one of the variables that were included in the model.

3. It is on that type of interpretation that the reader can note the analysis' refinement which provides the creation of dummy variables.

4. When this study was achieved, Whitsett and Land (1992) published the report of a study about the role strain felt by stepparents. This study has many things in common with ours, notably on a theoretical point of view.

REFERENCES

Ahrons, C. R. & Wallisch, L. (1987). "Parenting in the Binuclear Family: Relationships Between Biological and Stepparents," in *Remarriage & Stepparenting–Current Research & Theory*, edited by Pasley, K. & Ihinger-Tallman, M. New York: Guilford Press, 323 p.

Anderson-Kulman, R. E. (1986). "Working Mothers and the Family Context: Predicting Positive Coping." *Journal of Vocational Behavior*, 28(3), 241-253.

Baruch, G. K. & Barnett, R. C. (1986). "Consequences of Fathers' Participation in Family Work: Parent's Role Strain and Well-Being." *Journal of Personality and Social Psychology*, 51(5), 983-992.

Biddle, Bruce J. & Thomas, E. J. (1966). *Role Theory: Concepts and Research*. New York: John Wiley & Sons, Inc., 453 p.

Blackwell, J. M. (1984). "The Relationship between Sex Role Strain and Measures of Well-Being among Career Women and Homemakers." Thèse de doctorat, Université de Washington, 117 p.

Boisgelot, C. (1989). *T'es pas ma mère*! France: Olivier Orban, 194 p.

Burr, W., Hill, R., Nye, Y. F. & Reiss, I. L. (1979). *Contemporary Theories about the Families*, volume II. New York: The Free Press, 225 p.

Cherlin, A. (1978). "Remarriage as an Incomplete Institution." *American Journal of Sociology*, 84(3), 634-650.

Clingempeel, G. W., Brand, E. & Ievoli, R. (1984-a). "Stepparent-Stepchild Relationships in Stepmother and Stepfather Families: A Multimethod Study." *Family Relations*, 33(3), 465-473.

Clingempeel, G. W., Ievoli, R. & Brand, E. (1984-b). "Structural Complexity and the Quality of Stepfather-Stepchild Relationships." *Family Process*, 23(4), 547-560.

Clingempeel, G. W., Brand, E. & Segal, S. (1987). "A Multilevel-Multivariable-Development Perspective for Future Research on Stepfamilies," in *Remarriage & Stepparenting–Current Research & Theory*, edited by Pasley, K. & Ihinger-Tallman, M. New York: Guilford Press, 323 p.

Cuerrier, C. (1982). *Learning to Step Together*. Palo Alto, CA: Stepfamily Association of America, 117 p.

Duberman, L. (1973). "Step-Kin Relationships." *Journal of Marriage and the Family*, 35(2), 283-292.

Fast, I. E. & Cain, A. C. (1966). "The Stepparent Role: Potential for Disturbances in Family Functioning." *American Journal of Orthopsychiatry*, 36(3), 485-491.

Fine, M. A. & Schwebel A. I. (1991). "The Stepparent Stress: A Cognitive Perspective." *Journal of Divorce & Remarriage*, vol.17 (1-2), 1-15.

Furstenberg, F. F., Jr., & Spanier, G. B. (1984-a). "The Risk of Dissolution in Remarriage: An Examination of Cherlin Hypothesis of Incomplete Institutionalization." *Family Relations*, 33(3), 433-441.

Germain, D. (1986). "La famille reconstituée: Le deuil de l'idéal," in *Les nouvelles familles* edited by Gauthier, P. Québec: les éditions Saint-Martin, 135 p.

Giles-Sims, J. (1987). "Social Exchange in Remarried Families," in *Remarriage & Stepparenting–Current Research & Theory*, edited by Pasley, K. & Ihinger-Tallman, M. New York: Guilford Press, 323 p.

Glick, P. C. (1989). "Remarried Families, Stepfamilies, and Stepchildren: A brief Demographic Profile." *Family Relations*, 38(1), 24-27.

Goldstein, H. S. (1974). "Reconstituted Families: The Second Marriage and its Children." *Psychiatric Quarterly*, 48(3), 433-440.

Goode, W. J. (1960). "A Theory of Role Strain." *American Sociological Review*, vol. 25, no 4, p. 483-496.

Guisinger, S., Cowan, P. A. & Schuldberg, D. (1989). "Changing Parent and Spouse Relations in the First Years of Remarriage of Divorced Fathers." *Journal of Marriage and the Family*, 51(2), 445-456.

Hetherington, M. E., Arnett, J. D. & Hollier, A. E. (1988). "Adjustment of Parents and Children to Remarriage," in *Children of Divorce*, directed by Wolchik, S. A. & Karoly, P. New York: Gardner Press, Inc., 383 p.

Hobart, C. W. (1988). "Perception of Parent-Child Relationships in First Married and Remarried Families." *Family Relations*, 37(2), 175-182.

Hutchinson, R. L., Valutis, W. E., Brown, D. T. & White, S. J. (1989). "The Effects of Family Structure on Institutionalized Children's Self-Concepts." *Adolescence*, 24(94), 303-310.

Katz, M. H. & Piotrkowski, C. S. (1983). "Correlates of Family Role Strain among Employed Black Women." *Family Relations*, 32(3), 331-339.

Knaub Kain, P. & Hanna, S. L. (1984). "Strengths of Remarried Families." *Journal of Divorce*, 7(3), 41-55.

Marino, G. & Fortier, F. (1990). "Un modèle développemental pour l'intervention auprès des familles recomposées." *Service Social*, 39(3), 112-134.

Messinger, L. (1976). "Remarriage between Divorced People with Children from Previous Marriages: A Proposal for Preparation for Remarriage." *Journal of Marriage and Family Counseling*, 2(1), 193-200.

Pasley, B. K. & Ihinger-Tallman, M. (1989). "Boundary Ambiguity: Does Ambiguity Differentiate Degree of Marital Adjustment and Interaction?" *Family Relations*, 38(1), 46-52.

Pearlin, L. I. (1983). "Role Strains and Personal Stress," in *Psychosocial Stress–Trends in Theory and Research*, directed by Kaplan, H. B. New York: Academic Press, 346 p.

Roberts, T. W. & Price, S. J. (1985). "A System Analysis of the Remarriage Process: Implications for the Clinician." *Journal of Divorce*, 9(2), 1-25.

Roberts, T. W. & Price, S. J. (1987). "Instant Families: Divorced Mothers Marry Never-Married Men." *Journal of Divorce*, 11(1), 71-92.

Safilios-Rothschild, C. (1969). "Family Sociology or Wives' Family Sociology? A Cross Cultural Examination of Decision-Making." *Journal of Marriage and the Family*, 31(2), 290-301.

Saint-Jacques, M.-C. (1990). "Familles recomposées: qu'avons-nous appris au fil des ans?" *Service Social*, 39(3), 7-37.

SAS/STAT®. (1988). *User's Guide*, version 6.03, Cary, NC: SAS Institute, Inc., 1028 p.

Snarey, J., Friedman, K. & Blasi, J. (1986). "Sex Role Strain among Kibbutz Adolescents and Adults: A Developmental Perspective." *Journal of Youth and Adolescence*, 15(3), 223-242.

Statistique Canada. (1987). *Caractéristiques de la population et des logements, divisions et subdivisions de recensement*. Québec, partie 2, 94-110, Canada: Ministre des Approvisionnements et Services, 1561 p.

Stollman, W. (1985). *Familles reconstituées . . . avec succès*! Canada: Service à la famille, 94 p.

Szinovacz, M. E. (1983). "Using Couple Data as a Methodological Tool: The Case of Marital Violence." *Journal of Marriage and the Family*, 45(3), 633-644.

Van Meter, M. J. S. & Agronow, S. J. (1982). "The Stress of Multiple Role: The Case for Role Strain among Married College Women." *Family Relations*, 31(1), 131-138.

Visher, E. B. & Visher, J. S. (1978). "Common Problems of Stepparents and their Spouses." *American Journal of Orthopsychiatry*, 48(2), 252-262.

Visher, E. B. & Visher, J. S. (1979). *Stepfamilies: A Guide to Working with Stepparents and Stepchildren*. Secaucus, NJ: The Citadel Press, 280 p.

Visher, E. B. & Visher, J. S. (1989). "Parenting Coalitions after Remarriage: Dynamics and Therapeutic Guidelines." *Family Relations*, 38(1), 65-70.

Walonick, D. S. (1986). *StatPac–Statistical Analysis Package, Programs and manual*, version 6.0. Minneapolis: 298 p.

Whitsett, D. & Land, H. (1992). Role Strain, Coping, and Marital Satisfaction of Stepparents. *The Journal of Contemporary Human Services*, 2(1), 79-92.

Wilson, K., Zurcher, L. A., Claire, D. & Curtis, R. L. (1975). "Stepfathers and Stepchildren: An Exploratory Analysis from Two National Surveys." *Journal of Marriage and the Family*, 37(3), 526-536.

The Relationship of Remarriage to Post-Divorce Co-Parenting

Donna Hendrickson Christensen
Kathryn D. Rettig

SUMMARY. The purpose of this study was to examine the relationship between remarriage and indicators of post-divorce co-parenting. A sample of 372 women and 277 men contacted three years after their divorce was used. Marital status was a statistically significant predictor for eight of the twelve regression analyses that were conducted for the women and men. The regression equations indicated that remarriage was associated with less frequent co-parental interaction, less reported parenting support from the former spouse, and more negative attitudes about the other parent for both women and men; less parenting satisfaction and lower levels of involvement in children's activities for remarried men. These findings are discussed and the relationship between remarriage and post-divorce co-parenting is explored. *[Article copies available from The Haworth Document Delivery Service: 1-800-342-9678.]*

Donna Hendrickson Christensen, PhD, is Assistant Professor, University of Arizona, Family Studies, 210 Family and Consumer Resources, Tucson, AZ 85721. Kathryn D. Rettig, PhD, is Professor, University of Minnesota, Department of Family Social Science, 290 McNeal Hall, St. Paul, MN 55108.

The study was funded by the McKnight, Bush, St. Paul, and Bigelow Foundations; the Ramsey County District Court, the Department of Family Social Science at the University of Minnesota, and the Minnesota Agricultural Experiment Station. The methodologies and interpretations of results in this study are the responsibility of the authors and do not represent the views of any of the funding agencies. The project management of Lois Yellowthunder and research assistance of Carla M. Dahl and Wilma J. Ruffin are gratefully acknowledged.

[Haworth co-indexing entry note]: "The Relationship of Remarriage to Post-Divorce Co-Parenting." Christensen, Donna Hendrickson, and Kathryn D. Rettig. Co-published simultaneously in *Journal of Divorce & Remarriage* (The Haworth Press, Inc.) Vol. 24, No. 1/2, 1995, pp. 73-88; and: *Understanding Stepfamilies: Their Structure and Dynamics* (ed: Craig A. Everett) The Haworth Press, Inc., 1995, pp. 73-88. Single or multiple copies of this article are available from The Haworth Document Delivery Service [1-800-342-9678, 9:00 a.m. - 5:00 p.m. (EST)].

INTRODUCTION

Divorce and subsequent remarriage have become a common pattern in the lives of adults in current times, resulting in high numbers of children experiencing parental divorce and remarriage during their minority (Glick, 1989). The changing demographic pattern has prompted researchers to examine how parents approach shared parenting outside of marriage. An agreeable co-parenting arrangement following divorce has been found to be important to children's adjustment to parental divorce in regards to both degree of contact with the noncustodial parent (Hess & Camera, 1979; Hetherington, Cox, & Cox, 1982; Wallerstein & Kelly, 1980) and the amount of conflict between the parents (Emery, 1982; Hetherington et al., 1982; Johnston & Campbell, 1988).

The phrase "co-parenting" has been coined to describe the continuing relationship between divorced parents (Ahrons, 1981). Visher and Visher (1989) have suggested that "parenting coalition" is a more accurate descriptor when there are more than two adults parenting after divorce; such is the case after one or both of the parties remarry. Systems theory would suggest that cooperative parenting patterns and roles that were established between parents following divorce would be disrupted with the addition of a new system member. New patterns and roles must be established in the co-parenting relationship to account for the presence of the second spouse (Ahrons & Rodgers, 1987), so that a new cooperative parenting coalition between the children's households can be constructed (Visher & Visher, 1989).

Does remarriage negatively influence the ability to co-parent between divorced parties as theory might predict? Previous studies would seem to indicate that it does. Remarriage has been found to be negatively associated with co-parental interaction and discussion of the children (Ahrons & Wallisch, 1987; Ruffin, 1991; Seltzer, 1991), continued visitation with the children (Furstenberg & Nord, 1985; Seltzer, 1991), and parenting satisfaction (Ahrons & Wallisch, 1987; Ruffin, 1991). The unfavorable relationship between remarriage and post-divorce co-parenting has been found to be especially true if the husband had remarried (Ahrons & Wallisch, 1987; Seltzer, 1991).

Buehler, Hogan, Robinson, and Levy (1986) did not find parenting satisfaction related to remarriage status, however. The question still remains if remarriage is the key influence or are other factors often found in association with remarriage more influential in predicting the continued co-parenting relationship. For example, remarriage of fathers has been found to be associated with decreased levels of visitation by the noncustodial parent (Hetherington & Camara, 1984; Wallerstein & Blakeslee,

1989). Remarriage has also been found to be associated with increased economic well-being as measured by income for women (White, 1990). Economic well-being in turn has been found to be associated with social and emotional adjustment following divorce (Pett & Vaughan-Cole, 1986). There is also some evidence to suggest that overall well-being is higher for remarried individuals as compared with divorced persons (Mitchell, 1983); although others have found that likelihood of remarriage after divorce may be related to well-being after divorce (Spanier & Furstenberg, 1982).

It is reasonable to postulate that these other factors may be more influential than remarriage itself per se in understanding the deterioration of the co-parenting relationship following remarriage. Time needed for a new spouse may reduce visitation for a noncustodial parent, leaving him or her a less involved parent. Increased economic and overall well-being may allow for increased independence from a former spouse leaving the other spouse less open or feeling less need to co-parent.

The purpose of the present study is to examine the relationship of marital status to the post-divorce co-parenting relationship when allowing for the influence of other related factors, such as visitation, income, and recovery from the divorce. The central question is whether remarriage of men and women following divorce is associated with lower reports of cooperative parenting following divorce, increased parental conflict, lower parental satisfaction, and lower levels of involvement with children.

METHODS

Sample

Data from this study was obtained in the second phase of a longitudinal study on divorce. Phase I of the research collected data from 1,153 randomly selected court case records in ten Minnesota counties which represented the ten judicial districts in the state. These were divorces with final decrees in 1986 in which there were minor children. The cases in the sample represented 19% of the 6,117 divorces with minor children (8% of 14,411 total divorces) in Minnesota that year. The divorces in this sample most often involved families with one or two children in which the couples had been married an average of 10.6 years. The wives were approximately age 32 and the husbands were age 35.

Phase II of the research attempted to collect information from both adult parties of the Phase I cases. Updated addresses for both parties were obtained during the summer of 1989 and questionnaires were mailed in October, 1989 to the 909 women and 824 men whose addresses could be located. Completed questionnaires were received from 461 women and 364 men.

A comparison of Phase I data for respondents and nonrespondents to the Phase II questionnaire found that the nonrespondents had lower incomes at the time of divorce as compared with respondents. Men and women who responded to the questionnaire were approximately two years older and had been married nearly two years longer prior to divorce than nonrespondents. Men who responded were also more likely to have received both joint legal and joint physical custody at the time of divorce than were men who did not respond. A complete description of the sample is reported in Rettig, Yellowthunder, Dahl, Christensen, and Ruffin, 1990.

This article focuses on the 372 women and 277 men who had at least one dependent child at the time the Phase II questionnaire was completed and whose children currently were in the physical custody of the respondent, the respondent's ex-spouse, or in a joint or split custody arrangement. One hundred and six (28.5%) of the 372 women had remarried while 266 had remained single (71.5%). One hundred and six men (38.3%) had remarried in the three years since their divorce while 171 (61.7%) had remained single. The mean education level for the women was 13.6 years and 14.1 years for the men. The median gross household income for women in the sample was in the range of $15,000 to $19,999. The median range for gross household income for the men in the sample was $25,000-$29,999.

Both women and men had a median of two dependent children with a median age of 11 years old for the oldest dependent child. The women in the sample reported having sole physical custody of their children 84.4% of the time, the father having sole custody 5.1%, joint physical custody 7.5%, and split custody 3.0%. The men in the sample reported that mothers had sole physical custody 65.0%, they had sole physical custody themselves 15.2%, custody was joint 13.0%, and custody of the children split between the parties 6.8%.

Measures

Dependent variables. Dependent variables included several indicators of post-divorce co-parenting, parenting satisfaction, and involvement with children. Co-parenting after divorce was measured by four subscales developed by Ahrons' Binuclear Family Research Project (Ahrons & Wallisch, 1987). The co-parental interaction scale used a nine item 5-point Likert-type scale designed to assess how often respondents shared childrearing activities with their former spouse, such as making major decisions concerning the children or discussing the children's problems. The scale ranged from "never" (1) to "always" (5). A higher score reflected a greater amount of co-parental interaction. Ahrons and Wallisch (1987) reported a reliability of .94 for women and .93 for men using Cronbach's alpha. The alpha reliability for this sample was .94 for women and .95 for men.

The parenting support scale was comprised of 6 items which asked respondents how much they helped, supported, or received help or support from their former spouse in regards to childrearing matters. A higher score reflected a higher felt amount of support. Ahrons and Wallisch (1987) reported a reliability of .84 for women and .74 for men for this scale. The alphas for this sample were .89 for women and .86 for men.

The parenting conflict scale was comprised of three questions asking respondents how often they argued or disagreed with their former spouse about childrearing. A higher score reflected a higher level of conflict or disagreement. Ahrons and Wallisch (1987) reported alpha reliabilities of .84 for women and .88 for men. The reliability for this sample was .90 for women and .81 for men.

Parental attribution was measured using two of Ahrons' four items of attitude toward former spouse as a parent scale. This subscale asked respondents if their former spouse is a good and caring parent to the children. A higher score reflected a more positive attitude toward their former spouse as a parent. The alpha reliability for this sample was .93 for women and .90 for men.

Parental satisfaction was measured using three items developed by Ahrons' Binuclear Family Research Project. This scale asked respondents to assess their satisfaction with the custody arrangement, the amount of time they spent with their children, and the parenting relationship with their former spouse. A 5-point Likert-type scale ranging between "very dissatisfied" (1) to "very satisfied" (5) was used in conjunction with the items. The alpha reliability for this sample was .62 for women and .82 for men.

A modified version of Ahrons' Binuclear Family Research Project's Involvement with Children Scale was used to measure the respondents' involvement in their children's activities. A 17-item scale using a 5-point measure of involvement ranging from "never" (1) to "very often" (5) was employed. The reliability for this scale as measured by Cronbach's alpha was .89 for women and .95 for men.

Independent variables. The predictor of special interest was whether or not the respondent had remarried in the three years since their 1986 divorce. For the purposes of the regression analysis, marital status was coded as a dummy variable with 1 indicating the respondent had remained single and 2 indicating the respondent had remarried.

The independent variables were grouped into three categories: visitation and custody, economic well-being, and personal well-being.

A measure of visitation was controlled for by asking the number of days the dependent children spent in the respondent's household. Custody was controlled for by creating two dichotomous dummy variables. Situations in which the mother of the dependent children had sole physical custody were coded as 1; all other custody situations as 2. Custody situations in which physical custody was joint or split between the two parents was coded as 2; sole physical custody situations, 1. The omitted category for custody was situations in which the father of the children had sole physical custody.

Economic well-being was assessed by examining two variables: perceived income adequacy and gross annual household income. Perceived income adequacy was measured globally by asking respondents their perception of the adequacy of their income to meet their income needs. A 5-point scale ranging from "not at all adequate for the necessities" (1) to "afford about everything that was wanted and still save money" (5) was used to measure responses.

Personal well-being was measured by examining divorce stress recovery and overall life satisfaction. The respondent's recovery from the strain of divorce was measured by the stress recovery behaviors scale (Rettig, Bauer, & Danes, 1990). The original scale was reduced for the present study to 16 items representing cognitive, social, physical, and emotional behaviors which change as individuals recover from stress. The economic behaviors of the original scale were not included in the present study. The stress recovery scale asked respondents if they found it easier to concentrate (cognitive), were more interested in helping others (social), felt less depressed (emotional), and felt better physically now as compared with when their problems related to the divorce felt most severe. A six-point scale which ranged from "no change" (0) to "disagree strongly" (1) to "agree strongly" (5) was used. A higher score represented higher levels of agreement that the recovery-related behaviors were consciously observed in the life of the respondent. The alpha reliability for the 16-item scale was .94 for women and .95 for men. Life satisfaction was measured using a global measure of overall life satisfaction.

Data Analysis

A two-way ANOVA was conducted to compare the mean scores for the dependent variables by marital status and gender. Pearson correlations and multiple regression techniques were used to examine the relationship between marital status and indicators of post-divorce parenting. Correlation analyses were conducted for the dependent variables and control variables by gender. The six dependent variables were regressed on marital status and the control variables using a hierarchical regression procedure. The independent variables were entered in four blocks. First the visitation and custody variables were entered into the equation, followed by the measures of economic well-being and personal well-being. Marital status was entered as the last block to assess whether marital status was a significant predictor of the measures co-parenting after allowing for the influence of the control variables.

FINDINGS

Table 1 reports the results of the two way ANOVA on the dependent variables by gender and marital status. Significant main effects were found for gender on all of the measures of post-divorce co-parenting. Women, as compared with men, reported lower levels of co-parental interaction, $F (2, 649) = 18.82, p < .001$; parenting support, $F (2, 649) = 12.96, p < .001$; parenting conflict, $F (2, 649) = 13.09, p < .001$; and parenting attribution, $F (2, 649) = 39.18, p < .001$, and higher levels of parenting satisfaction, $F (2, 649) = 85.72, p < .001$, and involvement in activities, $F (2, 649) = 185.52, p < .001$.

Significant main effects were also found for marital status on all variables except involvement in children's activities. Single parents, as compared with remarried parents, reported higher levels of co-parental

TABLE 1. Mean Scores of Post-Divorce Co-Parenting Outcomes by Gender and Marital Status

	Gender		Marital status	
	Men (n = 277)	Women (n = 372)	Single (n = 437)	Remarried (n = 212)
Co-parental interaction	23.46	20.41	22.43	20.23
Parenting support	17.36	15.90	16.94	15.62
Parenting conflict	9.19	8.24	8.43	9.08
Parenting attribution	7.30	6.13	6.76	6.36
Parenting satisfaction	8.62	11.17	10.41	9.41
Involvement in activities	54.55	66.74	61.99	60.61

interaction, $F(2, 649) = 10.12$, $p < .01$; parenting support, $F(2, 649) = 9.36$, $p < .01$; attitudes toward former spouse as a parent $F(2, 649) = 6.53$, $p < .05$; and parenting satisfaction, $F(2, 649) = 6.63$, $p < .05$, and lower levels of parenting conflict, $F(2, 649) = 4.37$, $p < .05$.

Significant interaction effects were discovered for parenting satisfaction and parental involvement in children's activities. Remarried men as compared with single men reported lower levels of parenting satisfaction (mean = 7.45 for remarried men and 9.34 for single men, $p < .001$), and remarried women reported higher levels of involvement in children's activities as compared with single women (mean = 68.34 for remarried women and 66.15 for single women, $p < .05$). Significant differences were not found between remarried men and single men on involvement in children's activities and between remarried women and single women on parenting satisfaction.

Given the significant main effects for gender, correlation and regression analyses were conducted separately for men and women. Table 2 reports the results of the correlation analysis for men and women. In general, the measures of post-divorce co-parenting were correlated with the number of days the children spend in the father's household and perceived income adequacy for men. The greater number of days the children spend with the father, the lower the reported levels of parental conflict and parental attribution and the higher the reported levels of parenting satisfaction and parental involvement in children's activities. Greater perceived income adequacy was correlated with higher levels of co-parental interaction, felt parenting support, greater parenting satisfaction, and greater involvement in children's activities.

Gross household income, the number of days the children spend in the mother's household, and degree of stress recovery were generally correlated with the dependent measures of post-divorce co-parenting for women. Higher household income and greater reported stress recovery were associated with higher levels of reported cooperative co-parenting and involvement in children's activities. The greater number of days the children were in the mother's household was associated with lower levels of co-parenting interaction, felt parenting support, and parenting attribution and higher reported parenting conflict and involvement in children's activities.

Results of the multiple regression analyses are reported in Table 3 for both men and women. Co-parental interaction, support received by their former spouse, attitudes toward their former wife as a parent, parenting satisfaction, and involvement of fathers in their children's activities were predicted by marital status for men even when controlling for custody and

TABLE 2. Correlations of Independent and Dependent Variables for Men and Women

	1	2	3	4	5	6	7	8	9	10	11
1. Days in household		.28**	.13*	−.04	.11	.07	.06	−.17**	−.13*	.49***	.47***
2. Income adequacy	.02		.42***	.14*	.27***	.16**	.12*	−.07	−.03	.23***	.23***
3. Household income	−.02	.45***		.16**	.25***	.10	.08	.02	.06	.05	.23***
4. Stress recovery	.08	−.07	−.11*		.29***	.01	.02	.17**	−.07	−.05	.06
5. Life satisfaction	.07	.25***	.17**	.21***		−.02	−.01	−.01	−.09	−.12*	.09*
6. Co-parental interaction	−.31***	.06	.19***	−.14**	−.03		.72***	−.09	.50***	.41***	.36***
7. Parenting support	−.32***	.04	.19***	−.18**	−.04	.81***		−.13*	.61***	.44***	.30***
8. Parenting conflict	−.07	−.04	.10*	.09	−.03	.11*	.16**		−.07	−.38***	−.01
9. Parenting attribution	−.35***	.07	.19***	−.22***	−.07	.69***	.76***	.11*		.24***	.08
10. Parenting satisfaction	.19***	.10	.03	.00	.35***	.15**	.13*	−.33***			.35***
11. Involvement in activities	.23***	.05	.08	.22***	.24***	.03	−.04	−.00	−.09	.17**	

*p < .05, **p < .01, ***p < .001.

NOTE: The correlations on the top right are for men and on the bottom left are for women.

visitation, economic well-being, and personal well-being. The predictive influence of remarriage was negative in all cases with the change in the R^2 ranging from three to five percent. The regression equations would suggest, however, that visitation and custody status were better predictors of post-divorce co-parenting than was marital status.

For women, marital status predicted the degree of co-parental interaction, felt parental support, and attitudes toward former spouse as a parent even when controlling for the influence of custody status, visitation, economic well-being, and personal well-being. The amount of variance explained by marital status, however, was modest, ranging from one to two percent. The standardized beta's, as would the correlation matrix, suggest that days the children spent in the father's household, custody status, and

TABLE 3. Multiple Regression Analysis of Post-Divorce Co-Parenting Outcomes

	Women			Men		
	Beta	R^2 Change	F	Beta	R^2 Change	F
Co-Parental Interaction						
Days in houshold	−.36***			.28**		
Joint custody	.30***			.53***		
Mother custody	−.27*	.13***	17.81***	−.52***	.12***	12.55***
Income adequacy	−.04			.08		
Household income	.22***	.03**	13.85***	.11	.02	8.65***
Stress recovery	−.11*			−.01		
Life satisfaction	.01	.01	10.56***	.02	.00	6.29***
Marital Status	−.13**	.02**	10.26***	−.23***	.04***	7.56***
Parenting Support						
Days in household	−.40***			.17		
Joint custody	.29***			.30**		
Mother custody	−.31**	.13***	17.81***	−.30*	.04**	4.02**
Income adequacy	−.06			.09		
Household income	.22***	.03**	13.91***	.07	.01	2.96*
Stress recovery	−.16**			.01		
Life satisfaction	.01	.02*	11.46***	.03	.00	2.16*
Marital status	−.13*	.01*	10.96***	−.24***	.05***	3.73***
Parenting Conflict						
Days in household	−.08			−.04		
Joint custody	.00			.14		
Mother custody	−.01	.01	.71	−.18	.04*	3.76*
Income adequacy	−.10			.02		
Household income	.16**	.02*	2.02	−.05	.00	2.45*
Stress recovery	.13*			.17**		
Life satisfaction	−.06	.01	2.16*	−.06	.03*	2.90**
Marital status	.05	.00	2.01*	.10	.01	2.84**

TABLE 3 (continued)

	Women			Men		
	Beta	R^2 Change	F	Beta	R^2 Change	F
Parenting Attribution						
Days in household	−.36***			.21*		
Joint custody	.15			.40***		
Mother custody	−.13	.13***	18.40***	−.62***	.09***	9.10***
Income adequacy	−.01			.16*		
Household income	.20***	.03**	14.19***	−.02	.01	5.83***
Stress recovery	−.19***			−.07		
Life satisfaction	.01	.03**	12.58***	−.03	.01	4.84***
Marital status	.14**	.02**	12.15***	−.19**	.03**	5.46***
Parenting Satisfaction						
Days in household	−.07			.37***		
Joint custody	.34***			.02		
Mother custody	−.56***	.09***	12.75***	.09	.25***	30.36***
Income adequacy	.00			−.01		
Household income	−.04	.01	8.29***	.08	.01	19.37***
Stress recovery	−.14**			−.05		
Life satisfaction	.38***	.13***	15.28***	.15**	.01	14.20***
Marital status	−.04	.00	13.43***	−.25***	.05***	15.92***
Involvement in Activities						
Days in household	.01			.48***		
Joint custody	.29***			.15		
Mother custody	−.46***	.11***	14.56***	−.12	.25***	27.93***
Income adequacy	−.03			.18**		
Household income	.05	.01	9.25***	.01	.02*	18.95***
Stress recovery	.14**			.05		
Life satisfaction	.18***	.07***	11.24***	.03	.00	13.59***
Marital status	.09	.01	10.28***	−.15**	.02*	12.99***

$^*p < .05$, $^{**}p < .01$, $^{***}p < .001$.

household income were better predictors of post-divorce co-parenting than was marital status.

DISCUSSION

Marital status was a statistically significant predictor of post-divorce co-parenting for eight of the twelve regression analyses completed for women and men even when controlling visitation and custody, economic well-being, and personal well-being. The negative beta coefficients indicated that remarriage for both women and men was associated with less frequent co-parental interaction, less felt parenting support from former spouse, and more negative attitudes about the other parent. In addition, remarried men also experienced less parenting satisfaction and lower levels of involvement in their children's activities.

While marital status was influential in predicting post-divorce parenting for both men and women, marital status alone is not sufficient in understanding negative post-divorce co-parenting experiences given the relative size of its beta as compared with other variables and the overall variance accounted for by marital status in the regression equations.

Visitation and custody were consistent predictors of post-divorce co-parenting for both men and women, with more frequent contact with the father and joint custody arrangements important in understanding cooperative co-parenting. The direction of this influence, however, is debatable, as is the relationship between residential arrangement and co-parenting. Studies have found that fathers with joint custody have a greater amount of contact with their children, greater parental involvement, and more sharing of parenting responsibilities (Bowman & Ahrons, 1985; Leupnitz, 1986); however, custody arrangement has not been found to be related to the quality of co-parental communication (Bowman & Ahrons, 1985). Maccoby, Kepner, and Mnookin (1990) in their study of parents two years after divorce did not find the residential arrangement to be related to co-parenting. These conflicting results leave open the question as to whether joint custody parents are more motivated and better adjusted as compared with sole custody parents, and thus more likely to be cooperative co-parenters to begin with (Kelly, 1988) rather than assuming that the custody arrangement facilitates the co-parenting relationship.

The correlation between household income and co-parental interaction, parenting support, and parenting attribution was positive, that is, increased household income was related to increased reported co-parenting for women as determined by these three measures. In addition, the economic well-being measures were the only significant contributor to the regression equation for parenting conflict for women. These relationships were not true for men. Single women on average fell into the annual income range of $15,000-$19,999 while remarried women typically fell into an income range of $25,000 to $29,999 per year. As reported, remarriage has been found to be associated with increased economic well-being as measured by income for women (White, 1990). It is interesting to speculate as to the interaction between economic well-being and women's reports of co-parenting. Income is likely a continual conflict issue for divorced parents when economic well-being is more strained. The relationship between economic well-being and co-parenting also may bolster the idea that it is other variables that occur in concert with remarriage that refine explanations of how remarriage influences post-divorce co-parenting.

In general, the measures of personal well-being were not as important in understanding post-divorce co-parenting as were measures of visitation and custody for men and women and economic well-being for women. The exceptions were understanding reported parenting conflict for men and parenting satisfaction and involvement in activities for women. This may be explained by the correlations found between the measures of economic well-being and personal well-being and by the fact that the economic well-being variables were entered into the regression equations before the psychological well-being variables.

Men who had remarried reported lower parental satisfaction, but this was not true for women. The relationship between remarriage of men and lower parenting satisfaction is unclear. The correlations seem to indicate the answer may lie in visitation. A greater number of days children spent in their father's household was related to higher reports of parental satisfaction. Remarried men reported having their dependent children in their home an average of one day less a month than did single fathers (9.76 versus 10.73); although this difference was not statistically significant. Remarriage in its early stages in general does not produce consistently reduced reports of visitation. It does appear, however, parental satisfaction is likely decreased for those fathers whose visitation is reduced following remarriage. Parental satisfaction following remarriage seems contingent, to some degree, to the extent which the new marriage interferes with visitation. It is impossible to draw a firm conclusion from the data on this point without a longitudinal study design.

The ANOVA analysis indicated that single and remarried differed on their involvement in children's activities. The surprising result is the direction of the relationship. Remarried women reported higher levels of involvement with their dependent children than did single women. It could be predicted that the addition of the new spouse would decrease the time women would have available for their children since they would now need to spend time with their new spouse. This finding may show that women who have remarried may now have more time for their children even with the addition of the new household member, because they need to spend less time away from their children in dating and social activities and in producing income. Remarriage allows for easier integration of activities between the new spouse and the children of the former marriage and also reduces the economic burden for divorced women.

The relationship between remarriage and involvement with children drops out, however, when other variables were controlled for. It appears that residential arrangement and personal well-being are more important in understanding mother's post-divorce involvement with their children than is marital status. As reported, previous studies have found a relationship between remarriage and personal well-being (Mitchell, 1983; Spanier & Furstenberg, 1982). This finding may suggest that the interaction effect found between gender and marital status and mother's involvement with their children is better understood by examining the differences in personal well-being between single and remarried women after divorce.

Remarriage predicted involvement in their children's activities for men; however, the correlation matrix and regression equation would suggest that the number of days the father spends with their children is a much stronger predictor. The interaction of time spent with children and involvement in their activities may support the idea of parallel parenting forwarded by Furstenberg and Nord (1985), that is, that divorced parents often parent quite autonomously from each other rather than cooperatively following divorce. While remarriage may influence divorced parties' ability to parent cooperatively, it may not necessarily mean that remarriage by itself interferes with a divorced parent's autonomous parenting. Remarriage may only be influential in noncustodial parents' involvement in their children's lives when it interferes with visitation.

A portion of these findings could perhaps be explained by the newness of the remarriage. The duration of the remarriage in all cases was less than three years. It is possible that the altered family systems are still in the process of adapting to the changes brought on by the remarriage of either parent. Hetherington (1987) has pointed out the importance in distinguishing between the stages of remarriage. New roles and relationships in relation to the remarriage have not been established during the early stages of remarriage. Furstenberg (1987) has found, however, that time does not guarantee that family boundaries will be redrawn successfully. It is reasonable to expect some stability in these findings over time, that is, parenting coalitions may be difficult to form. The present study suggests that remarriage does influence divorced parents' ability to co-parent together as well as parenting satisfaction, particularly for men. This relationship, however, may be mediated by factors that often occur simultaneously with remarriage. The more complex relationship of remarriage and other related variables with post-divorce co-parenting deserves further exploration.

REFERENCES

Ahrons, C. R. (1981). The continuing coparental relationship between divorced spouses. *American Journal of Orthopsychiatry,* 51, 415-428.

Ahrons, C. R., & Rodgers, R. H. (1987). *Divorced families: A multidisciplinary developmental view.* New York: W. W. Norton.

Ahrons, C. R., & Wallisch, L. (1987). Parenting in the binuclear family: Relationships between biological and stepparents. In K. Pasley & M. Ihinger-Tallman (Eds.), *Remarriage and stepparenting: Current research and theory* (pp. 225-256). New York: Guilford Press.

Bowman, M., & Ahrons, C. (1985). Impact of legal custody status on father's parenting post-divorce. *Journal of Marriage and the Family, 47*, 483-488.

Buehler, C., Hogan, M. J., Robinson, B., & Levy, R. J. (1986). Remarriage following divorce: Stressors and well-being of custodial and noncustodial parents. *Journal of Family Issues*, 7, 405-420.

Emery, R. E. (1982). Interparental conflict and the children of divorce. *Psychological Bulletin*, 92, 310-330.

Furstenberg, F. F., Jr. (1987). The new extended family: The experience of parents and children after remarriage. In K. Pasley & M. Ihinger-Tallman (Eds.), *Remarriage and stepparenting: Current research and theory* (pp. 185-205). New York: Guilford Press.

Furstenberg, F. F., Jr., & Nord, C. W. (1985). Parenting apart: Patterns of childrearing after marital disruption. *Journal of Marriage and the Family*, 47, 893-904.

Glick, P. C. (1989). Remarried families, stepfamilies, and stepchildren: A brief demographic profile. *Family Relations*, 38, 24-27.

Hess, R., & Camera, K. (1979). Post-divorce family relationships as mediating factors in the consequences of divorce for children. *Journal of Social Issues*, 35, 79-96.

Hetherington, E. M. (1987). Family relations six years after divorce. In K. Pasley & M. Ihinger-Tallman (Eds.), *Remarriage and stepparenting: Current research and theory* (pp. 185-205). New York: Guilford Press.

Hetherington, E. M., & Camara, K. A. (1984). Families in transition: The process of dissolution and reconstitution. In *The family. Review of child development research, Vol. 7* (pp. 398-439). Chicago: University of Chicago Press.

Hetherington, E. M., Cox, M., & Cox, R. (1982). Effects of divorce on parents and children. In M. Lamb (Ed.), *Non-traditional families* (pp. 233-288). New Jersey: Lawrence Erlbaum.

Johnston, J. R., & Campbell, L. E. G. (1988). *Impasses of divorce: The dynamics and resolution of family conflict.* New York: Free Press.

Kelly, J. B. (1988). Longer-term adjustment in children of divorce: Converging findings and implications for practice. *Journal of Family Psychology*, 2, 119-140.

Leupnitz, D. A. (1986). A comparison of maternal, paternal, and joint custody: Understanding the varieties of post-divorce family life. *Journal of Divorce*, 9, 1-12.

Maccoby, E. E., Kepner, C. E., & Mnookin, R. H. (1990). Coparenting the second year after divorce. *Journal of Marriage and the Family*, 52, 141-155.

Mitchell, K. (1983). The price tag of responsibility: A comparison of divorced and remarried mothers. *Journal of Divorce*, 6, 33-42.

Pett, M. A., & Vaughan-Cole, B. (1986). The impact of income issues and social status on post-divorce adjustment of custodial parents. *Family Relations*, 35, 103-111.

Rettig, K. D., Bauer, J. W., & Danes, S. M. (1990). *Adjustments of farm families to economic stress: A two year study.* Minnesota Report 220-1900 (Item No. Ad-MR-3994). St. Paul, MN: Minnesota Agriculture Experiment Station.

Rettig, K. D., Yellowthunder, L., Dahl, C. M., Christensen, D. H., & Ruffin, W. (1990). *Economic consequences of divorce in Minnesota: Phase II research report.* St. Paul, MN: Department of Family Social Science, University of Minnesota.

Ruffin, W. J. (1991). *Paternal involvement of divorced fathers related to marital status, custody arrangements, and perception of adequacy of child support paid.* Unpublished doctoral dissertation, St Paul, MN: University of Minnesota.

Seltzer, J. A. (1991). Relationships between fathers and children who live apart: The father's role after separation. *Journal of Marriage and the Family*, 53, 79-101.

Spanier, G. B., & Furstenberg, F. F., Jr. (1982). Remarriage after divorce: A longitudinal analysis of well-being. *Journal of Marriage and the Family*, 44, 709-720.

Visher, E. B., & Visher, J. S. (1989). Parenting coalitions after remarriage: Dynamics and therapeutic guidelines. *Family Relations*, 38, 65-70.

Wallerstein, J., & Blakeslee, S. (1989). *Second Chances: Men, women, and children a decade after divorce.* New York: Ticknor & Fields.

Wallerstein, J., & Kelly, J. B. (1980). *Surviving the breakup: How children and parents cope with divorce.* New York: Basic Books.

White, L. K. (1990). Determinants of divorce. *Journal of Marriage and the Family*, 52, 904-912.

The Importance of Mother-Child Relations in Studying Stepfamilies

C. Ruth Solomon

SUMMARY. Increasing numbers of children are living in stepfamilies. The majority of such children are living with their biological mothers and a stepfather. When compared to children from nondivorced families they are overrepresented amongst the numbers of children manifesting social, emotional and behavior problems. Many of the children report themselves to feel less affection and warmth for their mothers than do children from nondivorced families. The author briefly summarizes the major findings concerning mother-child relations in stepfather families. She concludes that although logic would dictate that a solid positive relationship between mother and child might buffer the child against the possible negative effects of a series of important changes in the child's life, this essential factor has rarely been addressed. She argues for the need to conduct more research on mother-child relations and interactions in order to integrate the findings with other data concerning stepfamilies. This would lead to a better understanding of stepfamily functioning and its relation to positive and negative outcomes for children in remarried families. *[Article copies available from The Haworth Document Delivery Service: 1-800-342-9678.]*

The functioning of children in remarried or stepfamilies has aroused much interest given the increasing numbers of children living in such

---

C. Ruth Solomon, PhD, is on the faculty, Département de psychologie at the Université de Montréal, C.P. 6128, Succursale 'A', Montréal, Quebec, Canada H3C 3J7.

[Haworth co-indexing entry note]: "The Importance of Mother-Child Relations in Studying Stepfamilies." Solomon, C. Ruth. Co-published simultaneously in *Journal of Divorce & Remarriage* (The Haworth Press, Inc.) Vol. 24, No. 1/2, 1995, pp. 89-98; and: *Understanding Stepfamilies: Their Structure and Dynamics* (ed: Craig A. Everett) The Haworth Press, Inc., 1995, pp. 89-98. Single or multiple copies of this article are available from The Haworth Document Delivery Service [1-800-342-9678, 9:00 a.m. - 5:00 p.m. (EST)].

families. In 1987 in the U.S.A., there were 4.3 million stepfamilies with a child below the age of 18 (Glick, 1989). This number does not take into account the 2.3 million cases of cohabitation without marriage in 1986. Glick predicts that 33% of all children will probably live in a stepfamily before they reach the age of 18.

Whether stepfather or stepmother, simple (only one member of the couple has children) or complex (both members of the couple have children), the children have been through a series of difficult events, the separation of their parents, their divorce, adjusting to one parent family life and then adjusting anew to stepfamily life including a stepparent and in some cases stepsiblings. The divorce rate being higher in remarriage (Hetherington, 1989), some children go through these events more than once. For a good number of children these changes appear to have deleterious effects and they develop various problems and/or report less favorable relations with their mothers than do children from nondivorced families. Why only some of the children develop problems or less favorable attitudes remains unclear. Part of the answer to this question may lie in an analysis of custodial parent-child relations, an area of research which with some exceptions has largely been neglected in studies on stepfamily functioning, although researchers have pointed in that direction. Garmazy (1983) has emphasized the importance of a supportive family milieu as one of the buffers against the negative effects of stress in childhood. Hetherington (1989) has underlined the importance of the child's interpersonal relationships in determining the long-term effects of remarriage on children, especially the importance of a close relationship with one parent as the best protection against the adverse consequences of rejection by the other parent. Logically, it would seem that a solid positive relation between the custodial parent, usually the most stable figure in a child's life, and the child, would provide some protection against the potential negative effects of the multiple changes the child has had to face. Moreover, it would seem that this proposal would generate a great deal of research in a search for the protective factors which could characterize the parent-child relationship. It has not.

The following is a brief summary of the major research and clinical case study findings concerning the relations and interactions between custodial mothers and children and children's reactions to living in stepfamilies. There will also be presented some suggestions from the literature that the period of one parent family life may give rise to relations between mother and child that do not bode well for children's functioning in stepfather families. Some suggestions from the joint custody literature that seem to indicate the need to further investigate mother-child relations and interactions will also be presented.

Most of the research on stepfamilies has been conducted on the stepfather family which is the most common form of stepfamily, because 85-95% of the time the woman is awarded custody of the children. Several studies have addressed the problems which stepfamilies as a group face, especially the problems which stepparents face. Issues such as the children's loyalty conflicts, discipline problems, physical and psychological boundaries between children and stepfathers, sexual climate, role confusion of stepparents, negative stereotypes, and unrealistic expectations of parents and stepparents are amongst those that have been fairly widely studied in the clinical literature (Chilman, 1983; Gardner, 1984; Sager et al., 1983; Skeen et al., 1985; Visher & Visher, 1982). Amongst other issues, the child's reaction to the loss of the non-custodial parent, depression, anxiety, acting out and academic problems (Stollman, 1983; Wallerstein, 1987) and the effects of the divorced parents' style of relating have also received attention (Emery, 1982). However, there is extremely little information available about the quality of relations between custodial mother and child in stepfamilies and even less about interactional processes.

Hetherington (1989) reported the data from a 6-year follow-up of a longitudinal study of divorce and remarriage involving 304 nondivorced and mother custody families, 30 of them remarried, with the children 4 years old at the beginning of the study. The sample was drawn from a well-educated, middle-class white population. The researchers found that more than two years following remarriage, in many families mother-child relations were problematic, especially with girls, and many boys were disengaged from their families. Girls were more demanding, hostile, coercive, and less warm than girls in nondivorced families. They were sulky, resistant, and critical. Boys' behavior with their mothers, which was initially poor, improved over time if the remarriage occured before adolescence. However, both early adolescent boys and girls were exhibiting many behavior problems two years after their mother's remarriage.

Bray and Berger (1990) have been conducting a longitudinal study of how stepfamilies differ from nondivorced families. They reported that stepchildren, 6 to 9 years of age, had more behavioral problems after six months in a stepfamily than did comparably aged children in nondivorced families. After two-and-a-half years there were no differences in the behavioral adjustment of stepchildren, ages 8 1/2 to 11 1/2, compared to children in nondivorced families. After five years of remarriage, however, the children, now 11 to 14 years of age, were again having more problems than the comparison group children.

As to the interactions between mothers and children in stepfather families, Bray et al. (1987) report that after six months of remarriage mothers were more authoritarian or permissive in parenting in contrast to nondivorced mothers who were authoritative. When the children were pre-adolescent or adolescent, mothers from nondivorced families had decreased their level of control more than had remarried mothers. Hetherington (1989) found that in the first two years following remarriage mothers were not as successful as nondivorced mothers in controlling and monitoring their children's behavior, that is, in knowing where their children were or who they were with and what they were doing. Nonetheless, Hetherington reported that authoritative mothers, warm, firm and responsively controlling, had children, especially boys, with fewer behavior problems and greater social competency than had mothers who were authoritarian, disengaged or permissive. Hetherington also found that poor parenting practices, including verbal and physical attacks on the children, power assertion and withdrawal were associated with aggressive and insecure behavior in children no matter the family structure. Bray et al. (1991) used parent and child self-report scales, a child behavior check list, and a self-concept test for children as well as videotapes of family interactions in their study of 6- to 9-year-old children. They emphasized that remarried mothers' warmth, affection, levels of control and style of discipline play major roles in both boys' and girls' internalizing and externalizing problems, social competency and self-esteem, but in different ways. For boys, greater maternal affection, maternal warmth, and more monitoring and control and less punitive discipline were related to better behavioral adjustment, and more monitoring and control to later social competency. There were no predictors of self-esteem. For girls, warmth and mutual positive regard and monitoring were related to better behavioral adjustment, social competency and self-esteem. However, for girls both punitive and more rational discipline led to more externalizing problems, less social competency and lower self-esteem. The authors do not address the question of why more rational discipline would lead to problems in girls.

Concerning other apparent reactions to living in stepfather families, Lee et al. (1991) obtained survey data from several sources. They collected information from students, from one parent of each of the students (usually the mother), from administrators in the students' school and from two of their teachers. They also obtained the students' standardized achievement test scores in mathematics, science, reading and social skills. The results of their nationally representative sample of 22,000 American 8th graders showed that the majority of 8th graders exhibit neither serious school-identified behavioral problems nor emotional or adjustment problems.

However, when present, both types of problems were at least twice as common in stepfamilies and one parent families as in nondivorced families, with girls being more adversely affected by stepfamily structure than boys: girls living in stepfather families were more likely to exhibit school-related behavioral problems, and girls in stepmother families were more likely to exhibit both behavioral and emotional problems than were their counterparts in nondivorced families. In a much earlier study, Bowerman and Irish (1962) administered questionnaires to 2194 seventh to twelfth-grade students. They found that the levels of affection and closeness between children and their mothers were less in stepfather families than in nondivorced families. Parish and Dostal (1980), using questionnaires administered to 738 11- to 14-year-old children, found that those living in stepfather families evaluated their mothers less favorably than did children from nondivorced families. Nunn et al. (1983), using questionnaires and various scales with 566 fifth- and sixth-grade children including 99 stepfather families, also reported that the children in remarried families evaluate their mothers less favorably. Parish and Kappes (1980) reported similar results from university students. Santrock et al. (1982) analyzed videotapes of the interactions of 24 nondivorced families and 12 stepfather families with girls aged 6 to 11. They found the stepfamily girls to be angrier with their mothers.

Some investigators have suggested that the problems encountered in stepfamilies have their roots in events which occurred before the mother's remarriage. For instance, Kalter (1977) suggested that relations between mother and child are poor during the period which precedes the remarriage of the mother because the child may have identified earlier with the battling not yet divorced parents, and learned a hostile way of living and solving problems. This form of interacting then persists after the mother's remarriage. A different perspective is offered by several researchers who have found that some children gain status while living in a one parent family and this status is lost when the mother remarries. Visher and Visher (1982) reported a special relationship between mother and child during the time that the child lives in a one parent family. They found that the parent often turned to the child for emotional support. In response the child adopted a parenting role towards the parent. Bitterman (1986), Franke and Reese (1980) and Stollman (1983) have emphasized that during the time spent in a one parent family the parent and child establish a particularly close relationship. Hence when the parent remarries the child resents the loss of the privileged relationship and role, power and status. The child suffers a loss of self-esteem and reacts with, and to, feelings of loss and rejection, of abandonment and exclusion (Franke & Reese, 1980; Paris,

1984; Sager et al., 1983; Visher & Visher, 1982; Wallerstein & Kelly, 1980). Hetherington (1989) reported that in one parent families both boys and girls were allowed more responsibility and power in decision making than children from nondivorced families. In some cases this resulted in a mutually supportive relationship (in other families it resulted in resentment, rebellion or behavior problems).

Others have also suggested changes in mother-child relations that might cause problems in the stepfamily. Using clinical data as their basis Wallerstein and Kelly (1980) suggested that the mother pressures the child to shift allegiance from the biological father to the stepfather and this pressure causes problems. Crosby-Burnett and Ahrons (1985) made a similar suggestion. In addition they stated that children worry that they will be displaced when their mother has another child (which may imply a lack of sufficient reassurance offered to the child). They noted that following remarriage some mothers want the children to leave, to go and live with their biological fathers, because they perceive the children to be a threat to the new marriage. They also found that some mothers are jealous of the child-stepfather, especially daughter-stepfather relation, and react accordingly. They found other mothers to be suffering from role overload in trying to make everyone happy with poor success all around. Fox and Inazu's 1982 study also offers support for a change in mother-child relationships which the children view negatively. Using an interview technique they studied the response of 14- to 16-year-old girls, 211 from nondivorced families and 54 from stepfather families. A significant number of the girls felt that the presence of a stepfather had diminished the quality of their relationship with their mothers. Along the same lines, in questioning difficulties manifested in stepfather families, Hetherington (1989) found that closeness in the marital relationship and active involvement by the stepfather in parenting were associated with high levels of conflict between mother and daughter. While not directly examining before and after remarriage differences in mother-child relationships, Kain-Knaub and Hanna (1984) found that more than half of their 44 stepfamily subjects aged 2 to 22, wished to leave their custodial parent (88% mother) to live with their other parent at some point. Only 6 children, however, wished to do so often or all the time. Although this study does not offer evidence for a change in mother-child relations after remarriage, it underlines the importance of examining mother-child relations and interactions in order to understand childrens' motives for wanting to leave or not wanting to.

Turning now to the joint custody literature, McKinnon and Wallerstein (1986), in studying the motivations of divorcing parents for requesting joint custody of the children, found that their motivations were not always in the best interest of the child. They found that some parents had only a partial commitment to the child and were unwilling to make the child a priority over their working and social lives. Others found their commitment to the child diminished when they formed new relationships, especially romantic relationships. In making an analogy with stepfamilies, there is no reason to believe that all remarried mothers who were awarded custody of their children were uniquely motivated to obtain custody by the best interests of the child. On the contrary, anecdotal evidence repeatedly reveals the existence of other motivations in some parents (Solomon, 1991). These include revenge and punishment of the spouse as well as winning custody for winning's sake as prime motivators for obtaining child custody. Moreover, in some cases neither parent wants the children and one reluctantly agrees to take them.

In summary, the literature informs us that in many remarried families mother-child relations are initially poor, may improve for a time and then deteriorate again as the children reach preadolescence or adolescence. There are suggestions that mother-daughter relations are even more perturbed than mother-son relations. Some researchers and clinicians have suggested that a special relationship exists between mother and child before the mother's remarriage and that it is the rupture of this relationship that is the source of many of the post-remarriage problems. A different suggestion is that perturbed relations are carried from the time of difficult relationships in the original family, through the period of one parent life into the stepfamily. Whatever the sources of the problems, several investigators report that children in remarried families see their mothers less favorably than children in nondivorced families.

As to mother-child interactions, although there is some information available it is very broad general information which is insufficient to provide details as to how to provide or maintain buffers which might prevent the emotional and behavioral problems that children in remarried families develop in significantly greater proportions than do children from nondivorced families. Broad categories of parental child-raising styles such as authoritarian, authoritative, permissive and disengaged, parent behaviors such as monitoring and controlling, are good starting points but do not get at the nitty gritty of daily mother-child interaction. The relations between child temperament and remarried family functioning (Hetherington, 1989) and the relations between the kind and number of stress factors and remarried family functioning are very important to the understanding of remarried families. Certainly we need more broad-based ecological studies. However, we especially need to study individual patterns of mother-child interaction in remarried families using direct observations of interaction in various situations. We must obtain answers to many questions including the following questions: Why are children from remarried families angrier with their mothers? Why do they evaluate their mothers less favorably than do children from nondivorced families? Why do some children feel put aside and others do not? How does mother-child interaction change in the transitions from nondivorced to one parent to stepfather family? What do mothers say, do, and emotionally express that reassures the children while the mothers are establishing new relationships with spouse, new in-laws and perhaps stepchildren? What do mothers say and do about the children's loyalty conflicts? Do some daughters flirt with their stepfathers and, if so, how do their mothers react? Is the mother-child interaction related to a child's desire to leave, and, if so, how? Is it related to why some children do not want to leave? What are mothers and daughters saying and doing to each other that makes rational discipline lead to negative consequences?

We also need to include in our studies information concerning mothers' motivations for obtaining child custody in the first place, as well as their perceptions of how the child or children have helped or hindered them in getting on with their lives after the divorce from the children's father. We should also investigate further the children's perceptions of the mother's role in bringing about major changes in their lives.

Ever since the beginnings of psychoanalysis we have known that the mother-child relationship is central to child development and is narrowly related to child outcomes. We have since learned that fathers are very important, that systems are very important, and that all of society plays a role in the child's development (Bronfenbrenner, 1979). However, in our attempts to study all the factors that impinge on and affect a child's life we must not forget the mothers' central and crucial role, a role that may be even more crucial when a custodial mother remarries.

REFERENCES

Bitterman, C.M. (1968). The multi-marriage family. *Social casework, 49*, 218-221.

Bowerman, C.E., Irish, D.P. (1962). Some relationships of stepchildren to their parents. *Marriage and family living, 24*, 113-121.

Bray, J.H. (1987). Becoming a stepfamily. Symposium presented at the meeting of the American Psychological Association, New York.

Bray, J.H. (1991). Families in transition: what's in a name. *The Family Psychologist, Winter, 7*(1), 23-24.

Bray, J.H., Berger, S.H. (1990). The developing stepfamily. *The Family Psychologist, Summer, 6*(3), 31-32.

Bray, J.H., Berger, S.H., Pacey, K., Boethel, C.L. (1991). Longitudinal predictors of children's adjustment to divorce and remarriage. *Paper presented at the meetings of the SRCD*. Seattle, Washington.

Bronfenbrenner, U. (1979). *The ecology of human development*. Cambridge, Mass.: Harvard University Press.

Chilman, C.S. (1983). Remarriage and stepfamilies: research results and implications. *In* E.D. Macklin, R.H. Rubin (Eds): *Contemporary families and alternative lifestyles* (pp. 147-163). Beverly Hills: Sage.

Crosbie-Burnett, M., Ahrons, C.R. (1985). From divorce to remarriage: Implications for therapy with families in transition. *Journal of Psychotherapy and the Family, 1*(3), 121-137.

Emery, R.E. (1982). Interparental conflict and the children of discord and divorce. *Psychological Bulletin, 92*, 310-330.

Fox, G.L., Inazu, J.K. (1982). The influence of mother's marital history on the mother-daughter relationship in black and white households. *Journal of Marriage and the Family, 44*, 143-153.

Francke, L.B., Reese, M. (1980). After remarriage. *Newsweek*, February 11, p. 66.

Gardner, R.A. (1984). Counseling children in stepfamilies. *Elementary school guidance and counseling, 190*, 40-49.

Garmazy, N. (1983). Stressors of childhood. *In* N. Garmazy & M. Rutter (Eds): *Stress, coping, and development in children* (pp. 43-84). New York: McGraw-Hill.

Glick, P.C. (1989). Remarried families, stepfamilies, and stepchildren. A brief demographic profile. *Family Relations, 38*, 24-27.

Hetherington, M.H. (1989). Coping with family transitions: Winners, losers and survivors. *Child Development, 60*, 1-14.

Kain-Knaub, P., Hanna, S.H. (1984). Children of remarriage: Perceptions of family strengths. *Journal of Divorce, 7* (4), 73-90.

Kalter, N. (1977). Children of divorce in an outpatient psychiatric population. *American Journal of Orthopsychiatry, 47*, 40-51.

Lee, V.E., Zimiles, H., Ladewski, B., Burkham, D.T. (1991). Family structure and its effect on behavioral and emotional problems in young adolescents. *Paper presented at the meetings of the SRCD*, Seattle, Washington.

McKinnon, R., Wallerstein, J.S. (1986). Joint custody and the preschool child. *Behavioral Science and the Law, 4*, 169-183.

Nunn, G.D., Parish, T.S., Worthing, R.J. (1983). Perceptions of personal and familial adjustment by children from intact, single-parent and reconstituted families. *Psychology in the School, 20*, 166-174.

Paris, E. (1984). *Stepfamilies: Making them work*. Toronto: Avon Books.

Parish, T.S., Dostal, J.W. (1980). Evaluations of self and parent figures by children from intact, divorced, and reconstituted families. *Journal of youth and adolescence, 9*, 347-351.

Parish, T.S., Kappes, B.M. (1980). Impact of father loss on the family. *Social Behavior and Personality, 8*, 107-112.

Sager, C.J. et al. (1983). *Treating the remarried family*. New York: Brunner/Mazel.

Santrock, J.W., Warshak, R., Eliott, G. (1982). Social development and parent-child interaction in father-custody and stepmother families. *In* M.E. Lamb (Ed.): *Non-traditional families: parenting and child development* (pp. 284-314). Hillsdale: Erlbaum.

Skeen, P., Covi, R.B., Robinson, B.E. (1985). Stepfamilies: a review of the literature with suggestions for practitioners. *Journal of counseling and development, 64*, 121-125.

Solomon, C.R. (1991). A critical moment for intervention: After the smoke of the battle clears and custody has been won. *Journal of Divorce & Remarriage, 16* (3-4), 325-335.

Stollman, W. (1983). *Stepfamilies: Making yours a success*. Ottawa: Commoners' Publications.

Visher, J.S., Visher, E.B. (1982). Stepfamilies and stepparenting. *In* F. Walch (Ed.): *Normal family process* (pp. 331-353). New York: Guilford Press.

Wallerstein, J. (1987). Children of divorce: Report of a ten-year follow-up of early latency-age children. *American Journal of Orthopsychiatry, 57*, 199-211.

Wallerstein, J.S., Kelly, J.B. (1980). *Surviving the break-up: how children actually cope with divorce*. New York: Basic Books.

Influences on the Quality of the Stepmother-Adolescent Relationship

Donna S. Quick
Barbara M. Newman
Patrick C. McKenry

SUMMARY. This study identified the extent to which selected descriptors of relationship formation were related to the quality of the stepmother-adolescent relationship as perceived by both the stepmother and the adolescent stepchild. The reputational sample consisted of 50 stepfamilies who completed questionnaires in their homes. Correlational analysis indicated four significant predictors of relationship quality: the adolescent's perception of family's ability to acquire social support, the adolescent's perception of family's ability to reframe family problems, frequency of agreement between the stepmother and the father on how to raise the child, and stepmothers' satisfaction with the remarriage. A discussion of these findings are presented along with recommendations for intervention and policy formation. *[Article copies available from The Haworth Document Delivery Service: 1-800-342-9678.]*

Donna S. Quick, PhD, is Associate Professor of Family Studies, University of Kentucky, Lexington, KY 40506. Barbara M. Newman, PhD, and Patrick C. McKenry, PhD, are Professors of Family Relations and Human Development, Ohio State University, Columbus, OH 43210.

Funding for this project was provided, in part, by the Ohio Department of Mental Health and the Ohio Agricultural Research and Development Center (H-922).

[Haworth co-indexing entry note]: "Influences on the Quality of the Stepmother-Adolescent Relationship." Quick, Donna S., Barbara M. Newman, and Patrick C. McKenry. Co-published simultaneously in *Journal of Divorce & Remarriage* (The Haworth Press, Inc.) Vol. 24, No. 1/2, 1995, pp. 99-114; and: *Understanding Stepfamilies: Their Structure and Dynamics* (ed: Craig A. Everett) The Haworth Press, Inc., 1995, pp. 99-114. Single or multiple copies of this article are available from The Haworth Document Delivery Service [1-800-342-9678, 9:00 a.m. - 5:00 p.m. (EST)].

According to Martin and Bumpass (1989), approximately two-third's of first marriages today will end in divorce, and approximately 60% of these divorces will involve children under 19 (Glick, 1984). While the rate of remarriage has slightly declined in the 1980s, it is estimated that 70-75% of divorced persons remarry, and the majority of these remarriages occur within five years of the parental divorce. It is thus estimated that 35% of all children born today in the United States will spend part of their lives living in a stepfamily (Glick, 1984).

Understanding stepfamilies goes beyond the demographic tracking of numbers. As Furstenburg (1980) emphasized, behind the demographic shifts are complex social and kinship changes which necessitate a host of personal and interpersonal adjustments. Andrew Cherlin (1978) has labeled the stepfamily as an "incomplete institution," suggesting that these families are confronted with ambiguous social roles because society offers no institutional guidelines. Data do suggest that these family relationships may be more problematic than relationships in intact family structures. Yet we know less about stepfamilies than any other lifestyle (Herndon, 1982).

One relationship in stepfamilies that has been relatively unexplored is that of the stepmother-adolescent child, representing 5-10 percent of stepfamilies. Research assessing the adjustments and effectiveness of stepmothers indicates they do not fare as well as stepfathers; such reactions as anxiety, depression, and anger about family relationships appear to be common (Ihinger-Tallman & Pasley, 1987; Sauer & Fine, 1988). Moreover, role adjustments may be more difficult for stepmothers and children because women are expected to be the more loving, nurturant parents, yet the mother role is more difficult to replace. Also, the natural mother's absence may also represent a history of family problems (Ihinger-Tallman & Pasley, 1987).

In addition, the literature on stepfamilies has suggested that of all stepchildren, adolescents have the most significant adjustment problems (Chilman, 1983; Lutz, 1983). Yet little empirical data are available to support this claim. What does seem clear, however, is that parent-child relationships affect the relative ease with which the young person adjusts to the changed roles and new demands of adolescence. How the special nature and circumstances of the stepfamily influence these transitions is a critical research question for family scholars. Moreover, a better understanding of stepmother families with adolescents would not only shed more light on processes pertaining to stepfamilies, but would also contribute to a more comprehensive view of adolescent development in an evolving family form.

The purpose of this study was to investigate social and psychological influences that mediate the role strain thought to be inherent in the development of the stepmother-adolescent relationship. Remarried families are confronted with numerous structural changes including undertaking new roles and responsibilities, reorganization of household routines, and developing new attachments (Santrok & Sitterle, 1987) with few societal norms to guide them (Cherlin, 1987). According to role theory, whether the stepmother and the stepchild adjust to the stress involved in the formation of a new stepfamily depends, in part, upon resources that each individual brings to the situation as well as characteristics of the new family structure (Clingempeel, Brand, & Segal, 1987). Several factors have been identified in the stepmother-stepchild research as correlates of adjustment to these roles. Thus, based on a role adjustment perspective and related stepfamily literature, the following independent variables were examined: (a) age of stepmother at the time of the remarriage (Duberman, 1973); (b) adolescent's time in the current stepfamily (Papernow, 1984); (c) adolescent's perception of family coping patterns (McCubbin, Larsen, & Olson, 1982); (d) self-esteem of stepmother (Pearlin & Schooler, 1978); (e) marital quality (Brand & Clingempeel, 1987); (f) frequency of agreement between the stepmother and father on how to raise the stepchild (Messinger, 1976); (g) gender of the child as it interacts with the quality of the child's relationship with the non-residential mother (Clingempeel, Brand, & Ievoli, 1984). The latter variable was included because no studies heretofore have assessed the link between the adolescent's relationship with his or her non-residential mother and the quality of the relationship with his/her stepmother. However, studies that have examined this relationship with children have found that stepdaughter satisfaction with the stepmother is inversely related to the quality of relationship with the natural, non-residential mother, whereas for stepsons it is directly related (Clingempeel et al., 1984; Furstenberg & Nord, 1985).

METHODS

It has been argued that a major methodological weakness in the study of families in general has been the reliance upon one source of information regarding the entire family, usually the wife and/or mother (McKenry, Price-Bonham, & O'Bryant, 1981). Some researchers have labelled this "wives' family research" and proposed that we must move beyond this one family member point of view or perception of family functioning to designs that provide a "whole" family perspective. Multiple perception family research appears "to have the potential of gaining much valuable insight into the family as a 'unit of interacting personalities'" (Ball, McKenry, & Price-Bonham, 1983, p. 895).

This study was unique in that the key dependent variable was the quality of the stepparent-stepchild relationship, taking into account both the stepmother's and the adolescent's perceptions. In order to quantitatively reflect this relationship, data from both parties in the relationship were summed into a dyad score (Miller, 1986).

Sample

The sample used in this study consisted of 50 stepmothers and their adolescent stepchildren, custodial and non-custodial, between and including the ages of 12 and 18, residing in two large metropolitan areas of Ohio and Kentucky. For inclusion in this study, the children must either have lived with the stepmother and biological or adoptive father or visited regularly (at least once a month). All the adolescents' parents had previously divorced. Both the stepmother and adolescent stepchild participated in the survey. This sample was selected using a reputational sampling technique drawing upon stepfamily support groups as well as suggestions from colleagues and study participants.

The all-white sample consisted of 21 female adolescents and 29 male adolescents in the sample. The average age of the children was 15.26 years (SD = 1.71). The mean age of the stepmothers was 41.31 (SD = 1.93). The number of years the stepmothers had been married to their spouses ranged from one year to twelve years with a mean of 4.4 years (SD = 2.78). Twenty-four percent (n = 17) had been married for two years. Forty-two percent had been married between three and six years.

The level of education for both husbands and wives ranged from not completing high school through graduate degrees. Seventy-four percent of fathers had completed at least four years of college, and forty-eight percent had graduate degrees. Seventy-six percent of the stepmothers had completed four years of college, and thirty-four percent had graduate degrees.

All the fathers were employed full-time. Using Hollingshead (1957) criteria, 34% (n = 17) of the fathers were classified as business managers, proprietors of medium-sized businesses, and lesser professionals. The next largest group (32%, n = 16) included higher executives, proprietors of large concerns and major professionals. Ninety-eight percent of the stepmothers (n = 49) were also employed. Total family income ranged from $20,000 to more than $100,000, with 44% within the interval of $40,000 to $75,000. Twenty-two percent earned more than $100,000 per year.

Thus, the families tended to be highly educated, middle- to upper-middle-income families.

Data Collection

Stepmothers and their oldest adolescent stepchild were mailed a letter of introduction, inviting them to participate in the study. This letter was followed by a telephone call to give families the opportunity to ask further questions and to set up an appointment for a survey packet to be administered. Data were collected by the principal investigator as well as other trained personnel.

During the visit in the home, questionnaires were administered by the investigator to both the adolescent and his or her stepmother. Family members were requested to keep their written answers confidential. The investigator's presence assured that inappropriate sharing of responses between stepmother and stepchild did not confound the survey results; questionnaires were individually collected upon completion.

Instrumentation

Adolescent and stepparent versions of the questionnaire used in the study were composed of various standardized instrumentation chosen for their psychometric properties and relevance to a role transition/adjustment perspective. In addition, standard demographic and family background questions were included.

The dependent measure, *quality of the adolescent-stepmother relationship,* was assessed with the Parent-Adolescent Communication Scale (Barnes & Olson, 1982). The stepmother and adolescent scores were combined (summed). This created an index or joint evaluation of stepmother-adolescent relationship quality. This technique was used by Barnes and Olson to establish norms for the instrument.

Raw scores were used to assess the independent variables, *age of stepmother at the time of the remarriage, adolescent's time in the current stepfamily,* and *gender.* The Family Crisis Oriented Personal Evaluation Scale (F-COPES) (McCubbin et al., 1981) was used to measure the *adolescent's perception of family coping.* Three subscales were used: *family passivity, reframing family problems,* and *acquiring social support. Stepmother's self-esteem* was measured with the Rosenberg (1965) Self-Esteem Scale. The *stepmother's marital quality* was assessed using the Marital Comparison Level Index (Sabatelli, 1984). *Frequency of agreement between stepmother and the father* was assessed with a five-point rating scale ("always"–"never"). *Quality of time with the non-residential natural mother* was also assessed with a five-point rating scale ("very close"–"distant").

RESULTS

The relationship between the dependent variable and the independent variables was first investigated by bivariate correlation. In addition, simultaneous multiple regression was used to examine the variables found to be significant in the bivariate analysis. (To minimize the risk of a Type I error, multiple regression was conducted only with those variables found to be significant at the bivariate level.)

A contingency table revealed that while half the cases ($n = 25$) reported agreement between stepmother and adolescent on the quality of their relationship, half ($n = 25$) indicated a discrepancy in their combined perceptions of the quality of their relationship. For example, in sixteen cases the child indicated that the relationship quality was lower than did the stepmother. In nine cases the stepmother indicated the relationship quality was lower than the child indicated. Ideally, one would have examined the study variables in relation to those cases where discrepancy is apparent, but given so few cases ($n = 25$) a multiple regression analysis was not appropriate.

The zero order correlations for all the independent variables used in the regression analyses are presented in Table 1. The results of Pearson product-moment correlations (r) indicated significant relationships between the quality of the stepmother-adolescent relationship and (a) reframing family problems as perceived by the adolescent ($r = .24, p < .05$), acquiring social support as perceived by the adolescent ($r = .36, p < .01$), stepmothers' marital quality ($r = .30, p < .05$), and frequency of agreement between the stepmother and father on how to raise the stepchild ($r = .43, p < .01$). The correlation between the dependent measure and self-esteem of the stepmother approach significance ($r = .20, p < .10$).

A simultaneous regression analysis was run with all the independent variables to check for suppression effects. Data analysis revealed that those variables which were not significant at the bivariate level were also not significant in the multiple regression equation. Because the major independent variables were not highly intercorrelated, only the variables significant at the bivariate level were entered into the final multivariate regression equation.

The multiple regression procedure for the five variables selected from the bivariate analysis produced a significant R^2 of .35 ($F = 4.89$, $p < .001$),

TABLE 1. Zero Order Correlations Among Independent Variables

Independent Variable	1	2	3	4	5	6	7	8	9	10	11
1. Age of Stepmother	1.0	−.07	.00	−.03	−.24*	.14	.00	−.15	−.18	.11	.07
2. Years in Stepfamily		1.0	−.18	−.12	.24*	.20	−.15	.03	.14	−.11	.01
3. Acquiring Social Support			1.0	−.20	−.12	−.22	−.10	.01	.05	−.06	.36**
4. Family Passivity				1.0	−.23	.07	.04	.15	.00	−.11	.00
5. Reframing Family Problems					1.0	.15	.11	.19	.14	−.14	.24*
6. Self-Esteem of Stepmother						1.0	.29*	.53**	.02	−.08	.20
7. Marital Quality							1.0	.27*	−.02	−.06	.30*
8. Frequency of Agreement on How to Raise Child								1.0	−.20	.13	.43**
Interaction Between Quality of Child's Relationship with Non-Residential Mother and Being:											
9. Male									1.0	−.87**	−.12
10. Female										1.0	.12
11. Quality of Stepmother-Adolescent Relationship											1.0

*$p < .05$, **$p < .01$

indicating the amount of variation in the dependent variable explained by the independent variables equaled 35 percent. The findings of this analysis are summarized in Table 2. The multiple regression analysis revealed that only two of the five predictors were significant: *acquiring social support* (beta = .38, $p < .05$) and *frequency of agreement between the stepmother and the father on how to raise the child* (beta = .33, $p < .05$).

DISCUSSION

The findings of this study provide support for viewing the quality of the stepmother-adolescent relationship more as a function of characteristics of the new family unit as compared to individual characteristics of either the stepmother or the adolescent. All four significant variables in the correlational analyses were descriptors of aspects of stepfamily functioning. Because the stepfamily is a relatively recent family form and the role of the stepmother is particularly ill defined, the process of adjustment for all family members is rather nebulous. Because there are so few guidelines for proper role behavior, a variety of factors appear to influence the transition and adjustment to the role. The factors identified in this study would be consistent with Clingempeel, Brand, and Segal's (1987) multilevel-multivariable-developmental approach to the study of stepfamily formation and adjustment; these authors suggest that insufficient attention has been given to the variety and complexity of factors that may influence the quality of stepfamily life.

Examination of the norms developed for the dependent measure indicates that the combined parent-child mean score for this sample was lower than reported norms. The average combined score for the stepmother and adolescent on Barnes and Olson's (1982) Parent-Adolescent Communication Scale was 125.4. The norm given for this combined scale was 142.1. It is not surprising that the study sample had a lower mean score as the families used in the Barnes and Olson study were first-married families with adolescents, whereas the sample in this study utilized stepfamilies with adolescents that had been together for an average of only four years and are probably still in transition in terms of establishing a quality relationship with the stepmother.

Adolescent's perception of family's ability to reframe family problems. While no studies to date have examined coping strategies within the stepfamily as perceived by the adolescent, it appears that the ability to reframe or redefine a stressful event is an important coping dimension. Because the role of stepmother and stepchild is not clearly defined and society offers no clear guidelines as to what can be expected in that role (Cherlin, 1978),

TABLE 2. Multiple Regression Analysis of Influences on the Stepmother-Adolescent Relationship

Independent Variables	Unstandardized Regression Coefficient	Standard Error	Standardized Regression Coefficient (Beta)	*F*
Reframing Family Problems as Perceived by the Adolescent	8.55	5.30	.20	2.61
Acquiring Social Support as Perceived by the Adolescent	5.32	1.80	.38	8.70*
Self-Esteem of the Stepmother	.20	.79	.04	.06
Marital Quality	.11	.12	.12	.83
Frequency of Agreement on How to Raise the Child	11.81	5.33	.33	4.91*
(constant)	2.75			

$R = .60$
$R^2 = .35$
Adjusted $R^2 = .28$
$F = 4.89$, $p = .001$

*$p < .05$

each family member must work out his or her own definition of how to behave. This process can pose particular challenges for some stepfamilies, especially those with stepmothers. The purported ambiguity of steprelationships would suggest that the tolerance of that ambiguity and the ability to redefine stressful family situations in a more positive framework is a family characteristic that may be an important predictor of relationship quality in stepfamilies.

Adolescent's perception of family's ability to acquire social support. Clinical literature suggests that many adolescents and their families turn to friends for support during this transition period (Visher & Visher, 1982). It may be that many of these adolescents are still adjusting to painful losses in their family–the loss of a parent by divorce, moving to a new neighborhood, leaving friends and familiar routines, needing to share one's room and other physical spaces, and a loss in the amount of individual attention received. Moreover, the child's parents often are not emotionally available during these transitions because of their own adjustments. Adjusting to these changes often takes time and understanding. The expression and acceptance of hurt, anger, fear, and guilt are a normal part of this healing process. It appears that the family's ability to acquire support from relatives, friends, and neighbors is an important resource for stepfamilies. Considerable anecdotal data collected in the present study also suggest that social support is an important component of the quality of parent-adolescent relationships in remarried families.

Stepmother's satisfaction with the remarriage. This finding is partially consistent with the findings of Brand and Clingempeel (1987) which stated that marital quality was associated with more positive stepmother relationships for boys, but not for girls. In the present study the average score on Sabatelli's (1984) Marital Comparison Level Index was 144.56. The normative score which indicates that expectations are being met is 128. Thus, the stepmothers in the current study indicated that the marital relationship more than met their expectations. It appears that a quality marital relationship is related to the quality of the stepmother-adolescent relationship and could serve as a resource to the family. It is important to note that in a correlational design these relationships could be interpreted conversely, i.e., a quality parent-child relationship could also enhance the parents' marriage.

Even though the remarried couple is usually enthusiastic about their new family, some of the children and relatives may be less than enthusiastic. Studies of first-married families have pointed out the potential importance of the marital relationship as a source of help to individuals in times of stress (e.g., Coombs, 1991). In stepfamilies the strength and health of the marital bond may be particularly important. In these stepfamilies individuals, often from different backgrounds, find themselves suddenly living together in the intimacy of a family. Furthermore, there are typically former spouses, assorted relatives, and friends of various affiliations who continue to have input into and influence on the family unit. In this complicated set of relationships, the stepmother again finds herself in a situation that lacks clear role guidelines. A happy marriage could serve as a support system for the stepmother role and also provide the stepchildren with exposure to a positive model of marital interaction. A positive marital atmosphere may also send a clearer message to the children that a reconciliation between the child's former parents is no longer possible. This, in turn, may promote the children's ability to accept reality and help them focus on the positive aspects of their current family situation. Making a commitment to a strong marriage, creating new rules, roles, and family routines may further serve the adjustment to new roles that facilitate the quality of the stepmother-stepchild relationship.

Frequency of agreement on how to raise the stepchild. Disagreements over stepchildren appear to be a frequent problem in stepfamilies (Albrecht, Bohr, & Goodman, 1983; Duberman, 1973; Messinger, 1976; Visher & Visher, 1982). Although studies regarding the stepmother's role in disciplining the children are practically non-existent, studies of stepfathers do indicate that disagreements related to enforcement of rules and discipline strategies are a source of stress for parents and children. Because of the more salient role of mother as parent, stepmothers are often expected to be more involved in parenting than stepfathers. It does appear from the results of the present research that successful parental efforts to work out issues related to parenting expectations and strategies are related to the quality of the stepmother-adolescent relationship and could serve as a resource to the stepmother. It seems reasonable to expect that as the stepmother and father experience more cooperation and agreement on issues related to child rearing, the role strain associated with the unclear nature of how the stepmother is supposed to function in this disciplinary role would be reduced. It appears that a "united front" of both parents regarding discipline and child guidance contributes to a quality relationship between the stepmother and stepchild.

Self-esteem of the stepmother. While the findings of this study indicated that the self-esteem of the stepmother was only marginally significant, there is reason to think that this factor is perhaps more important as a predictor of the quality of her relationship with an adolescent stepchild. Although several studies have assessed the child's self-esteem in terms of adjustment to stepfamily living, no studies to date have examined self-esteem of the stepmother as a component of family functioning. Small (1988) among others has found that in first-married families the mother's self-esteem was highly related to better communication with her adolescent child. The role of the stepmother has typically been depicted as self-centered, uncaring, and even evil, yet there are societal expectations that these women share in childrearing duties. It may be that a strong sense of self-worth allows the stepmother to more effectively and realistically cope with the ambiguity and negative connotations of this role.

CONCLUSIONS

Several study variables were not predictive of the quality of the stepmother-adolescent relationship as hypothesized. The relatively small sample size would, in part, account for the lack of statistical significance in these hypothesized relationships. Similarly, the relatively small variation in some of the variables, e.g., age of stepmother, length of time in stepfamily, relationship with the natural, non-residential mother, would minimize statistical significance. A larger, more representative sample would not only have increased statistical power and generalizability of the findings, but also permitted the inclusion of additional theoretically relevant variables and an examination of predictors of stepmother-adolescent discrepancy in perceptions. Nevertheless this study does represent one of the larger samples of stepmother families and is one of the very few to include more than one family member. In addition, the findings of this study suggest some interesting questions for further research as well as important implications for family practitioners.

IMPLICATIONS FOR PRACTICE AND POLICY

It can well be argued that the most pressing content area for future research is that of focusing more on healthy stepfamily development (Giles-Sims & Crosbie-Burnett, 1989). This study is a preliminary step in that skills have been identified as associated with reducing stress associated with stepfamily living (i.e., acquiring social support and the frequency of agreement between the stepmother and father on how to raise the child). These findings suggest means of building strong stepfamilies because the identified skills and strengths can be learned.

The family's ability to acquire support from relatives, friends, neighbors, and extended family can be a valuable resource for helping adolescent children cope with the changes and stressors involved in the formation of a relationship with a stepparent. The significant increase in the number of individuals and families affected by divorce in recent years has not been accompanied by widespread societal support that might ease the transition to a remarried lifestyle (Price & McKenry, 1988). Most societal efforts have focused on divorce prevention, not facilitation of post-divorce lifestyle. The importance of the families' use of other social support networks including church and religious resources, community resources, neighborhood agencies and programs such as counseling services could be emphasized by family life educators and family therapists as resources for families and children in the transition from a single parent family to a stepfamily and also during the period of relationship formation. Support groups provided by high schools for adolescents experiencing divorce and/or remarriage might be helpful in providing yet another situation where the adolescent can share his or her experiences in a supportive atmosphere of peers and teachers.

This study indicated that maintaining open communication and cooperation between the stepmother and father on discipline strategies used with the adolescent was a major factor in the quality of the stepmother-adolescent relationship. Expectations regarding parenting roles should be discussed in preparation for remarriage when children are involved. Additionally, there needs to be an emphasis on preparation for remarriage classes where parenting as well as other stepfamily issues are discussed. Further, information for preparation for remarriage could be provided through newspaper articles, magazines, and prepared lists of recommended readings for parents and children. Special workshops on issues related to stepfamily living such as one product developed by the American Personnel and Guidance Association called *Strengthening Stepfamilies* (1986) are also suggested. Participation in a workshop on communication and/or problem solving is highly recommended, as is setting aside time each week or month to discuss family problems and solutions.

This study does lend support to the fact that the family's ability to reframe problems as perceived by the adolescent is also related positively to the quality of the relationship with his or her stepmother. Helping the family and child to develop the ability to redefine stressful events in order to make them more manageable also serves as a resource for dealing with the remarriage of the child's father and subsequent addition of a stepmother. It is further recommended that the thoughts and beliefs of the adolescent be entertained regarding having a stepmother, and that negative perceptions of that event be replaced with more positive, realistic expectations.

Family life educators and therapists should be trained to help stepfamilies understand that stepfamily living often brings a larger number of people into the closeness and intimacy of sharing a common family life. This increase in close interpersonal relationships creates an abundance of opportunities to put others first, to express patience and kindness, and to learn communication and problem-solving skills. It is important to reframe these difficulties as challenges and opportunities instead of seeing them only as hassles or problems that are without purpose or benefit.

Recommendations for family life educators and practitioners regarding stepfamilies include providing information, training, and support for a strong couple relationship (Quick & Quick, 1986). This study lends support to the notion that a healthy, growing, flexible marriage actuated by a two-way commitment to common goals and values is the cornerstone of successful stepfamily living. In stepfamilies, the strength and health of the marital bond is particularly important. Incorporating regular periods of marriage-enriching activities is recommended.

Family counselors may need training to help them to better understand the uniqueness of stepfamily living (Quick & Quick, 1991). Negative, unrealistic attitudes and values regarding remarriage and stepfamilies need to be assessed. Family professionals should familiarize themselves not only with stepfamily characteristics and concerns, but stepfamily strengths as well.

This research also suggests recommendations for family policy. Stepparents under the current family law are not provided with clear and comprehensive rules associated with their responsibilities to the stepchild (Fine, 1989). This legal ambiguity can further contribute to role strain. There is need for legislation that is more sensitive to the legal status (or lack of, as the case may be) of stepfamily members and to further consider the interplay between legal issues and parent-child relationship and adjustments in stepfamilies.

REFERENCES

Albrecht, S., Bohr, H., & Goodman, K. (1983). *Divorce and remarriage: Problems, adaptations, and adjustments.* Westport, CT: Greenwood.

American Personnel and Guidance Association. (1986). *Strengthening stepfamilies.* Washington, DC: American Personnel and Guidance Association.

Ball, D., McKenry, P. C., & Price-Bonham, S. (1983). Use of repeated-measure designs in family research. *Journal of Marriage and the Family, 45,* 885-896.

Barnes, H., & Olson, D. H. (1982). Parent-adolescent communication. In D. H. Olson et al. (Eds.), *Family inventories.* St. Paul, MN: Department of Family Social Science, University of Minnesota.

Brand, E., & Clingempeel, W. G. (1987). Interdependence of marital and stepparent-stepchild relationships and children's psychological adjustment: Research findings and clinical implications. *Family Relations, 36,* 140-145.

Cherlin, A. (1978). Remarriage as an incomplete institution. *American Journal of Sociology, 86,* 636-650.

Chilman, C. S. (1983). Remarriage and stepfamilies: Research results and implications. In E. D. Macklin & R. H. Rubin (Eds.), *Contemporary families and alternative lifestyles: A handbook on research and theory* (pp. 147-163). Beverly Hills, CA: Sage.

Clingempeel, W. G., Brand, E., & Ievoli, R. (1984). Stepparent-stepchild relationships in stepmother and stepfather families: A multimethod study. *Family Relations, 33,* 465-473.

Clingempeel, W. G., Brand, E., & Segal, S. (1987). A multilevel-multivariate developmental perspective for future research in stepfamilies. In K. Pasley & M. Ihinger-Tallman (Eds.), *Remarriage and stepparenting: Current research and theory* (pp. 65-93). New York: Guilford.

Coombs, R. H. (1991). Marital status and personal well-being: A literature review. *Family Relations, 40,* 103-105.

Duberman, L. (1973). Step-kin relationships. *Journal of Marriage and the Family, 35,* 283-292.

Fine, M. A. (1989). A social science perspective on stepfamily law: Suggestions for legal reform. *Family Relations, 38,* 53-58.

Furstenberg, F. F., Jr. (1980). Reflections on Remarriage. *Journal of Family Issues.*

Furstenberg, F. F., Jr., & Nord, C. W. (1985). Parenting apart: Patterns of childrearing after marital disruption. *Journal of Marriage and the Family, 47,* 893-904.

Giles-Sims, J., & Crosbie-Burnett, M. (1989). Stepfamily research: Implications for policy, clinical intervention, and further research. *Family Relations, 38,* 19-23.

Glick, P. C. (1984). Marriage, divorce, and living arrangements: Prospective changes. *Journal of Family Issues, 5,* 7-26.

Herndon, A. (1982). Do we know enough about the predominant family form of the 21st century? *Wake Forest,* 36-37.

Hollingshead, A. B. (1957). Two factor index of social position. (Available from August B. Hollingshead, 1965 Yale Station, New Haven, CT.)

Ihinger-Tallman, M., & Pasley, K. (1987). *Remarriage.* Newbury Park, CA: Sage.

Lutz, P. (1983). The stepfamily: An adolescent perspective. *Family Relations, 32,* 367-375.

Martin, T. C., & Bumpass, L. L. (1989). Recent trends in marital disruption. *Demography, 26,* 37-51.

McCubbin, H. I., Larsen, A., & Olson, D. H. (1981). Family crisis oriented personal evaluation scales (F-COPES). In D. H. Olson (Ed.), *Family inventories.* St. Paul, MN: Department of Family Social Science, University of Minnesota.

McKenry, P. C., Price-Bonham, S., & O'Bryant, S. (1981). Adolescent discipline: Different family members' perception. *Journal of Youth and Adolescence, 10,* 327-337.

Messinger, L. (1976). Remarriage between divorced people with children from previous marriages: A proposal for preparation for remarriage. *Journal of Marriage and Family Counseling, 2,* 193-200.

Miller, B. C. (1986). *Family research methods.* Newbury Park, CA: Sage.

Papernow, P. O. (1984). The stepfamily cycle: An experimental model of stepfamily development. *Family Relations, 33,* 355-364.

Pearlin, L. I., & Schooler, C. (1978). The structure of coping. *Journal of Health and Social Behavior, 19,* 2-21.

Price, S. J., & McKenry, P. C. (1988). *Divorce.* Newbury Park, CA: Sage.

Quick, D. S., & Quick, J. S. (1986). *Building strong blended families: Sixteen key elements.* Lexington, KY: University of Kentucky Cooperative Extension Service.

Quick, J. S., & Quick, D. S. (1991). *Creating healthy blended families.* Lexington, KY: University of Kentucky Cooperative Extension Service.

Rosenberg, M. (1965). *Society and the adolescent self-image.* Princeton, NJ: Princeton.

Sabatelli, R. M. (1984). A marital comparison level index: A measure for assessing outcomes relative to expectations. *Journal of Marriage and the Family, 46,* 651-662.

Santrock, J. W., & Sitterle, K. A. (1987). Parent-child relationships in stepmother families. In K. Pasley & M. Ihinger-Tallman (Eds.), *Remarriage and stepparenting: Current research and theory* (273-299). New York: Guilford.

Sauer, L. E., & Fine, M. A. (1988). Parent-child relationships in stepparent families. *Journal of Family Psychology, 1,* 434-451.

Small, S. A. (1988). Parental self-esteem and its relationship to childrearing practices, parent-adolescent interaction, and adolescent behavior. *Journal of Marriage and the Family, 50,* 1063-1072.

Visher, E. B., & Visher, J. S. (1982). Children in stepfamilies. *Psychiatric Annals, 12,* 832-841.

Adolescents from Stepfamilies, Single-Parent Families and (In)Stable Intact Families in The Netherlands

A. P. Spruijt

SUMMARY. This article examines the effects on intimate relationships, relational attitudes, and well-being of growing up in: stepfamilies after divorce, single-parent families, instable intact families, and stable intact families. Data are used from the national panel study USAD (Utrecht Study of Adolescence Development), a study of developments as they occur in the life course of young people during the 1990s. Results are presented from 2,064 respondents between 15 and 25 years of age, about their well-being and their development in intimate relationships and their views on (marriage) relationships. On a number of topics their parents are interviewed as well.

From the analysis, it is clear that young people who lived in single-parent families and in stepfamilies significantly differ from young people who lived in stable intact families. Young people from single-parent families are more likely to start their relational career sooner and reported more problems with intimate relations than youngsters from stable intact families. Youngsters from stepfamilies have more modern views on relations than people from intact families. Adolescents from instable intact families have moderate scores. Most of these effects remain when the results are adjusted for differences in social class, family income and the parental views on family life. *[Article copies available from The Haworth Document Delivery Service: 1-800-342-9678.]*

A. P. Spruijt, PhD, is Senior Lecturer, Department of Youth, Family and Life Course, Utrecht University, Heidelberglaan 2, P.O. Box 80.140, 3508 TC Utrecht, The Netherlands.

[Haworth co-indexing entry note]: "Adolescents from Stepfamilies, Single-Parent Families and (In) Stable Intact Families in The Netherlands." Spruijt, A. P. Co-published simultaneously in *Journal of Divorce & Remarriage* (The Haworth Press, Inc.) Vol. 24, No. 1/2, 1995, pp. 115-132; and: *Understanding Stepfamilies: Their Structure and Dynamics* (ed: Craig A. Everett) The Haworth Press, Inc., 1995, pp. 115-132. Single or multiple copies of this article are available from The Haworth Document Delivery Service [1-800-342-9678, 9:00 a.m. - 5:00 p.m. (EST)].

INTRODUCTION

"Further studies in which simple comparisons of children from different family structures are made are generally not needed," Ganong and Coleman (1993) conclude in a meta-analytic comparison of the self-esteem and behaviour problems of stepchildren to children in other family structures. They base this conclusion on the fact that stepchildren generally do not differ greatly from children in other family structures. Nevertheless, we present here the results of new research into differences between youngsters from various types of families. Firstly, because Ganong and Coleman's study still leaves many unanswered questions, for example, that they find few differences between children from stepfamilies and children from single-parent families. McLanahan and Bumpass (1988) conclude in their study concerning the intergenerational consequences of family disruption that women who spend part of their childhood in a single-parent family experience problems with relations. And, secondly, because they only study the effects of the family structure on problems related to self-esteem and behaviour. We are particularly interested in the effects of family disruption on the relational views and behaviour of youngsters. Moreover, we have added an important family type to the study: instable intact families, which is a more interesting group for the purpose of comparison than the stable intact families.

This article reports on an empirical investigation into growing up in different kinds of families in The Netherlands. The study examines the effects on well-being, intimate relationships and relational attitudes of growing up in four different family types: stepfamilies, single-parent families, instable intact families and stable intact families. The stepfamilies and the single-parent families in this study are 'new', i.e., families formed after divorce of the parents. Data were used from the USAD (Utrecht Study of Adolescence Development) national panel study, a longitudinal survey, the results of the first set of measurements of the study being available at the time of writing.[1] The total number of stepfamilies in The Netherlands (population 15 million) in 1994 is about 150,000 (married and unmarried partners); the number of single-parent families is about 350,000 (Van Delft and Niphuis-Nell, 1988). In the period 1987 to 1993, about 30,000 divorces were pronounced per year in The Netherlands and 20,000 remarriages celebrated (C.B.S.: Central Bureau of Statistics, 1991: 40).

De Graaf (1991) has reported on the influence of divorce of the parents on the demographic behaviour of the women in The Netherlands. He concludes that a clear effect can be observed, even after allowing for the influence of a number of background characteristics. It turns out that women from single-parent families leave the parental home at a younger age, live together earlier without getting married, break up relationships more often and tend to have a more negative opinion about their personal relationships. Ganong and Coleman (1984: 401) conclude that there was in general little evidence that children in stepfamilies differ from children growing up in other family structures, but some studies do report more problems with stepchildren. Dutch research carried out in 1989 on stepfamilies (Spruijt et al.) shows that particularly adolescents in divided stepfamilies (the parent and the stepmother or father disagree on a number of matters) mention many problems, while in most other stepfamilies things go fairly well. Following the study of Cherlin et al. (1992) we also turned our attention to children in families with serious problems but where there was, so far, no divorce. We made a difference here between stable and instable intact families. Instable intact families are families where the parents are considering divorce: the 'almost divorced' families.

Just how great are the effects of family disruption on relational variables? When examining the literature on divorce and the forming of a stepfamily, it is important to differentiate between two sorts of publications: the clinical and the empirical. Ganong and Coleman (1987: 105) state, "The research literature, for the most part, has not reported significant difference between stepchildren and children from other family structures. The clinical literature, on the other hand, has generally reported that stepchildren and their families are beset by problems and difficulties." Differences such as these are also found in The Netherlands between clinical and empirical research among non-clinical populations (Spruijt and Hendrickx, 1993). It is not surprising to find that in clinical research, among persons seeking help from specialized organizations, for example, many problems are recorded, in the case of children of divorced parents as well. It is important for this kind of research to be carried out in order to gain more insight into the problems following divorce and the measures which can be taken to help. But it is not correct to generalize data from this kind of research and apply the results to a greater population of non-clients. It is therefore necessary to carry out empirical research among a broader population.

Insight into the differences between youngsters from stepfamilies, single-parent families and intact families can make it clear whether the ongoing concern about the consequences of divorce is in fact justified. Is it more difficult for the young people who have experienced major disturbances in their life (divorce of parents or formation of a stepfamily) to get along in today's society, than others? All children are increasingly confronted with the results of modernization and individualization in society. This means greater emphasis on being responsible for your own decisions, in the area of personal relations as well. Du Bois-Reymond (1992: 32) talks about the development from standard lifecourse to chosen pattern. Is the chosen pattern extra-complicated in the case of a young person who, as a child, experienced the divorce of his parents or their problematic marriage?

The formulation of the problem discussed in this article is:

> What are the differences between children from stepfamilies, single-parent families, instable intact families and stable intact families with respect to their well-being and their (attitude towards) relationships? Can the differences be explained by the (divorce) experience in the family?

In Section 2 we discuss what effects of family disruption are defined in the literature and what are the theoretical lines of approach for describing and accounting for the differences between children from the various family types. Section 3 gives a short description of the USAD project, which is the source of the empirical data used in this article. The research data are presented in Section 4 and they include allowance for the effect of a number of background variables. The paper closes with the conclusions.

CONSEQUENCES OF FAMILY DISRUPTION ON YOUNGSTERS IN THE LITERATURE

Kitson and Morgan (1990) are left with a question: Why is there in America such continuing societal concern about divorce and its consequences? They assume the reasons are: the long Judeo-Christian heritage of antipathy to divorce, the world-wide trend toward conservatism and religious fundamentalism, the (negative) effects of divorce on individuals and society, and the possible long-term consequences for society. Kitson and Morgan stress the fact that we still do not know what the long-term implications of divorce are for adults or children. However, if the goal of the society is to produce appropriately socialized and trained individuals who, in turn, marry and reproduce, the long-term effects of divorce and remarriage raise important questions for the future. In The Netherlands, Van Gelder (1989) carried out a literature study on the long-term effects of divorce. He establishes that children of single-parent families have somewhat more doubts with respect to future married and family life. They are more active in forming relationships with the opposite sex and at the same time also more critical. Van Gelder also reports that children of divorced parents more often give birth to children outside marriage, get married a little earlier and get divorced more often. Finally, they are more critical about their marriage relationship.

Amato and Keith (1991) have conducted a meta-analysis of studies dealing with the long-term consequences of parental divorce for adult well-being. Effect sizes were calculated for 15 outcome variables across 37 studies involving over 81,000 individuals. They conclude that parental divorce has significant negative effects on the well-being of the children in their adulthood. A number of variables such as teenage pregnancy, teenage marriage, social well-being, the quality of marriage, divorce and physical health are concerned. This pessimistic conclusion must be tempered, however. The effect sizes are generally significant, but weak. Moreover, effect sizes were significantly stronger in clinical studies than in studies based on community samples.

Various authors (including Demo and Acock, 1988) point out rightly that in much research into the effects of divorce, the two-parent family is implicitly or explicitly the norm. This is in accordance with the Freudian approach, that both a father and a mother are necessary for normal development of a child. Many researchers apply this norm, partly because other theories related to personality development (such as, for example, structural functionalism, the theory of social learning and symbolic interactionism) are also based on the presence of two parents of different sexes. The theoretical explanations which are put forward for the occurrence of differences between children of single and two-parent families mostly assume a family with a biological father and a biological mother as starting point. Amato and Keith (1991) recognize three commonly adopted theoretical approaches for the explanation of differences between children in single and two-parent families. The first approach stresses the economic decline experienced by many single-parent (mother only) families. The difficult financial situation has a negative effect in many different ways on the views and behaviour of the children. The second approach concentrates on divorce as a stressful experience for children. Divorce often means a long drawn-out period of family conflict and, moreover, problems rarely come singly. In addition to the divorce, children often have to deal with a number of other stressful matters such as moving to another house, changing school and losing touch with friends, grandparents and other family members. The third approach emphasizes the significance of the changed family structure after the divorce. Not only is one parent not in a position to do as much as two but, also, the daily example of a parent of the one sex is missing. In addition, contact with the parent who has left may well be difficult.

McLanahan and Bumpass (1988) distinguish between three approaches similar to Amato and Keith but, with respect to the third approach, put greater stress on the socialization aspect. In a single-parent (mother only) family the emphasis may be more on the absence of the (socializing) father or on the presence of the (socializing) mother. The fact that many daughters of single mothers become single mothers themselves could mean that the daughters have learnt that women can run a family perfectly well on their own. The positive approach to the characteristics of children of single-parent families is interesting here. Glenn and Kramer (1987) seek the explanation for "intergenerational transmission of marital instability" in various directions: the absence or failure of the example of the husband role, the inadequate social control of family and neighbourhood, the low resistance to divorce, getting married young, and growing up under difficult economic circumstances. These possible explanations for differences between children from stepfamilies, single-parent families and intact families can in principle be illustrated according to the schema of Amato and Keith.

One explanation should, however, be added to the list. Bosman and Louwes (1988: 6) mention "the mentality with respect to single-parent families which continues to be characterized by lack of acceptance and preconceived notions." Dronkers (1992: 35) concludes that "part of the reason for children from single-parent (mother only) families being behind at school, is the negative image of mother-only families in our society, as expressed in this case in the (negative) assessment by the teacher of the future possibilities of children with only a mother." The negative stereotype as far as stepchildren are concerned is well-enough known. Coleman and Ganong (1987) conducted research into this negative stereotype in the United States in a number of different professional groups. It appeared that teachers, social workers, lawyers, students and others in the social sector all had a negative stereotyped image of stepchildren; only experienced therapists did not share the preconception. It is likely that the continuation of the negative preconceived notions about stepchildren has something to do with the incomplete institutionalization of stepfamilies (after divorce), observed by Cherlin as long ago as 1978 and still in existence. Amato (1991: 67) also carried out research into the existence of negative stereotypes with respect to children of divorced parents. He observed that the negative image of children of divorced parents is still very widespread in (American) society. Moreover, he demonstrated that in this case as well such negative stereotypes lead to respondents remembering negative information about children of divorced parents and forgetting the positive things about them.

Altogether, this means that globally speaking, four theoretical viewpoints exist for studying the long-term effects of family disruption:

- negative financial results of divorce
- occurrence of stress situations
- changed family structure after divorce and remarriage
- negative image forming with respect to single-parent and stepfamilies.

In the following sections we will, based on data from the USAD project, first examine what differences exist between children from the four differentiated family types in The Netherlands at the beginning of the 90s. We will then attempt to throw some light on the tenability of possible theoretical explanations for the differences.

METHOD: THE USAD PROJECT

Our answers to the questions which arise from our definition of the problem are based on data provided by the USAD project. In the period September-November 1991, 2918 young people, aged from 12 to 24 years, answered a large number of questions, both oral and written, about their development and way of life. The following aspects were dealt with, amongst others: physical and psychological well-being, breaking loose from parents and becoming independent, relationships, sex, going steady and leaving home, and the relations between generations. One of the parents of the young people concerned was also interviewed.[2] Presented here are data concerning 2140 individuals aged 15-24 years.[3]

With respect to the youngsters in question, it is known whether or not their parents are divorced. We also know if the divorced parents are living together with someone else or have remarried. The non-divorced parents of the young people were asked: Have you thought seriously about splitting up any time during the last five years? Marriages of persons who answered 'yes, often' or 'yes, on occasion' were designated as 'instable'. Those who answered 'no' or 'yes, once' were described as having a 'stable' marriage. The kinds of family from which the young people came were divided up as follows (Table 1):

After a divorce, children often remain with their mother: of the single-parent families after divorce, 91% are single-mother families and 9% single-father families. Of the stepfamilies, 93% are stepfather families and 7% stepmother families. Analysis of the correlations between youngsters per family type and a number of background variables (sex, age, educational level, social class) indicated that they are not strong and mostly not

TABLE 1. Young People by Family Type

stepfamily after divorce:	79	(3.8%)
single-parent family after divorce:	175	(8.5%)
instable intact family:	193	(9.4%)
stable intact family:	1617	(78.3%)
Total	2064	(100%)*

*The total (2064) is less than the total number of 15 - 24 year-olds who participated in the study (2140) since some family types have not been considered here; the most important category in this respect is the single-parent family after death of one parent (n = 45).

significant ($p > .05$).[4] The connection between family type and sex is significant but not strong ($p = .03$): there are somewhat more girls in single-parent families than boys. This fact confirms the results of the study carried out by Morgan, Lye and Condran (1988) that parents of girls get divorced more often than parents of boys. The divorce in the two family types after divorce took place on average 10 years earlier, and living together again or remarriage of the stepfamilies, 8 years earlier on average; we can therefore talk of research into long-term effects of parental change.

RESULTS

Relational Career

The age at which young people begin the process of becoming relationally adult has become lower and lower during the last decades. From 1959 to 1989, the average age of the first coitus dropped from 22.5 to 17.5 years (Van der Vliet, 1990). Data from the USAD project indicate a further drop in age to 17.0 years. This means that period during which young people can experiment with relationships and sexuality, before entering into a more or less permanent relationship by way of marriage or (long-term) cohabitation, has continuously grown. 't Hart, Meeus and Kox (1993: 15) talk of "the origin and lengthening of the relational moratorium and, together with the educational moratorium, of a formidable lengthening of the period of youth." Is there any difference between young people from the various family types as far as the beginning of that relational moratorium is concerned (see Table 2, lines 1 to 3)?

Young people from stepfamilies and those from single-parent families have their first sexual experience at a younger age than young people from stable intact families. Young people from single-parent families have the most experience in relationships. They also go to bed with someone more often than the others. Sixty nine percent of the offspring of single-parent families have had some kind of sexual experience and 31% none; for children from the other family types the figures are 49% and 51%, respectively. We also asked if sex the first time was with a steady girl or boyfriend or a one-night stand. A significant difference was also found here (p = .000): 29% of young people from stepfamilies and 34% from single-parent families had sex the first time with a casual partner, while this figure is 21% for young people from intact families. Young people from single-parent families thus differ significantly on a number of points in comparison with young people from stable intact families; they go to bed

TABLE 2. Summary of Mean Scores of Young People Derived from the Four Family Types.

	(a) step-family	(b) single-parent family	(c) instable intact family	(d) stable intact family	F value	p value	significant contrasts*
Relational career							
1. age first coitus	16.5	16.5	17.0	17.2	F(3.1029)=7.096	p=.000	a,b - d
2. number of (past) relations	2.25	2.51	2.40	2.23	F(3.2039)=4.996	p=.002	b - d
3. sex experience (yes=1)	1.51	1.31	1.49	1.52	F(3.2036)=8.745	p=.000	b - a,c,d
Well-being							
4. physical health	7.78	7.50	7.80	8.02	F(3.2031)=9.089	p=.000	b - d
5. psychological health	22.9	21.9	22.5	23.4	F(3.2030)=19.983	p=.000	b,c - d
6. suicide thoughts (yes=1)	1.81	1.69	1.89	1.89	F(3.2059)=10.942	p=.000	b - d
Leaving home							
7. age leaving home	18.6	18.2	19.3	19.3	F(3.0324)=6.086	p=.001	a,b - d
8. cohabiting (yes=1)	1.95	1.79	1.96	1.90	F(3.2030)=9.901	p=.000	b - a,c,d
9. divorce experience (yes=1)	1.98	1.95	1.99	1.99	F(3.2026)=3.732	p=.010	b - c,d
Relational opinions							
10. child planning (yes=1)	2.35	2.16	2.10	1.96	F(3.2026)=8.723	p=.000	a,b - c,d
11. role division (modern=1)	2.41	2.55	2.64	2.83	F(3.1948)=7.793	p=.000	a,b - d
12. relational views (modern=1)	2.14	2.16	2.24	2.39	F(3.2039)=9.448	p=.000	a,b,c - d

*This column indicates which young people significantly differ from others according to the Scheffé procedure; a,b - d means that children from stepfamilies and single-parent families differ significantly from children from stable intact families.

with someone at a younger age and more often have a casual sexual partner. Children of stepfamilies take up an in-between position. Young people from stable intact families score as the most 'traditional'.

Well-Being

What is the long-term effect of divorce or conflicts between parents and the well-being of their children? Table 2 (lines 4 to 6) shows that children from single parents score lowest on well-being and children from stable intact families highest. Children from stepfamilies score better on well-being variables than children from single-parent families.

Leaving Home

About 15% of the young people who participated in the USAD project have left the parental home. These young people are, however, not divided equally among the various family types. Children of single-parent families leave the parental home at a significantly younger age (18.2 years) than those of intact families (19.3 years) and children from stepfamilies are in between (18.6 years). The reasons for leaving home for the four categories of young people do not differ greatly. The most important are: to study (35%), to live together with boy or girlfriend (32%) and to get married (12%). A striking result from the USAD data is that youngsters from single-parent families significantly more often give 'other' as the reason for leaving home. This may have something to do with problems in the parental home. The next step in the relational career of many young people is to go and live together with a partner. About two-thirds of the young people who were living outside the parental home during the research period live together with a partner, that is, about 10% of all the respondents. Young people from single-parent families live together from an earlier age than other young people (see Table 2, line 8); they also have more experience in breaking up relationships.

Relational Opinions

Experiencing friction in the parental home, the divorce of the parents and the possible arrival of a new, important person in the family–the stepparent–undoubtedly influences the opinions of youngsters on relations and family life. Our expectation is that experiencing family problems have made the youngsters more critical about relationships. In this study, young people are asked for their opinions on three aspects of relationships: whether or not to have children, role division in a relationship and opinions about alternative family structures. Scales were developed for these aspects based on a number of items.[5] The scales run from 'modern (1)' to 'traditional (5)'. Choosing for children is also measured by way of a five-point scale. This scale goes from 'absolutely not' to 'certainly'. Absolutely not choosing for children is therefore considered as modern and certainly choosing for children as traditional.[6] The scores are given in Table 2 (lines 10 to 12).

Children from stepfamilies hesitate the most when it comes to having children, even more than children of single-parent families. Children from stable intact families have a more traditional view about the division of roles in a relationship than children from single-parent families and stepfamilies. Children from instable intact families appear to adopt an in-between position. Children from single-parent and stepfamilies have themselves experienced what it is like to live in a 'new' family structure. Does this mean then that they have a more positive view about other forms of cohabitation or have they just learnt the hard way and are, on the contrary, more traditional in their views than young people from intact families?

Young people from stable intact families have the most traditional views about new forms of cohabitation and children of stepfamilies are the most progressive. It would seem that the experiences of children whose parents have divorced contribute to a modern way of thinking about relationships and family structures.

The Influence of Some Background Variables

At the beginning of the 90s in The Netherlands, some significant differences seem to exist between children from stepfamilies, single-parent families and instable and stable intact families with respect to their well-being and relational career and their vision of (marriage) relationships. The results of the USAD project summarized in Table 2 show that the most significant differences exist between children from single-parent families and children of stable intact families. Children from stepfamilies often adopt an in-between position, except where views on relationships are concerned. They do not take it so much for granted to have children and are the most modern in their opinions about role division in relationships and alternative family structures.

The first question arising from the formulation of the problem has thus been answered, but the (second) question concerning the possible explanation for the differences, has not. Before proceeding with the various explanations (see Section 2 on consequences), we wish to check the correlations found, given in Table 2, against some background characteristics. This is done for the variables 'social class' and 'how modern are the views of the parents'. The question is whether, after allowing for the effect of social class and views of the parents, there is still a correlation between family background and (ideas about) relationships of the young people. Social class is measured on a five-point scale, how modern the views of the parents are is measured by way of questions on opinions about new forms of cohabitation. The programme 'anova' is used to first determine the correlation between the covariates social class and parental opinions and the relational variables, and thereafter what the remaining correlation is between the categories of young people and the relational variables (see Table 3).

Table 3 shows that–after allowing for the effect of two background variables–two of the twelve connections between the four categories of youngsters and differences in well-being and (opinions about) relationships, are no longer significant. The connection with social class is signifi-

TABLE 3. Summary of F and p Values of the Relations Between Relational Variables and the Four Kinds of Youngsters after Control of the Covariates Social Class and Parent Opinions.*

		p value belonging to the covariates	
		social class	parental opinions
Relational career			
1. age first coitus	F(3.0839)=3.222 (p=.022)	p=.099	p=.144
2. number of (past) relations	F(3.1855)=4.049 (p=.007)	p=.083	p=.041
3. sex experience (yes=1)	F(3.1855)=5.565 (p=.001)	p=.000	p=.018
Well-being			
4. physical health	F(3.1827)=6.764 (p=.000)	p=.268	p=.051
5. psychological health	F(3.1828)=16.864 (p=.000)	p=.017	p=.107
6. suicide thoughts	F(3.1854)=8.333 (p=.000)	p=.579	p=.059
Leaving home			
7. age leaving home	F(3.0115)=1.098 (p=.353)	p=.002	p=.019
8. cohabiting (yes=1)	F(3.1834)=1.280 (p=.280)	p=.996	p=.930
9. divorce experience (yes=1)	F(3.1826)=3.068 (p=.027)	p=.090	p=.944
Relational attitudes			
10. child planning (yes=1)	F(3.1840)=5.666 (p=.001)	p=.637	p=.003
11. role division (modern=1)	F(3.1764)=7.410 (p=.000)	p=.000	p=.000
12. relational views	F(3.1855)=4.027 (p=.007)	p=.001	p=.002

*The variable 'family income' was also taken into account. Only three p values turn out to be significant: sex experience, thoughts of suicide and experience of divorce. This means that the influence of the family income is less than that of social class and parental opinions.

cant five times and the connection with parental opinions, six times. This means that the opinions of the parents about relationships and the social environment also influence the relational career and relational opinions of the young people. The connection with family background is clearly demonstrated.

CONCLUSIONS

Central to this article are questions about the long-term effects of family disruption on the well-being, relational behaviour and relational views of young people. Just how important is the parental example of a relationship for a child? This question is important with respect to the future, apart from anything else. How are the increasing numbers of children from divorced or remarried parents going to give form to their relational career?

Our data have demonstrated that significant relational differences exist between the four types of youngsters. As far as the actual relational career is concerned, children from single-parent families are in the lead and children from stable intact families trailing behind the rest. Children from single-parent families are the first to leave home on average and also the youngest when first living together with a partner. The sense of well-being of children from single-parent families is the lowest of all categories. Children from stepfamilies adopt an in-between position as far as their relational behaviour is concerned and their sense of well-being. As far as views about relationships are concerned, children from stepfamilies are clearly the most modern: they hesitate the most about having children, are the strongest in their support for equality between the sexes in terms of role division and are the most open for new forms of living together. Children from stable intact families are in every respect the most traditional and the most healthy.

Family disruption exerts an influence on the relational career and the ideas about relationships of young people, even after allowing for social background, parental opinions and family income. The results of the children from instable intact families point to the same result: these youngsters adopt an in-between position on many points. The results indicate that it is important to look at more than just the significance of divorce and take into account the effects of the conflicts of parents on the verge of divorce as well. However, the effects clearly become stronger when the parents are in fact divorced.

Which of the four theoretical explanations mentioned in Section 2 for differences between young people (negative financial consequences of a divorce, occurrence of stress situations, the changed family structure after divorce and remarriage, and the negative image-forming of single-parent families and stepfamilies) seems to be the most plausible? The last column of Table 2 shows which categories of youngsters differ significantly from each other. Summarized in brief, children from stable intact families are the most traditional and children from single-parent families the most modern. However, the scores of children from stepfamilies show them as the most modern in their relational views and the question is to what extent, with the second and third sets of measurements in the USAD project, they will continue to demonstrate such modern behaviour. They have in any case experienced the most parental change. As far as the sense of well-being is concerned, children from single-parent families are the worst off.[7] Children from stepfamilies do not deviate much from children from instable intact families.

The most important conclusion must probably be that there is no one single explanation. The first explanation of Amato and Keith (1991) (decline in the financial position of the single-parent family) cannot be rejected entirely, although no clear connection with income could be found (see footnotes in Tables 2 and 3). The social class of the parents of the youngsters does, generally speaking, seem to be connected with a number of relational variables (see Table 3). Amato and Keith's second explanation concerning the significance of stressful events with respect to behaviour and views of young people is partly supported and partly rejected by the results. Partly rejected because children from stepfamilies, who have experienced at least two stressful events, do not score very differently from children from single-parent families. Partly supported because children from stable intact families strikingly demonstrate the most traditional behaviour and have the most traditional opinions and young people from instable intact families adopt an in-between position. The third explanation concerns the changed family structure after divorce and the forming of a stepfamily. The in-between position adopted by children from a stepfamily might indicate that structural variables in the family (absence of father and husband role, less social control) do indeed play a role in explaining the differences between the four types of youngsters. In the stepfamily, the structure of the family changes again and tends to resemble once again the structure of an intact family. It is difficult to draw conclusions about whether or not the labelling theory can be applied. This fourth theoretical approach is grounded in the negative stereotype of children in single-parent and stepfamilies. It appears, however, that these two categories of youngsters also differ from each other. Children of single-parent families in our society are possibly more stigmatized than children with a stepmother or father, even if just because a stepfamily looks from the outside more like an intact family. But the research results do not provide much support for the stigmatization theory.

There is a tendency in the literature to ascribe automatically the (negative) characteristics of children of divorced parents to the divorce, in single-parent and also in stepfamilies. It should not be forgotten, however, that it appears from the USAD project, amongst other sources, that 5% to 20% of all young people have problems anyway (Meeus & 't Hart, 1993). The problem of the category of children of divorced parents, which most certainly exists, must, however, be seen in the right proportions. This does not signify in any way a refusal to acknowledge that individual children of divorced parents can indeed experience major problems. It is important to note in this respect the conclusion of Amato and Keith (1991) that systematic clinical research does (of course) paint a worse picture of the effect of divorce than sociological research. This conclusion is supported by the results recorded in this paper: the actual differences in this empirical study are significant, but not very great. There are undoubtedly some worrisome aspects about the differences between the various types of youngsters, but it may be a positive that young people from stable intact families are the most traditional in their thinking and children from single-parent families the most modern. It appears that children of divorced parents probably reflect more critically on their relationships. The future sets of measurements taken within the framework of the USAD project will show whether they do in fact act more critically as they grow older and more relational choices have to be made.

NOTES

1. The next sets of measurements were planned for the end of 1994 and the end of 1997.

2. This interview round was the first in a series of three: the same young people and their parents were asked again certain questions in 1994, and will be asked them in 1997 ('t Hart, Meeus & Kox, 1993).

3. The random selection was based on statistics on households and young persons living independently, from the National Script Panel and the National Mini Census ('t Hart, Meeuw & Kox, 1993). At the most, two persons aged 15-24 per household were selected. A total of 3525 households were approached. The percentage of refusals was 26.1% and the total of non-response from among the households, 35.9%. Control calculations indicate that the random selection of young people deviates slightly from information known about young people based on other sources. There are two important areas of deviation: the percentage of those living on their own is too low and those of different racial background are hardly represented at all. These two matters must be taken into account in interpreting the data.

4. The SPSS programme, version 4.0.1., was used for calculating the data. Various subprogrammes were worked with, in every case a p value of .05 was

applied as criterium for an identified difference as lower level (see also Meeus & 't Hart, 1993).

5. The role division scale comprises 3 items (for example: caring for children is more important for a woman than a job outside the home) and has an alpha of 0.81; the scale for opinions about alternative family structures comprises 8 items (for example: I think it is acceptable for a couple to live together without being married) and has an alpha of 0.88 (see, further, Meeus & 't Hart, 1993).

6. There is also a significant connection between 'choosing for children' and 'sex of the respondent': 76% of the girls and 68% of the boys choose to have children (probably or certainly). The connection between young people per family type and choosing for children remains significant, even after allowing for the sex of the respondent variable (p = .000).

7. This result is despite the fact that the divorce happened ten years ago on average. This connection remains even after allowing for income.

REFERENCES

Amato P.R. & B. Keith (1991), Parental divorce and adult well-being: a meta-analysis. *Journal of Marriage and the Family, 53*, pp. 43-58.

Amato P.R. (1991), The "child of divorce" as a person prototype: Bias in the recall of information about children in divorced families. *Journal of Marriage and the Family, 53*, pp. 59-70.

Bois-Reymond, M. du (1992), *Jongeren op weg naar volwassenheid.* Wolters-Noordhoff, Groningen.

Bosman, R. & W. Louwes (1988), Eenouder-en tweeoudergezinnen en school-loopbanen. *Mens en Maatschappij, 63*, pp. 5-23.

C.B.S. (1991), *Maandstatistiek van de bevolking*, nr. 7.

Cherlin, A.J. (1978), Remarriage as an incomplete institution. *American Journal of Sociology, 84*, pp. 634-649.

Cherlin, A.J., F.F. Furstenberg, P.L. Chase-Landsdale, K.E. Kiernan, P.K. Robins, D.R. Morrison & J.O. Teitler (1992), Longitudinal studies of effects of divorce on children in Great Britain and the United States. *Science, 252*, pp. 1386-1389.

Coleman, M. & L.H. Ganong (1987), The cultural stereotyping of stepfamilies. In K. Pasley & M. Ihinger-Tallman (eds.), *Remarriage and stepparenting*. Guilford Press, New York, London.

Delft, M. van & M. Niphuis-Nell (1988), *Eenoudergezinnen: ontstaan, leefsituatie en voorzieningengebruik*. Sociale en Culturele Studies–9, Sociaal en Cultureel Planbureau, Rijswijk.

Demo, D.H. & A.C. Acock (1988), The impact of divorce on children. *Journal of Marriage and the Family, 50*, pp. 619-648.

Dronkers, J. (1992), Zullen wij voor de kinderen bij elkaar blijven? De veranderende effecten van eenoudergezinnen op de schoolloopbanen van de kinderen. *Mens en Maatschappij, 67*, pp. 23-44.

Furstenberg, F.F. (1988), Child care after divorce and remarriage. In E.M. Hetherington & J.D. Arasteh (eds.), *Impact of divorce, single parenting and stepparenting on children*. Lawrence Erlbaum Associates, Hillsdale, New Jersey, pp. 245-261.

Ganong, L.H. & M. Coleman (1984), The effects of remarriage on children: a review of the empirical literature. *Family Relations, 33*, pp. 389-405.

Ganong, L.H. & M. Coleman (1987), Effects of parental remarriage on children. In K. Pasley & M. Ihinger-Tallman (eds.), *Remarriage and stepparenting*. Guilford Press, New York, London.

Ganong, L.H. & M. Coleman (1993), A Meta-Analytic Comparison of the Self-Esteem and Behavior Problems of Stepchildren to Children in Other Family Structures. *Journal of Divorce & Remarriage, 19*, pp. 143-163.

Gelder, K. van (1989), *Kinderen van de rekening?* Eenouderkinderen in de onderzoeksliteratuur. NIMAWO, 's-Gravenhage.

Glenn, N.D. & K.B. Kramer (1987), The marriage and divorces of the children of divorce. *Journal of Marriage and the Family, 49*, pp. 811-825.

Graaf, A. de (1991), De invloed van echtscheiding van de ouders op demografisch gedrag van de vrouw. *Maandstatistiek van de bevolking, 8*, pp. 30-38. CBS, 's-Gravenhage.

Hart, H. 't, W. Meeus & W. Kox (1993), Jongeren in Nederland: achtergronden en opzet van een nationaal survey. In W. Meeus & H. 't Hart (red.), *Jongeren in Nederland. Een nationaal survey naar ontwikkeling in de adolescentie en naar intergenerationele overdracht.* Academisch uitgeverij Amersfoort.

Kitson, G.C. & L.A. Morgan (1990), The multiple consequences of divorce: a decade review. *Journal of Marriage and the Family, 52*, pp. 913-924.

McLanahan, S. & L. Bumpass (1988), Intergenerational consequences of family disruption. *American Journal of Sociology, 94*, pp. 130-152.

Meeus, W. & H. 't Hart (red.) (1993), *Jongeren in Nederland.* Een nationaal survey naar ontwikkeling in de adolescentie en naar intergenerationele overdracht. Academisch uitgeverij Amersfoort.

Morgan, S.P., D.N. Lye & G.A. Condran (1988), Sons, daughters, and the risk of marital disruption. *American Journal of Sociology, 94*, pp. 110-129.

Spruijt, A.P. (red.) (1989), *Stiefgezinnen: gewoon of anders?* Giordano Bruno, Amersfoort.

Spruijt, A.P. & J. van der Meer (1991), Het tweede huwelijk: een nieuwe kans? In A.P. Spruijt (red.), *Psychologie van het gezin; zicht op huwelijk en relaties.* Teleac Utrecht, p. 243-260.

Spruijt, A.P. & J.J.P. Hendrickx (1993), Problemen en positieve ervaringen in stiefgezinnen: gezinssociologisch onderzoek en klinische implicaties. In *Systeemtherapie, 5*, pp. 15-29.

Spruijt, A.P. (1993), Relaties: feiten, opvattingen en problemen. In W. Meeus & H. 't Hart (red.), *Jongeren in Nederland.* Een nationaal survey naar ontwikkeling in de adolescentie en naar intergenerationele overdracht. Academisch uitgeverij Amersfoort, p. 56-78.

Thornton, A. (1991), Influence of the marital history of parents on the marital and cohabitational experiences of children. *American Journal of Sociology, 96,* pp. 868-894.

Vliet, R. van der (1990), De opkomst van het seksuele moratorium. In G. Hekma, B. van Stolk, B. van Heerikhuizen & B. Kruithof (red.), *Het verlies van de onschuld.* Wolters-Noordhof, Groningen, pp. 51-69.

Using Social Construction Therapy with the REM Family

Joan D. Atwood
Renée Zebersky

SUMMARY. It is estimated that currently one child in five under the age of eighteen is a stepchild and that by the year 2000, the remarried (REM) family will outnumber all other family forms. Historically, American society defines any form of family life that does not conform to the traditional nuclear family as problematic. Family researchers have generally been consistent with society's negative views, using a problem-oriented approach to studying the REM family (Hoffman, 1991; Duncan and Brown, 1992; Coleman, Ganong, and Gingrich, 1985). In so doing they have focused on documenting the difficulties of the REM family. This paper attempts to rectify these issues by first exploring the typical problems associated with the REM family focusing on social constructionist themes and therapy which serve to shift the focus of a problem-oriented approach toward a search for the strengths and positive characteristics of the family. Social constructionism focuses on the sociocultural and the individual relationship influences of language, family and culture. In addition, the paper proposes a six-stage therapeutic model based on Social Constructionist Theory (Gergen and Gergen, 1983). The six stages of therapy with a remarried family are: (1) Joining the Family

Joan D. Atwood, PhD, is Coordinator, Graduate Programs in Marriage and Family Therapy, Hofstra University, Hempstead, NY 11570. Renée Zebersky, PD, at the time of writing this article, was a Marriage and Family Therapist at Hofstra. She is now in private practice and works with special education students at Oceanside School District, Oceanside, NY.

[Haworth co-indexing entry note]: "Using Social Construction Therapy with the REM Family." Atwood, Joan D., and Renée Zebersky. Co-published simultaneously in *Journal of Divorce & Remarriage* (The Haworth Press, Inc.) Vol. 24, No. 1/2, 1995, pp. 133-162; and: *Understanding Stepfamilies: Their Structure and Dynamics* (ed: Craig A. Everett) The Haworth Press, Inc., 1995, pp. 133-162. Single or multiple copies of this article are available from The Haworth Document Delivery Service [1-800-342-9678, 9:00 a.m. - 5:00 p.m. (EST)].

Meaning System, (2) Proposing the Notion of a Socially Constructed Family Meaning System, (3) Learning the Family's Meaning System, (4) Challenging the Family's Meaning System, (5) Amplifying the New Meaning System, and (6) Stabilizing the New Meaning System. It allows the REM family the ability to construct new meanings around their problems in living in order that they might find workable family solutions. *[Article copies available from The Haworth Document Delivery Service: 1-800-342-9678.]*

INCIDENCE

The United States has the highest divorce in the world: there are approximately 1.2 million divorces each year in the United States involving 2.4 million adults and more than a million children (Furstenberg and Spanier, 1984, p. 37). Coupled with this high divorce rate is a high rate of remarriage: eighty percent of those who divorce remarry with over three-fourths remarrying within 3-5 years of their divorce (Norton and Glick, 1976). More than forty percent of marriages in any given year are remarriages for one or both partners (Duncan and Brown, 1992). Visher and Visher (1988) report that 79% of divorced men and 75% of divorced women remarry and that 60% of these have children. The more recent USA Today Gallop poll (August 15, 1989, p. 1) revealed that the incidence of remarriage among men was now closer to 83% of men and 76% for women. Remarriage does not presuppose a lasting marriage as divorce rates are slightly higher among the REM (60%) as compared to first time marriages (57%) (Furstenberg and Spanier, 1984, p. 45; Pasley and Ihinger-Tallman, 1987; Visher and Visher, 1988).

The National Center for Health Statistics reports that since 1980 there has been a 50% increase in marriages involving single women and divorced men. Those involving single men and divorced women have increased 60%. An examination of the households in the United States indicates that of the 64.5 million households, 50.7 million have a spouse living in the house, and 9 million, or one fifth, were comprised of remarried couples where one or both parties had been previously divorced (Furstenberg and Spanier, 1984, p. 39). There are 72.8 million natural or adopted children and 3.8 million stepchildren in these homes. Stepchildren constitute 1.5% of the total population in the United States. Glick (1989) estimated that forty percent of married couple households are projected to become remarried families before the youngest child turns 18. It is estimated that at this time one child in five under the age of 18 is a stepchild and "that by the year 2000 this type of family will actually outnumber all other kinds of American families" (Glick, 1984; Glick and Lin, 1986).

DEFINITIONS OF REMARRIED FAMILIES

A stepfamily is defined "as a household in which there is an adult couple at least one of whom has a child from a previous relationship" (Visher and Visher, 1988, p. 9). Coleman and Ganong (1985) refer to the stepfamily as a two-parent unit initiated by the legal remarriage of a divorced or widowed person. Other adjectives such as "blended," "REM," "reconstituted," "merged," "recouped," "reorganized," and "synergistic" have been used to describe this family structure (Hayes and Hayes, 1986; Prosen and Farmer, 1982; Visher and Visher, 1979, 1988; Walsh, 1992). Sager (1981) used the letters "REM" to stand for the REM family and McGoldrick and Carter (1989) recommend the term ". . . to emphasize that it is the marital bond that forms the basis for the complex arrangement of several families in a new constellation" (p. 400). The term REM families is used in this article to refer to remarried families (unless quoted from other sources).

Negative Definitions of REM Families

American culture presently considers any form of family life that does not conform to the traditional politically correct nuclear family as problematic. The media has created negative definitions of REM families (Perkins and Kahn, 1979; Visher and Visher, 1979), along with folklore (Fast and Cain, 1966; Jones, 1978). Coleman and Ganong (1987) state that "folk tales have facilitated either the development or the maintenance of beliefs about stepmothers and stepchildren" (p. 35). Smith (1953) studied cases in which reading or hearing about fairy tales negatively colored children's images of stepfathers, stepmothers or stepfathers. For example, children's stories and fairy tales, such as Cinderella, Snow White and Hansel and Gretel portray stepmothers and stepsisters as wicked and mean. Thus, attitudes toward REM families in this society have generally been unfavorable (Duncan and Brown, 1992).

The lack of language used to describe REM families may also contribute to the negative image. Prosen and Farmer (1982) view the words stepfamily, reconstituted family, and merged family as "inappropriate because they conjure images that may denigrate the structures or individuals involved" (Walsh, 1992, p. 709). This negative image is so pervasive that even in Webster's Seventh New Collegiate Dictionary the definition of the word stepchild is "one that fails to receive proper care or attention." The term "step anything" suggests neglect (Coleman and Ganong, 1987). An example of this was recently given when a Marriage and Family Counseling graduate student recently referred to Human Resources as the "stepchild" of the corporation, meaning less respected, or less loved. In addition, several studies have shown that college students have a negative perception of stepparents (Ganong and Coleman, 1983, p. 83); human service professionals also have been found to hold this view (Bryan, Ganong, Coleman, and Bryan, 1985, p. 83). Basically, the language needed to describe remarriage relationships has not yet been developed (Messinger and Walker, 1981; Wood and Poole, 1983). In this sense, the stepfamily labels serve as the bases for socially constructed stepfamily assumptions and stepfamily stereotypes.

FAILURE OF RESEARCH

With the above statistics in mind indicating the prevalence of REM families in the United States society, it would seem that there would exist a wealth of research in the area of divorced and REM couples. Unfortunately this is not the case. Ganong and Coleman (1984) believe that the quality of research on the REM family is poor. Most studies looked at minor aspects of divorce and remarriage. According to these theorists, researchers failed to look at interpersonal relationships or the emotional experiences of stepfamily members. In addition, there is no satisfactory research available on the process of remarriage or the adjustment to it (Carter and McGoldrick, 1980, p. 267). There have been no longitudinal studies of REM families in formation, and the normal process of reconstituting a family has not really been defined.

Perhaps the most blatant problem is that most REM family research is based on intact first families. Family researchers have generally been consistent with society's negative views, using a problem-oriented approach to studying the REM family (Coleman, Ganong, and Gingrich, 1985; Duncan and Brown, 1992; Hoffman, 1991). For example, researchers compare REM families to intact nuclear families in an attempt to understand these newly formed relationships. Inherent in this type of research approach is the assumption that the intact family is the "normal" family and anything outside this range is less than or negative. This creates the construction for researchers to perceive REM families within a problem oriented framework, or within a deficit model. For example, family researchers have examined role confusion, loyalty issues, loss and mourning (Furstenberg, Nord, Lutz, and Jacobs, 1985). In so doing they have focused on documenting the difficulties of the REM family.

Ignoring the strengths of the REM family and focusing on the problems that REM families experience may create a negative self-fulfilling prophesy in that since there is such an emphasis on, resulting in the documentation of, the problems, REM families may come to accept that problems are "normal" and to be expected. In fact, family researchers may be in part responsible for "behavioral confirmation" in that beliefs about a group of people (constructions about the REM family) may influence their behaviors (Snyder and Swan, 1978). "Seek and ye shall find." W. I. Thomas believed that if men define situations as real, they are real in their consequences. When a person believes something is true, s/he is likely to act as though it is true, and the action then further confirms the belief. Beliefs can facilitate solutions to problems or impede them. They can create problems where none exist and where the solutions create more problems (Watzlawick et al., 1974). Although researchers are beginning to abandon the nuclear family comparison, it still appears to be the most popular model. Nearly one half the studies reported by Coleman and Ganong (1989) included a nuclear family comparison, focusing on the problems associated with REM families.

The identification of strengths in the REM family is a relatively new concept. Only since the middle 1980s has there been any empirical research concerning what makes REM families work (Duncan and Brown, 1992). For example, of the fifty self-help books evaluated by Coleman and Ganong (1989), only four of the books mentioned potential strengths (Duncan and Brown, 1992; Knaub, Hanna, and Stinnett, 1984) and Brown and Duncan (1992) report that they were only able to find one research study which related to the strengths of the REM family.

COMMON REM FAMILY ISSUES

In this paper REM family problems are regarded mainly as realities that have been created by society which are incorporated into the expressed language and which serve to reinforce the ongoing social definitions.

Remarriages are not like first marriages, whether or not children are involved. When a couple marries there is usually an adjustment period for a couple bond to form before the arrival of children (Prosen and Farmer, 1982). That luxury does not exist with the REM couple. REM families are instant families (Felker, 1981; Hayes and Hayes, 1986; Martin and Martin, 1992; Meyer, 1992; Thies, 1977; Visher and Visher, 1979, 1982, 1988; Walsh, 1982, 1992). A bachelor may become a husband and a stepfather at once, or a single mother of two may suddenly become a wife and a stepmother of four and perhaps even a grandmother!

REM families usually plunge into instant multiple roles; in many cases, there is no honeymoon period. There is little time to deal with relationship issues that could be present in the new marriage such as power, conflicts, independence and dependency needs and struggles, family of origin issues, and struggles around intimacy and closeness (Martin and Martin, 1992; Visher and Visher, 1988; Walsh, 1992). In addition, the REM family lacks the history of shared events and tradition that creates a sense of belonging (Hansen and Messinger, 1982). Reinhart-Kompara (1980) discussed difficulties in the socialization process of stepparenting. One problem in step socialization is the lack of specific norms for role behavior in the stepfamily. Inconsistent cultural expectations of the roles may give rise to role ambiguity and role conflict.

Walsh (1992) identified issues in REM families as falling into four main categories: (1) Initial family problems, (2) Developing family problems, (3) Feelings about self and others, and (4) Other adult problems (p. 709). These categories, representative of typical REM issues, are discussed below.

Problems with the Initial Family

Issues with the initial family refers to the time period prior to the onset of the REM relationship. The transition into remarriage involves dealing with residual issues from the first marriage, the divorce, and the single parent period, as well as meeting the challenge involved in forming a functional REM family system. This category also incorporates the initial mourning of losses associated with the original family (Visher and Visher, 1992). Transitions generally involve loss and this is especially true of divorce (Belovitch, 1987; Block, 1979; Goldsmith, 1980; Hayes and Hayes, 1986; Huntington, 1982; Issacs, Montalvo, and Abelsohn, 1986; Levinger and Moles, 1979; Martin and Martin, 1985; Visher and Visher, 1979, 1982, 1988; Walsh, 1982, 1992). Visher and Visher (1982) contend that a REM family is "a family born of loss, because important interpersonal losses have preceded the formation of the family" (p. 344). The members of a REM family must resolve the losses associated with the dissolution of previous family structures prior to the construction of a successful REM family (Felker, 1981; Hayes and Hayes, 1986; Meyer, 1992; Thies, 1977; Visher and Visher, 1979, 1982, 1988; Walsh, 1982, 1992).

The continuing conflict or residue of feelings between natural parents may prevent the REM family from adjusting to their new lives (Wallerstein and Kelly, 1979) and the newly developing REM family. In these cases, the children may be used by the adults for revenge or to hurt the other parent (Kupisch, 1987; Wallerstein and Kelly, 1979). This can place considerable stress upon the children (Strother and Jacobs, 1984; Wallerstein and Kelly, 1980). Also, during this stage, in children, the fantasy (if there is one) of biological parental reconciliation may begin to dissipate as the new marriage approaches and this could be painful for the children (Hayes and Hayes, 1986; Martin and Martin, 1992; Skeen et al., 1981; Turnbull and Turnbull, 1983; Visher and Visher, 1979, 1982, 1988; Walsh, 1982, 1992). Also in this stage, issues as simple as a name for the new parent can become problematic. Here the use of appropriate terminology is usually decided by individual families with little guidance found in literature or research (Walsh, 1992).

Additionally, children involved in REM families may have to adjust to having two biological families and one or two stepparents, as well as a host of siblings, biological and step. Two positively related factors to REM family adjustment are the quality of the REM couple relationship and the degree of acceptance of the new REM family by the absent biological parents (Kleinman, Rosenberg, and Whiteside, 1979; Lutz, 1983; Visher and Visher, 1979; Walsh, 1992). Another common situation issue arising in the REM family is one where one of the children may have taken on added responsibilities and developed a greater maturity during the single parent family system and now must relinquish some or all of these responsibilities. The child, although probably happy to be relieved of the burden of responsibilities, may not easily move back to a less responsible, more dependent position (Whiteside, 1982).

Problems with the Developing Family

Problems with the developing family refers to the types of problems that arise in the REM family after its initial formation. Included in this category are the overlapping issues that can range from confusion over family roles, sibling conflict, competition for time, extended kinship network, sexual conflicts, changes over time, and exit and entry of children (Walsh, 1992, p. 710). When a family absorbs a new member, that new member must adapt to the system's rules, and the old system must be modified to include each new member. There is a tendency to maintain the old patterns, which places a stress on the new member and may cause him or her to increase his/her demands (Minuchin, p. 64). Subsystems, alliances, and individual roles had been established in the previous families (Felker, 1981; Hayes and Hayes, 1986; Meyer, 1992; Thies, 1977; Visher and Visher, 1979, 1982, 1988; Walsh, 1982, 1992), and the stepparent and step-siblings are often defined as intruders. The built-in ambiguity of boundaries and membership in REM families defies simple definition, and our culture lacks any established patterns, guidelines, traditions, or rituals to help families with this transition. Walker and Messinger (1979) contend that the boundaries of the REM family are more permeable and the roles of family members are more ambiguous than in a nuclear family. The couple must first define their own boundaries as a couple. There must be clear boundaries between the couple subsystem and the child/stepchild subsystem. This helps alleviate the problematic triangulation of the children that is often seen in REM families.

Affection for the new stepparent and the non-custodial parent are dealt with at this time. Often displays of affection are related to feelings of loyalty to the natural parent (Hayes and Hayes, 1986; Visher and Visher, 1979, 1982, 1988; Walsh, 1982, 1992). Frequently, because of loyalty, children in REM families stifle any initial displays of affection toward the stepparents (Hayes and Hayes, 1986; Turnbull and Turnbull, 1983; Visher and Visher, 1988). Another common issue is the physical movement of the children between their permanent home and the home of the non-custodial parent. Walsh (1992) explains that the turmoil of the exit and entry extends beyond the time of the visitation because there is a mental and physical preparation and a recovery time after the children return. During the initial stages of the REM family formation, this may be difficult. Discipline may present a problem. Discipline by the stepparent is often listed as a major conflict in REM families (Felker, 1981; Kupisch, 1987; Maddox, 1975; McClenahan, 1978; Messinger, 1976). The single parent family may have adapted to maintaining firm, effective discipline procedures and now with the remarriage, the stepparent role is often undefined. A problem arises also if there is not initially a strong positive relationship between the stepparent and the child. It is important for the couple to work out the rules in advance and support one another when the rules need to be enforced (Felker, 1981; Martin and Martin, 1992; Turnbull and Turnbull, 1983).

Financial issues can also be a source of conflict in REM families (Belovitch, 1987; Martin and Martin, 1992; Visher and Visher, 1988; Walsh, 1992). These include child support, alimony, and the distribution of property between stepchildren and biological children (Kirkwood, 1983; Sager, Brown, Crohn, Engel, Rodstein, and Walker, 1983). Fishman (1983) suggests that the manner in which finances are handled may reflect the commitment expressed by REM couples to each other and to each other's children.

Problems with Feelings About Self and Others

The third category relates to social definitions of the REM family. These sociocultural opinions and stereotypes, most of them negative, have ramifications for the REM family as a whole as well as each family member individually (Hayes and Hayes, 1986; Skeen, Covi, and Robinson, 1985). "Language is both a reflection of and a determinant of beliefs" (Lewis, 1980) and as stated earlier, there is not an adequate vocabulary for many REM family relationships. In addition, Visher and Visher (1979) point out that stepparents' expectations of themselves are often unrealistically high or low. Many times, the REM family's self-concept is often that of a deviant, deficient, inadequate family (Ganong and Coleman, 1984). These unrealistic beliefs (both positive and negative) held by REM family members can be reinforced by the inaccurate terminology (Visher and Visher, 1988).

Individual family members may experience psychological conflict in response to these socially created negative definitions (Kupisch, 1987). The fairy tale idea of the "wicked stepmother" is sometimes incorporated into a stepparent's and/or stepchildren's self-concept and reactions (Amato, 1987; Kupisch, 1987). These stereotypes and the resultant negative feelings are resolved with the establishment of stable intimate relationships (Amato, 1987). Therapists can notice and emphasize these bonds to the family.

Problems with Other Adults

The extended family of the REM family has also been affected by the divorce and the remarriage. This last section of issues relates to the other adults in the REM family. Visher and Visher (1988) refer to this structure as the "REM family's suprafamily system." They discuss the continuing links with other households that result in numerous relationships, a collection of subsystems, and more than two parenting adults. As a first marriage joins two families, a second marriage involves the interweaving of three, four, or more families, whose previous family life cycle course has typically been disrupted by death or divorce (Carter and McGoldrick, 1980). There is a network of people and relationships created through the prior divorce(s) and the new formalization of the REM marriage. These include former spouses of one or both of the REM adults (alive or dead), the families of origin of all the adults (alive or dead), and the children of each of the adults. Grandparents, aunts, uncles, cousins, and step-grandparents are a part of this network as well. Thus the REM family is a subsystem of the REM supra system. This supra system is made up of the network of the different individuals and functionally related people (subsystems) who have influence on REM members. Some of these subsystems may cross two or more households. The complexity of this family system is obvious when one attempts to draw a genogram.

According to Stern (1978) and Visher and Visher (1988), satisfactory REM family integration generally takes years to achieve. Visher and Visher (1979) believe it takes about two years for basic reorganization in a REM family whereas Anderson and White (1986) presume that it could take closer to twelve years for a REM family to "appear as cohesive as a biological family" (Walsh, 1992). It is important to note that the labels put on families and the problems assigned to different family types and the adjustment times given are all socially constructed and value laden. All family traits and types can be labeled good or bad dependent on one's socially constructed worldview.

LIFE CYCLE CONSIDERATIONS

When considering the REM family, one must consider life cycle transitions. A REM family is subject to pressure from within each developmental change in its own members and from the outside pressures of other social institutions. These pressures require a constant shift of the position of family members in relation to one another. Originating with the first marriage, through the divorce or death of a spouse, through the single parent family, and through the remarriage, all family members have experienced these transitional periods. Within each developmental stage are certain relationship tasks. A family must accomplish the tasks of a stage before they are capable of coping with the tasks of the next (Whiteside, 1982). The resolution of each stage establishes patterns for coping and dealing with each succeeding stage. In each of these family groups, different organizations develop in terms of family boundaries, the roles within the family, any legal ties, and all the emotional relationships. More specifically, as a family moves from one family organization to the next, each transition requires significant description and change. In addition, the successful solution to the family needs of each phase may be different from, and perhaps contradictory to, the necessary solution to similar family needs in the succeeding phase (Whiteside, 1982). Through the transitional periods where the stability of the family system and the roles of each member are in transition, family members may experience heightened feelings of tension, anxiety and confusion (Whiteside, 1982). The REM family is composed of two separate families and each family might be at different stages of the life cycle, adding to the complexity of tasks, role allocations, and emergent possibilities.

It is helpful for therapists to redefine both the dilemmas of the REM family as normal problems in living occurring in response to a stressful readjustment period. In the initial stages of life cycle therapy it is critical to establish the boundaries of treatment. Key tasks involve reaching out to the family, identifying and reframing the problem in family terms, and setting appropriate goals. Helping the family come to terms with the different role changes necessary and the development of the couple subsystem are the basis of the therapeutic work with the REM family. Another principle important to working with REM families is that of clarifying the perceptions and expectations of client system constituents. The potential for miscommunication and misperception may be particularly germane in the context of REM families. Because the norms for REM families are so ambiguous and REM family issues are so complex, it is not surprising that the need for clarification of roles and norms is so important. In this sense, family therapy with REM families represents a wealth of opportunities for all members.

The genogram is a useful tool in predicting or pointing out to the family their alliances, coalitions, boundaries, roles, rules, expectations, myths, patterns and many more characteristics that will show the family where each of them are and why they behave the way they do in relation to other family members. Plotting the genogram links old patterns with what is going on in the family life today. It also provides the opportunity to acknowledge the many strengths and important truths in their family. As the therapist is gathering information, questions may also open up new areas of communication (Marlin, 1989).

SOCIAL CONSTRUCTIONIST THEORY AND THERAPY WITH THE REM FAMILY

Social Construction Theory

Early theories of family therapy were based upon notions of cybernetics which include recursive and self-regulating loops that were believed to maintain a system's equilibrium (Goolishian and Anderson, 1987). "As a result of this early work, problem behavior or symptoms were conceptualized as serving a function: conserving stability or family homeostasis and the symptom was described as feedback in a cybernetic loop of mutual causality and circularity" (Anderson and Goolishian, 1987, p. 529). White

(1986) claims that "cybernetic theory provides a negative explanation of events in systems" (p. 169). He maintains that it restrains the family from seeking new and different solutions.

A newer approach to family therapy is found in social construction theory (Gergen and Gergen, 1985). Taking this position means challenging the original concepts of the homeostatic system held by cybernetics. In contrast to other theories, "the social constructionists see ideas, concepts and memories arising from social interchange and mediated through language. This new viewpoint has been labeled "the interpretive turn" (Hoffman, 1991, p. 4) and it is within this context that a number of family therapists have "defected" (Anderson, Goolishian, Gergen, Hoffman, De-Shazer, White, Lax). In this new approach, the central metaphor for therapy changes to conversation, and an emphasis is placed on the role of language and dialogue in the social construction of meaning. In this sense individuals construct the worlds they do because they participate in language and social practices (Anderson and Goolishian, 1992, p. 12). Therapy may now be seen as co-constructed conversation, not as intervention. It is this co-constructing which is distinctly different from the original structural and cybernetic thinking.

At the forefront of this paradigmatic shift is Gergen (1985) who states that Social Constructionism holds the following metatheoretical assumptions: (1) what we take to be experience of the world does not in itself dictate the means by which the world is understood; (2) the terms in which the world is understood are social artifacts, products of historically situated interchanges among people and the process of understanding is the result of an active, cooperative enterprise of persons in relationship; (3) the degree to which a given form of understanding prevails or is sustained across time is not fundamentally dependent on the empirical validity of the perspective in question; and (4) forms of negotiated understanding are of critical significance in social life because they are integrally connected with many other activities in which people engage.

According to Lax (1989), the following are theoretical guidelines and basic assumptions that have evolved from social construction family therapy theorists:

- Problems are viewed as existing in the domain of meanings.
- Problems generate systems rather than systems create problems.
- People cannot change under a negative connotation.
  Emphasis is on positive connotations.
- There is a recursive relationship between meanings and action; as meanings change, behavior may be altered.

- Reality is observer defined and the therapist is a participant in the construction of the therapy system's reality.
- There are no right views but only ones that fit the system and are acceptable to it.
- Therapy is viewed as maintaining a lateral position between therapist and client rather than a hierarchical one.

In social construction therapy, the focus of therapy is increasingly on "the storied basis of human life and the social construction of meaning" (Goolishian and Anderson, 1992). Inquiry is principally concerned with unfolding the processes by which people come to describe, explain, or otherwise account for the world (including themselves) in which they live. When persons seek therapy, an acceptable outcome would be the identification or generation of alternative stories that enable them to perform new meanings. New meanings that persons have experienced or find more helpful, satisfying and without limits (White and Epston, p. 15). People can only participate in a conversation to the extent of their own repertoire of interactions and ideas. A stuck family system is thus limited by its range of ideas and meanings. In order to get "unstuck," new ideas must be introduced in order for the family to further evolve. These new ideas, distinctions or differences which facilitate change must fit with the family system (Lax, 1989).

Social construction theory puts forth an evolving set of meanings that emerge unendingly from the interactions between people (Gergen, 1985, p. 267). Social construction therapy shifts the focus of a problem oriented approach toward a search for the strengths and positive characteristics of its clients. "A family strengths approach helps REM families identify and build upon the strengths of positive characteristics they already have or would like to develop" (Duncan and Brown, 1992, p. 152). "When families realize they have special strengths and are responsible for their enhancement, they are more likely to feel capable and motivated to achieve the kind of family life they want" (Duncan and Brown, 1992, p. 153).

The Role of the Therapist

In Social Construction Therapy, the role of the therapist is crucial. It has been argued that early family therapists viewed their influence over the family as necessary for their work. Hoffman (1991) agrees and further claims that early family therapists supported the idea of therapists' control. By supporting hierarchy and control, Hoffman (1991) suggests that therapists "keep clients at a distance and do not share the thinking of the clinician" (p. 10). The clients are in effect being observed by the therapist.

In social constructionism, the therapist does not act upon the system but rather works from within the system of therapist and client. This eliminates the "hierarchy and control" of the earlier family therapies. Within this context, the therapist's hierarchical position changes. S/he is now seen as a real person who is part of the ever-evolving narrative described by the individual family members. In social constructionist therapy, the therapist plays the role of "participant facilitator" (Real, 1990, p. 259). The therapist takes the position of not knowing; the therapist yearns to be told more. The therapist is always on his/her way to understanding, but never understands. "By not knowing, the therapist adopts a stance that relies on the continuing analysis of experience as it occurs within the logical dialogical context" (Hoffman, 1991, p. 120). Since the stories presented change constantly, the therapist and client are continually learning and changing. They are always in the process of becoming. The therapist facilitates dialogue in order to learn how the client experiences the world. When the client is ready to learn and incorporate new information, the therapist then discusses alternative concepts and ideas with the client that challenge their reality. This theory of conversation and continual learning contrasts sharply with the "hierarchical and unidirectional" therapy of the early family therapists (Hoffman, 1991, p. 12).

"Within this new meaning system a reorganization of mutual respect and reciprocity begins with self-disclosures made possible through our communicative action, dialogue and discourse" (Anderson and Goolishian, 1992, p. 12). The therapist's role is now that of a participant observer as well as a collaborator with the family, mirroring, summing up, and getting a true feeling of what the family is experiencing. This new position assists the therapy toward a process in which all members (including the therapist) can be open to change. The family and the therapist begin to create new realities together. Thus, therapy is a process where new stories can be told which allow for new meanings, realities, and new narratives (Anderson and Goolishian, 1992, p. 11). The therapist's role is to be the master architect of conversation, assisting and maintaining dialogue which is informed only by the family. The therapist's dominant discourse does not prevail. S/he maintains a genuine interest and openness to the family's reality and ever-evolving narrative, while ". . . maintaining a sense of coherence" (Atwood, 1993).

SOCIAL CONSTRUCTION THERAPY

Since society's expectations of the REM family have been shown to be generally negative (Duncan and Brown, 1992; Ganong and Coleman, 1983; Bryan, Ganong, Coleman, and Bryan, 1985), therapists cannot help but be influenced by the findings of research and/or the media. As a result, most therapists use an approach that seeks out problems in the REM family (Coleman, Ganong, and Gingrich, 1985a), and as such may play a key role in implementing a self-defeating attitude. When family therapists adhere to deficit or problem focused assumptions, they remain "stuck" in their view of stereotyping the negative dynamics of the REM family life, as well as limiting awareness of the strengths of these newly formed families. As Duncan and Brown (1992) point out, "This would lead us to pinpoint problems and appropriate interventions to solve them." By asking clients to present a problem for treatment, not only does the therapist request that some description of simple action be categorized as a problem (White, 1986); but, it is also possible that REM families adjust themselves to fit into the negative script. In this sense, these families are coerced into believing that they may have problems that previously had not been considered negative (Coleman et al., 1985a). In addition, by holding the comparison of the REM family and the first married family, therapists help to perpetuate the negative stereotype of remarriages and undermine their strengths. It is in this sense that family therapists and therapies are shapers of the REM families' problematic realities.

REM families who come for therapy are experiencing problems. Many of the issues that bring them into therapy were noted earlier in this paper. These families have tried a myriad of solutions, many of them unsuccessful. The problems they are experiencing have a negative effect on the family. In social construction therapy, the therapist's job is to understand what the family's belief systems are, assess which beliefs have created and maintained the problems, understand how the resulting solutions based on the belief systems have created more difficulties, and co-construct with the family new solutions that contain a lifestyle without the problems.

Social Construction Therapy explores the family meanings that incidents, behaviors, and encounters with REM families have for individuals and how these are determined by the sociocultural environment. The sociocultural environment equips them with methods and ways of understanding and making judgments about aspects of REM families ranging from how they feel about their new stepparent/stepchild to social family values. These ways of making sense of experiences are embedded in a meaning system which is accepted as reality by the social group and in the scripts (ways of behaving) that are a part of the family's meaning system. The dialectical relationship between the individual realities, the family realities, and the socially constructed meanings around the REM family is the focus of this section.

1. Joining the Family Meaning System

Using the above as a backdrop for doing therapy with the REM family, the therapist joins the family's meaning system. Joining is crucial. Through joining, a workable reality can be constructed. It is the dynamic interplay of joining and constructing a workable reality that initiates the process of change. This process involves the shift that occurs when the problem is transformed from a paradigm of individual causality to a paradigm of family interaction. The family's own language is used by the therapist in a reflective facilitation to create a comfortable environment in which change can take place. In the role of curious observer, the therapist elicits the family's expert knowledge surrounding their story (the problem) (White, 1989).

2. Proposing the Notion of a Family Meaning System

Therapy with REM families can be divided into three different stories: the families' story about their families of origin (the origination of the development of the meaning system); the story about their present family (the maintenance of the meaning system); and the story about their future vision (what changes can be envisioned). These stories provide the primary frame for making sense of the family's experiences and for shaping their lives. The telling of these stories allows the family to observe and gain insight about the frame of the problem.

Bruner (1986) likens these stories to landscapes; one of action, the other of consciousness. Events are connected in a particular order through past and present and future according to certain themes in the landscape of action. These provide the individual with a perspective or frame to explain experiences over time. The interpretation of the characters themselves within the story is considered the landscape of consciousness. This constitutes the meanings attributed to the characters as they experience the landscape of action. White (1993) explains that the landscape of consciousness is constructed of one's speculations concerning the perceptions of the desires and preferences of the characters. The individual reflects on their personal and relationship characteristics and qualities with an intent to understand and clarify their motives and purposes. Once the values and beliefs of the characters are substantiated, they blend into commitments of a way of life. The stories that are constructed are culturally determined. Hoffman (1990) states that, "Problems are stories that people have agreed to tell themselves (p. 3), then we have to persuade them to tell themselves a different, more empowering story, have conversations with them, through the awareness that the findings of their conversations have no other reality than that bestowed by mutual consent" (p. 4).

Here REM families are asked about what the problems associated with being a REM family mean to them in their given sociocultural contexts. The notion of "Remarried Family" is treated as a symbol invested with meaning by society. The approach to the family's problem is thus a matter of symbolic analysis and interpretation. The family problem is seen as emanating from various forms of action or practice within the family's life.

Exploring the Past

In REM families there is no common past. Only some of the family members have a common history from which to draw experiences. Even the family's sociocultural experiences have a different reservoir from which their reality is extracted. If the family feels there are unresolved issues from the prior marriage contributing to their current problems or if the family feels like they "really don't know each other," the therapist can use "the rubber band method" to help the family move back in time. To a child: "If I were to take a rubber band and stretch it back to when you were living with your original family, could you tell your stepDad/Mom what it was like for you? Could you tell Mom/stepDad what you would like to remember most about that family? Could you tell Mom/stepDad what you would like to forget about that family? Could you tell Mom/stepDad how they could help you with this? What meanings did you give to these experiences? What did you learn about yourself from these experiences? What strengths did you develop during that time? What other strengths? And Mom/stepDad, could you reflect that back?" Similar questions could be asked of the parent: "Could you tell your son/daughter what wishes and desires you had for them when they were first born? Your fears and concerns? And son/daughter, can you reflect that back?" To the stepDad: "Could you tell Jimmy what kind of relationship you envisioned for both of you when you first met him?" The same questions are then asked to the other family members. These questions could be used to ask questions about the first marriage, the divorce, the single parent phase and the remarried time. This phase is only used if the family feels there are old unresolved issues that they would like to settle or if they feel they want to know more about each other. The focus of this phase is not to determine truth but rather to put the perceptions in perspective, along with recognizing that different family members hold different perceptions of the same event. It assists the family with exploring any "unfinished business" from the past while at the same time educating the new family members as to some of the history. In so doing, the REM family's intimacy level is enhanced.

Putting the Past in Perspective

After both parents and children have explored the story of the past, the past can be put in perspective. This can be facilitated by a ritual. The family members can write down all the important events that relate to the explored issues, both the positive and negative, and place the paper in a shoe box and bury it (i.e., symbolically burying the past). Family members may wish to write letters to each other, forgiving them for their mistakes and thanking them for the gifts (kindnesses, caretaking, strengths) they gave them. They can set the original family experience free (if appropriate) by symbolically setting a balloon or a kite free at the beach. Or, they may want to design a ritual to signify the beginning of their new REM family. They could designate a yearly holiday signifying the anniversary of the REM family. On this day, they could generate a list of their vision for the family, how they would like it to be for the following year.

3. Learning the Present Meaning System

Once REM family members have discussed their individual stories, they can tell their current story. Here the therapist attempts to obtain as complete an understanding as possible of the family's story about the problem. In so doing, s/he pays careful attention to linguistic symbolizations such as family myths, legends, rites, and metaphors, slowly uncovering the family meaning system. Here the family and the therapist learn what information the family selects out of their environment and how they then fit that information into an already existing meaning system so as to reinforce that system. For example, in a REM family, differentiating the fine line between being a member of a family and being a member in a REM family becomes particularly important. It will make a great difference for how the family member sees him/herself, especially if the person has incorporated the negative social definitions. Here the family and the therapist learn how the family's patterned conversations and attempted solutions (many of which were not successful) reflect this meaning system. When families learn about their meaning systems and connect them to the way they see their problems, they gather information about how they have inadvertently participated in the perpetuation of the problem.

Once it is accepted that a family's meaning is socially constructed, it then becomes possible to deconstruct it. The following sections elaborate on the processes by which the family's meaning system can be uncovered and then challenged in order to "make room" for new experiences. Choice arises as the family learns that it is their decision whether to keep the uncovered meaning system or change it. Some ways of amplifying the family's process are tracking, circular and reflexive questions. Tracking is where the therapist focuses on the symbols, metaphors, themes, and language of the couple in order to help the couple better understand their transactional processes. Circular questioning is where the therapist invites one member to comment on the relationship of two other members. Through circular questioning, a view of the meaning the problem holds for the family emerges that allows both the therapist and the family to appreciate its interconnectedness and circular nature. Reflexive questions are questions which enable the family's own healing processes to emerge. "If you made no changes in your relationships, what do you think the consequences would be? What would have to happen in order for you to realize that the problem was getting a little better?"

In this phase, practical issues are also addressed. The therapist helps the family get "unstuck" by reinforcing old coping skills, teaching new skills, and providing education–about the complexity of the REM family.

4. Challenging the Family's Meaning System

Once the notion of a family meaning system is accepted by the family, and the individual family meaning systems are uncovered, a competing meaning system can be introduced. It is not apparent to most individuals that there are alternative ways of behaving. Our meaning systems make areas outside the dominant ones appear invisible. This invisibility serves to maintain and foster adherence to the dominant definitions. In fact, the function of socialization and of the sanctions against moving outside the dominant script is to keep individuals within it. This is particularly relevant in the REM families where negative social definitions impinge on the family's definitional system. To find, name, focus on, and help the family experience alternative meanings and scripts is the intention of this section.

Behavior that is incongruous with the individual's meaning system will result in a change in the person's perceptual view. There are numerous scripts available to us for examination. Here the role of the therapist is to notice competing constructions or exceptions in the family's meaning system. Change requires a two-sided perspective and a therapist may seek to construct a relational definition by developing two (or complementary) descriptions of the problem (White, 1986). Complementary questions are derived and introduced to challenge or help to deconstruct the dominant explanation and to assist families in achieving a relational or double description of the problem. The therapist reinforces alternatives to the dominant description of the problem–helping to make visible areas outside the dominant meaning system. The double description then provides the source of new responses (Atwood and Levine, 1991; White 1986). The family's explanation, or frame, begins to overlap the frame offered by the therapist (like two overlapping Venn diagrams), and it is in this overlap that there is the possibility for change.

Here the therapist assists the family by focusing on and amplifying exceptions in the person's description of his or her world, times in the family's life when the problem is NOT happening (DeShazer, 1991). The family is encouraged to describe the influence of the problem on the family and the influence of the family on the problem (1989). Questions are employed to map out the problem's realm of influence (White, 1989). These questions also serve the purpose of allowing the family members, with the therapist's assistance, to notice exceptions to the influence of the problem in their lives or as White (1989) refers to them, "unique outcomes" (p. 37). Then the family can construct a new description of the problem or a "redescription" (White, 1989, p. 43). White (1989) gives an example of a direct question that can elicit these responses, "Can you recall an occasion when you could have given in to the problem but didn't?" (p. 41). An indirect question is "What do you think it is about the events that you have related that tells me you still have some influence in the life of the problem?" (White, 1989, p. 42).

The social constructionist REM family therapist focuses on challenging the family's view of the problem, confusing their definition of the problem and the significance the problem (and its maintenance) has for the family. Using the family's language, the problem is externalized (White, 1989). In this process the family objectifies the problem which allows the family to view the problem as a separate entity and thus outside the family and the REM family relationships. The use of metaphors and reframing help the family in finding exceptions to the problem, leading to its deconstruction. In so doing, s/he begins to undermine what previously had been specifying and justifying the family's reality (Amundson, 1990). This paves the way for transformation.

White (1989) explains that now the family can describe themselves from a "new and non-problem-saturated perspective" (p. 5). An alternative story can be developed. The problem can be reframed in a new meaning system and this new meaning system can then be amplified. The

REM family can now be viewed as a family with a solution instead of a family with a problem.

5. Amplifying the New Meaning System

Bateson (1972) believed that the amplification of the exception is essential for triggering the new construction which holds the possibility for new solutions. Here the therapist amplifies the competing constructions in the family's meaning system. "When the problem is not there, how are your relationships? If you were to enjoy your relationships more often, how would you notice? What would be different? What else would be different? How would that be for you?" By helping the REM family to deepen the experience of their relationships, the therapist facilitates a new construction, that of more positive relationships, which hold new meanings for the family. In this way, the therapist creates an environment that amplifies the family's strengths, resources, and solutions (Lipchick, 1988).

6. Stabilizing the New Meaning System

At this point, alternative meaning systems are available to the family, holding possibilities for new solutions. Now the family can begin to focus on the future. As Penn (1985) suggests, questions should seek out future trends. According to Atwood (1990), projection into the future allows individuals, couples, or families to participate in a deliberate choice for their future direction (p. 48). She suggests the future may be rendered even more real by marking its arrival in some ritualized manner.

Future focus helps the family visualize a future without the problems. DeShazer (1988) uses the Miracle Question to access this future without the problem and help stabilize the family's new meaning system. "Suppose that one night, while you were asleep, there was a miracle and this problem was solved. How would you know? What would be different?" (p. 5). How will each member of the family know? Questions like, "If you could stretch the rubber band three years into the future and the problem was gone, what would your family look like? What would your relationships be like? How would your relationships with one another be different? How else would they be different?" (Atwood, 1993). These questions open up and stabilize new possibilities for the REM family.

CASE MATERIAL: THE REAL FATHER

Betsy B., a divorced woman with two children ages 6 and 10, married Mathew, a bachelor, 6 years her senior. Prior to this marriage, when the youngest child was one year old, his father abandoned the family, running off with another woman. The family never heard from him again. When Betsy married Mathew, he claimed he wanted a ready-made family. The marriage went well until Betsy gradually noticed that her husband had no interest in supplying any guidance for the children. He apparently vacillated between identifying with her two sons as their buddy and being envious of the time and attention that his wife gave to them. Betsy began to feel increasingly that she had three competing male children on her hands. When the family came for therapy, they expressed great concern over the tension and hostility that existed in the home.

In the first stage of therapy with this REM family, the therapist joins their meaning systems. When joining the family's meaning systems, the therapist provides a safe environment for the family to explore their process. As a curious observer, the therapist listens and learns the family's language and story about the problem and then uses this language to join and create a safe, comfortable environment. The therapist listens to Betsy's definition of the problem as well as Mathew's and the children's. The therapist validates and reflects the statements back to the family members, adding new questions to expand the story ever so slightly. "So, Betsy, you see Mathew as participating in the children's play and not taking on a parental role. It must be hard for you to be a parent to the three of them. How does Mathew teach you to play?"

The second stage of therapy involves proposing the notion of a family meaning system. To do this, the therapist needs to understand the B. Family's frame of the problem and to point out the different views of the problem. When exploring Mathew and Betsy's story, the therapist and the couple learn what information the couple selects out of their environment and how they fit that information into an already existing meaning system in order to reinforce that system. This is when the therapist and the family learn how their patterned conversations and previous attempted solutions (scripts) reflect their view of the problem and how the REM family problem became scripted into their relationship.

Mathew and Betsy's story about the effects of the REM problem are explored. The couple tells their present story, how they combined their individual meaning systems and scripts to co-create a couple script. Their discussion then centers around how the problem became scripted into the couple relationship, at both the individual and couple level (Atwood and Dershowitz, p. 207). Here Betsy disclosed her present frustration about Mathew not taking on the parenting role. Here the therapist explores how Mathew defines his role as a stepfather. Mathew believes "that stepfathers are looked at negatively and he doesn't want the boys to hate him" so he decided that he would not discipline the boys. He wanted to be a pal to them so that they would like him. When the boys were asked about their story, they said they never felt like Mathew was like a real father to them. They felt he never corrected them, or punished them like their friend's fathers did. When asked what this meant to them, they said this meant he didn't love them because otherwise he would punish them. They weren't a real family because in real families, "kids got yelled at and punished." Mathew realized that even though he was playing with the boys, he was relating with them in a very unrealistic way.

Once the therapist has an understanding of Mathew, and Betsy, and the children's present story, their meaning system can be challenged to create new experiences. Techniques used to amplify the couples process can be used. Using amplification, the therapist chooses an idea, affect, theme or behavior sequence from the system, and through attention evokes more of it (Real, 1990). When challenging the system, it is important for therapists to find exceptions to the problem. For example, the therapist might ask Betsy, "Was there ever a time when Mathew acted like a parent to your children?" When the therapist finds the exception, s/he wants to amplify the exception by saying, "Tell me more about that." The therapist could ask Mathew, "Could you remember a time when your wife gave you attention and you did not feel envious of her children?" Again the therapist explores deeper into the exception and amplifies it. The therapist is facilitating a new construction, that of a more positive relationship.

The third story deals with the future of the REM family. The original meaning system has been replaced by a new description. This is where the new meaning system is stabilized. By asking Mathew and Betsy questions around the future, the therapist makes the future more real. "What would your relationships be like with each other, with the children, if the frustrations were not there? How would your relationships be different? How else would they be different?" After a few therapy sessions, Mathew began to tell the boys when they were behaving inappropriately and once even punished one of them when he hit his brother. He began to treat the boys in a more realistic manner, punishing them for misbehavior and rewarding them when they behaved. After approximately five sessions, the family reported that the tension level had decreased and there was a major change in Mathew's involvement with the children's discipline and caretaking. As a result, the boys believed that he loved them because he was more like a "real" father. They now felt like they were a "real" family. New information was taken into their meaning system, causing them to redefine their stepfather. Changes in the narratives that couples hold about their scripts can lead to opportunities for change in their meaning systems which can ultimately reorganize the way they "see" their lives.

CONCLUSION

Belovitch (1987) reports on twelve different family structures operating in the United States. Even though statistically, dramatic changes in what is considered the "normal family" have been taking place over the last few decades, in this society, socially constructed negative definitions are applied to any family form different from the traditional breadwinner father, homemaker mother, and dependent biological children family. Statistically, these "other" types of families are no longer alternative families consisting of a small minority of the population; they have become dominant family structures in the United States. Yet, these families still experience the negative culturally based definitions. These negative definitions are especially evident when examining the REM family.

The REM family is not an alternative family but a normative family with unique characteristics (Furstenberg and Spanier, 1984; Martin and Martin, 1992; Skeen, Covi, and Robinson, 1985; Visher and Visher, 1988; Wald, 1981). Research on the REM family has generally been negative. It has focused on the problems while ignoring the REM family strengths (Duncan and Brown, 1992). "Most studies have focused on a narrow range of research issues" (Clingempeel, Brand, and Segal, 1987) and have incorporated the "deficit-comparison" model which may have served to further amplify this negative theme (Ganong and Coleman, 1984). The assumption of this model is that REM families are less adequate than first marriage families (Duncan and Brown, 1992). In many ways, the negative definitions serve to create problem behaviors as these families "fit" themselves into the already existing negative script. However, it is not only REM families who absorb these definitions; family therapists hold these views also. It is in this way that family therapy and family therapists facilitate the process by which these families incorporate and adopt the negative views.

In an attempt to address this situation, this paper presented a six-stage model of social constructionist therapy with the REM family. See Figure 1. Social constructionist therapy provides clinicians with a therapy form that mobilizes the resources, competencies, and strengths of the REM family while deemphasizing family deficits. After reviewing the literature, research, and therapeutic approaches to REM families, the remarks made by Ihinger-Tallman (1984) reflect the state of the field with regard to the REM family, "There is much to do, but we have a beginning."

FIGURE 1. Summary of Social Constructionist Therapy

SOCIAL CONSTRUCTION THERAPY WITH THE REM FAMILY

JOINING THE FAMILY MEANING SYSTEM

↓

PROPOSING THE NOTION OF A FAMILY MEANING SYSTEM

↓

LEARNING THE FAMILY'S MEANING SYSTEM

↓

CHALLENGING THE FAMILY'S MEANING SYSTEM

↓

AMPLIFYING THE NEW MEANING SYSTEM

↓

STABILIZING THE NEW MEANING SYSTEM

REFERENCES

Ahrons, C. R., & Perlmutter, M. S. (1982). The relationship between former spouses: A fundamental subsystem in the remarriage family. In J. Hansen & L. Messinger (Eds.), *Therapy with remarriage families* (pp. 31-46). Rockville, MD: Aspen System Corporation.

Amato, P. R. (1987). Family processes in one-parent, stepparent, and intact families: The child's point-of view. *Journal of Marriage and Family*, 49, 327-337.

Amato, P. R., & Ochiltree, G. (1987). Child and adolescent competence in intact, one-parent, and stepfamilies: An Australian study. *Journal of Divorce*, 10, 75-96.

Andersen, T. (1987). The reflecting team: Dialogue and meta-dialogue in clinical work. *Family Process*, 26, 415-428.

Anderson, T. Z., & White, G. D. (1986). An empirical investigation of interaction and relationship patterns in functional and dysfunctional nuclear families and stepfamilies. *Family Process*, 407-422.

Atwood, J. (1993). Social Constructionist Couple Therapy. *The Family Journal: Counseling and Therapy for Couples and Families*, 1(2), 116-130.

Atwood, J., & Dershowitz, S. (1992). Constructing a sex and marital therapy frame: Ways to help couples deconstruct sexual problems. *Journal of Sex & Marital Therapy*, 18(3), 196-217.

Atwood, J. D., & Meyer, G. (1990). 10 Necessary steps in stepfamily integration. *Marriage Encounter*, 20-25.

Beavers, W. R., & Hampson, R. B. (1990). *Successful families: Assessment and intervention*. New York: Norton.

Belovitch, J. (1987). *Making remarriage work*. Lexington, MA: Lexington Books.

Block, J. (1979). *To marry again*. New York: Grosset & Dunlap.

Cade, B., & O'Hanlon, W. H. (1993). *A brief guide to brief therapy*. New York: Norton.

Capaldi, F., & McRae, B. (1979). *Stepfamilies: A cooperative responsibility*. New York: New Points/Vision Books.

Cavan, R. (1964). Subcultural variations and mobility. In H. T. Christensen (Eds.), *Handbook of marriage and the family* (pp. 535-584).Chicago: Rand McNally.

Chang, J., & Phillips, M. (1993). Michael White and Steve DeShazer: New Directions in Family Therapy. In S. Gilligan & R. Price (Eds.), *Therapeutic conversations* (pp. 95-111). New York: Norton.

Coleman, M., & Ganong, L. H. (1985). Remarriage myths: Implication for the helping professions. *Journal of Counseling and Development*, 64, 116-120.

Crohn, H., Sager, J., Brown, H., Rodstein, E., & Walker, L. (1982). A basis for understanding and treating the remarried family. In J. C. Hansen & L. Messinger (Eds.), *Therapy with remarriage families* (pp. 161-186). Rockville, MD: Aspen System Corporation.

DeShazer, S. (1982). *Patterns of brief family therapy*. New York: The Guilford Press.

DeShazer, S. (1985). *Keys to solution in brief therapy*. New York: Norton.

DeShazer, S. (1988). *Clues: Investigating solutions in brief therapy*. New York: Norton.

D'Zurillz, T. J. (1986). *Problem-solving therapy: A social competence approach to clinical intervention*. New York: Springer Publishing Company.

Elkaim, M. (1990). *If you love me, don't love me*. New York: Basic Books.

Ellison, E. S. (1983). Issues concerning parental harmony and children's psychosocial adjustment. *American Journal of Orthopsychiatry*, 53, 73-80.

Epston, D. (1991). "I am a bear": Discovering discoveries. *Family Therapy Case Studies*, 6(1), 11-20.

Felker, E. H. (1981). *Raising other people's kids: Successful child-rearing in the restructed family*. Grand Rapids, MI: William B. Eerdmans Publishing Company.

Fishman, B. (1983). The economic behavior of stepfamilies. *Family Relations*, 32, 359-366.

Freedman, J., & Combs, G. (1993). Invitations to new stories: Using questions to explore alternative possibilities. In S. Gilligan & R. Price (Eds.), *Therapeutic conversations* (pp. 291-308). New York: Norton.

Furman, B., & Ahola, T. (1992). *Social talk: Hosting therapeutic conversations*. New York: Norton.

Furstenberg, F., & Spanier, G. B. (1984). *Recycling the family: Remarriage after divorce*. Newbury Park, CA: Sage.

Ganong, L. H., & Colman, M. (1984). The effects of remarriage on children: A review of the empirical literature. *Family Relations*, 33, 389-406.

Garfield, R. (1982). Mourning and its resolution for spouses in marital separation. In J. C. Hansen & L. Messinger (Eds.), *Therapy with remarriage families* (pp. 1-16). Rockville, MD: Aspen System Corporation.

Gergen, K. J. (1985). Social constructionist inquiry: Context and implications. In K. J. Gergen & K. E. Davis (Eds.), *The social construction of the person* (pp. 3-18). New York: Springer-Verlag.

Gergen, K. J. (1991). *The saturated self.* New York: Basic Books.

Glick, P. (1980). Remarriage: Some recent changes and variation. *Journal of Family Issues*, 1, 455-478.

Goldenberg, I., & Goldenberg, H. (1991). *Family therapy: An overview.* (3rd ed.). Pacific Grove: Brooks/Cole Publishing Company.

Goldner, V. (1982). Remarriage family: Structure, system, future. In J. C. Hansen & L. Messinger (Eds.), *Therapy with remarriage families* (pp. 161-186). Rockville, MD: Aspen System Corporation.

Goldsmith, J. (1980). The relationship between former spouses: Descriptive findings. *Journal of Divorce*, 4, 1-20.

Goolishian, A., & Anderson, H. (1992). Strategy and intervention versus nonintervention: A matter of theory? *Journal of Marital and Family Therapy,* 18(1), 5-15.

Greene, B. L. (1981). *A clinical approach to marital problems; Diagnosis, prevention and treatment.* Springfield, IL: Charles C Thomas, Publisher.

Haley, J. (1987). *Problem solving therapy.* San Francisco, CA: Jossey-Bass, Publishers.

Hammond, J. M. (1979). Children of divorce: A study of self-concept academic achievement and attitudes. *Elementary School Journal,* 80, 54-62.

Hansen, J., & Messinger, L. (eds.) (1982). *Therapy with remarriage families.* Rockville, MD: Aspen System Corporation.

Hayes, R. L., & Hayes, B. A. (1986). Remarriage families: Counseling parents, stepparents, and their children. *Counseling and Human Development*, 18, 1-8.

Hodges, W. F., Wechsler, R. C., & Ballantine, C. (1979). Divorce and the preschool child: Cumulative stress. *Journal of Divorce*, 3, 55-67.

Hoffman, L. (1981). *Foundation of family therapy.* New York: Basic Books.

Hoffman, L. (1991). A reflexive stance for family therapy. *Journal of Strategic and Systemic Therapies*, 10 (3&4), 4-17.

Huntington, D. S (1982). Attachment, loss and divorce: a reconsideration of the concepts. In J. C. Isaacs, M. B. (1982). Facilitation family restructuring and relinkage. In C. Hansen & L. Messinger (Eds.), *Therapy with remarriage families* (pp. 121-143). Rockville, MD: Aspen System Corporation.

Isaacs, M. B., Montalvo, B., & Abelsohn, D. (1986). *The difficult divorce: Therapy for children and families.* New York: Basic Books.

Jacobson, N. S., & Margolin, G. (1979). *Marital therapy: Strategies based on social learning and behavior exchange principles.* New York: Brunner/Mazel.

Jensen, L. C., & Jensen, J. M. (1981). *Stepping into stepparenting: A practical guide.* Palo Alto, CA: R & E Research Associates, Inc.

Johnson, S. (1990). Six characters in search of an author: A constructivist view. *Family Process*, 29, 297-308.

Kalter, N. (1990). *Growing up with divorce.* New York: Signet.

Kirkwood, G. (1986). Blended families: America's confusing phenomenon. *Colorado State Magazine*, 41-43.

Kleinman, J., Rosenberg, E., & Whiteside, M. (1979). Common developmental tasks in forming reconstituted families. *Journal of Marriage and Family Therapy*, 5, 79-86.

Kupisch, S. (1987). Children and Stepfamilies. In A. Thomas & J. Grimes (Eds.), *Children's needs: Psychological perspectives.* Washington, DC: National Association of Psychologists.

Lax, W. D. (1989). Systematic family therapy with young children and their families: Use of the reflecting team. *Children in Family Therapy: Treatment and Training*, 56-60.

Levant, R. (1984). *Family Therapy: A Comprehensive Overview.* New Jersey: Prentice Hall.

Lewis, H. C. (1980). *All about families: The second time around.* Atlanta, GA: Peachtree.

Lutz, P. (1983). The Stepfamily: An adolescent perspective. *Family Relations*, 32, 367-375.

Maddox, B. (1975). *The half-parent.* New York: New American Library.

Martin, D., & Martin, M. (1992). *Stepfamilies in therapy: Understanding systems, assessment, and intervention.* San Franciso, CA: Jossey-Bass, Inc., Publishers.

McClenahan, C. (1978). Group work with stepparents and their spouses. *Unpublished manuscript.*

McGoldrick, M., & Carter, E. (1980). Forming a remarried family. In E. Carter & M. McGoldrick (Eds.), *The changing family cycle: A framework for family therapy* (pp. 399-432). New York: Gardner Press.

McLean, C, & Fifield, M. (1991). Broadening the problem definition: A case of a woman's unconfidence. *Family Therapy Case Studies*, 6(1), 29-34.

Messinger, L. (1976). Remarriage between divorced people with children from previous marriages. *Journal of Marriage and Family Counseling*, 2, 193-200.

Meyer, G. (1992). Family therapy with divorcing and remarried families. In J. D. Atwood (Ed.), *Family therapy: A systemic approach* (pp. 159-172). Chicago: Nelson-Hall.

Minuchin, S. (1974). *Families and family therapy.* Cambridge, MA: Harvard University Press.

Minuchin, S., & Fishman, H. C. (1981). *Family therapy techniques.* Cambridge, MA: Harvard University Press.

Norton, J., & Glick, P. (1979). Marital instability in America. In G. Levinger & O. Moles (Eds.), *Divorce and separation: Content, causes, and consequences* (pp. 3-60). New York: Basic Books.

O'Hanlon, W. H., & Weiner-Davis, M. (1989). *In search of solutions.* New York: Norton.

Parish, T. S., & Taylor, J. C. (1979). Impact of divorce and subsequent father absence on children's and adolescents' self-concepts. *Journal of Youth and Adolescence*, 8, 427-432.

Pasley, K., & Ihinger-Tallman, M. (1982). Stress in remarried families. *Family Perspective*, 16(4), 181-190.

Piercy, F. P., & Sprenkle, D. H. (1986). *Family Therapy Sourcebook*. New York: Guilford Press.

Prest, L., & Carruthers, M. (1991). The case of the sneaky sleep thief. White's externalizing technique within a broad strategic frame. *Journal of Strategic and Systemic Therapies*, 10 (3&4), 66-75.

Prosen, S. S., & Farmer, J. H. (1982). Understanding stepfamilies: Issues and implications for counselors. *The Personnel and Guidance Journal*, 60, 393-397.

Raschke, H. J., & Raschke, V. J. (1979). Family conflict and children's self-concept: A comparison of intact and single-parent families. *Journal of Marriage and the Family*, 41, 367-374.

Robson, B. (1982). A developmental approach to the treatment of children of divorcing parents. In J. C. Hansen & L. Messinger (Eds.), *Therapy with remarriage families* (pp. 59-78). Rockville, MD: Aspen System Corporation.

Sager, C. J., Brown, H. S., Crohn, H., Engel, T., Rodstein, E., & Walker, L. (1983). *Treating the remarried family*. New York: Brunner/Mazel.

Sager, C. J., Brown, H. S., Crohn, H., Engel, T., Rodstein, E., & Walker, L. (1983). Therapy with the remarried family system. In M. R. Textor (Ed.), *Helping families with special problems* (pp. 209-226). New York: Jason Aronson.

Satir, V., & Baldwin, M. (1983). *Satir: Step-by-step. A guide to creating change in families*. Palo Alto, CA: Science and Behavior Books.

Schaefer, C. E., Briesmeister, J. M., & Fitton, M. E. (1984). *Family therapy techniques for problem behaviors of children and teenagers*. San Francisco, CA: Jossey-Bass, Publishers.

Selvini-Palazzoli, M., Boscolo, L., Cecchin, G. F., & Prata, G. (1978). *Paradox and counterparadox: A new model in the therapy of the family in schizophrenic transaction*. New York: Aronson.

Skeen, P., Covi, R. B., & Robinson, B. E. (1985). Stepfamilies: A review of the literature with suggestions for practitioners. *Journal of Counseling and Development*, 64, 121-125.

Speed, B. (1991). Reality exists, O.K.? An argument against constructivism and social constructionism. *Family Therapy*, 13, 395-409.

Stern, P. N. (1978). Stepfather families integration around child discipline. *Issues in Mental Health Nursing*, 1, 326-332.

Stewart, K., & Kulka, C. (1991). The deconstruction of a violent story: Untangling certainties; theirs and ours. *Family Therapy Case Studies*, 6(1), 35-45.

Strother, J., & Jacob, E. (1984). Adolescent stress as it relates to stepfamily living: Implications for school counselors. *The School Counselor*, 32, 97-103.

Tessman, L. (1978). *Children of parting parents*. New York: Aronson.

Thies, J. M. (1977). Beyond divorce: The impact of remarriage on children. *Journal of Clinical Child Psychology*, 6, 59-61.

Tomm, K. M. (1984). One perspective on the Milan approach: Part I. Overview of development, theory, and practice. *Journal of Marital and Family Therapy*, 10, 113-125.

Turnbull, S. K., & Turnbull, J. M. (1983). To dream the impossible dream: An agenda for discussion with stepparents. *Family Relations*, 32, 227-230.

Visher, E. B., & Visher, J. S. (1979). *Stepfamilies: A guide to working with stepparents and stepchildren*. New York: Brunner/Mazel.

Visher, E. B., & Visher, J. S. (1982). Stepfamilies in the 1980's. In J. C. Hanson & L. Messinger (Eds.), *Therapy with remarriage families* (pp. 105-119). Rockville, MD: Aspen Systems Corporation.

Visher, E. B., & Visher, J. S. (1982). Stepfamilies and Stepparenting. In F. Walsh (Ed.), *Normal Family Process* (pp. 331-353). New York: The Guilford Press.

Visher, E. B., & Visher, J. S. (1987). *Old loyalties, new ties: Therapeutic strategies with stepfamilies*. New York: Brunner/Mazel.

Wald, E. (1981). *The remarried family; Challenge and promise*. New York: Family Service Association of America.

Walker, K. N., & Messinger, L. (1979). Remarriage and divorce: Dissolution and reconstruction of family boundaries. *Family Process*, 18, 185-192.

Wallerstein, J. S., & Kelly, J. B. (1980). *Surviving the break-up: How children actually cope with divorce*. New York: Basic Books.

Walsh, F. (1982). Conceptualizations of normal family functioning. In F. Walsh (Ed.), *Normal Family Process* (pp. 3-42). New York: The Guilford Press.

Walsh, F. (1991). Promoting healthy functioning in divorced and remarried families. In A. S. Gurman & D. P. Kniskern (Eds.), *Handbook of family therapy*. Volume II (pp. 525-545). New York: Brunner/Mazel.

Walsh, W. (1993). Twenty major issues in remarriage families. *Journal of Counseling & Development*, 70(6), 709-715.

Watzlawick, P. (1984). *The invented reality*. New York: Norton.

White, M. (1989). Anorexia nervosa: A cybernetic perspective. In M. White, *Selected papers* (pp. 65-75). Adelaide: Dulwich Centre Publications (Reprinted from Eating Disorders, 1986).

White, M. (1989). The process of questioning: A therapy of literary merit? In M. White, *Selected papers* (pp. 37-46). Adelaide: Dulwich Centre Publications. (Reprinted from Dulwich Centre Newsletter, 1987, Spring).

White, M. (1989). The externalizing of the problem. In M. White, *Selected papers* (pp. 5-28). Adelaide: Dulwich Centre Publications. (Reprinted from Dulwich Centre Newsletter, 1988/9, Summer).

White, M. (1993). Commentary: The histories of the present. In S. Gilligan & R. Price (Eds.), *Therapeutic Conversations* (pp. 121-135). New York: Norton.

White, M., & Epstein, D. (1990). *Narrative means to therapeutic ends*. New York: Norton.

Whiteside, M. F. (1982). Remarriage: A family developmental process. *Journal of Marital and Family Therapy*, 59-64.

Witkin, S. L. (1989). Scientific ideology and women: Implications for marital research and therapy. *Journal of Family Psychology*, 2(4), 430-446.

Stepfamily Assessment: An Integrated Model

Katalin Morrison
Wilma Stollman

SUMMARY. The increase in the number of stepfamilies in our society is reflected in the high number of stepfamilies requesting help in mental health facilities and social agencies.

The rationale for developing a model for assessing remarried families comes from an awareness of the complexities of remarried families and of the difficulty therapists have in assessing and organizing all relevant information.

We do not imply any particular method to assess the families; we are simply suggesting a format which needs to be in the mind of the therapist when interviewing the family or a family member. Our model emphasizes particular aspects of remarried family life that play a crucial role in the successful adjustment of the remarried family, such as the resolution of the previous relationship, the influence of the outside parent, the co-parental relationship, the mobility of the children between households, and the integration of the new partner.

Katalin Morrison, MD, FRCP, is Assistant Professor, University of Ottawa, Department of Psychiatry, and in private practice, 2249 Carling Avenue, Ottawa, Ontario, Canada K2B 7E9. Wilma Stollman, MSW, is Senior Program Manager on the staff of the Family Service Centre.

The authors wish to thank Dr. Paul Steinhauer for his advice after reading the manuscript, Dr. Robert Morrison for major editing work, Pat Koeslag and Shirley White for typing assistance, the Queensway Carleton Hospital for its financial contribution and the clients and patients who helped us understand the problems and strengths of remarried families.

[Haworth co-indexing entry note]: "Stepfamily Assessment:: An Integrated Model." Morrison, Katalin, and Wilma Stollman. Co-published simultaneously in *Journal of Divorce & Remarriage* (The Haworth Press, Inc.) Vol. 24, No. 1/2, 1995, pp. 163-182; and: *Understanding Stepfamilies: Their Structure and Dynamics* (ed: Craig A. Everett) The Haworth Press, Inc., 1995, pp. 163-182. Single or multiple copies of this article are available from The Haworth Document Delivery Service [1-800-342-9678, 9:00 a.m. - 5:00 p.m. (EST)].

Our assessment model is divided into two parts: (1) The psychosocial history completed by the family; (2) The assessment of the stepfamily by the therapist. This includes the assessment of the functioning of the stepfamily based on Steinhauer's Process Model.

Our model helps therapists to conceptualize the problems and the strength of the stepfamily. The active participation of the stepfamily in the process of assessment facilitates the development of treatment goals and the therapeutic contract.

This paper only includes the functional assessment of the stepfamily. The psychosocial history questionnaire is available from the authors upon request. *[Article copies available from The Haworth Document Delivery Service: 1-800-342-9678.]*

INTRODUCTION

Stepfamilies are coming in increasing numbers to mental health facilities. The rationale for developing a model for assessing remarried families comes from an awareness of the complexities of remarried families and of the difficulty therapists have in assessing and organizing all relevant information.

It was felt that in a busy clinical practice where assessment must be accomplished in one or two sessions due to time and money limitations, a brief structured assessment can be most valuable for the families and for the therapist–whatever theoretical orientation she or he may have, regardless of their educational background (social work, psychology, psychiatry, nursing, etc.).

We assume that the therapist is familiar with the differences in structure and function between nuclear, single parent and remarried families. These issues are documented well elsewhere (Visher and Visher 1979, 1983; Sager 1983, 1985; Messinger 1981; McGoldrick 1985; Morrison et al. 1986a, 1986b). We do not imply any particular method to assess the families; we are simply suggesting a format which needs to be in the mind of the therapist when interviewing the family or a family member.

Our model consists of two parts:

The first part is the psychosocial history of the stepfamily questionnaire. It has to be completed by the stepfamily and has been tested and proven useful to integrate essential information about the stepfamily.

The second part is the therapist's assessment of the stepfamily functioning. For this part, we have used Steinhauer's (1984) Process Model of family functioning, and applied this model to the assessment of the stepfamily.

The model includes those particular aspects of remarried family life that play a crucial role in the successful adjustment of remarried families, such as:

1. Resolution of the previous partnership–and the influence of the outside parent (the ex-spouse) on the present relationship.
2. Co-parental relationship both between the ex-spouses and between the present partner and the stepparent. When we refer to the co-parental relationship we include the degree of consensus and the ability to work out childrearing issues.
3. Mobility of the children between households.
4. Integration of the different family cultures in a remarried family.

This paper addresses the assessment of the stepfamily function by the therapist. (The psychosocial questionnaire is available from the authors upon request.)

LITERATURE REVIEW

Stepfamily research has been so far the "stepchild" of family research–both in theoretical and in clinical areas. The complexity of the structure and function of the stepfamily contributes to the reluctance of studying this family form. Challenges for researchers regarding these problems are summarized by Ihinger-Tallman and Pasley (1987). Visher and Visher (1979) laid the foundation to the understanding of remarried families–their functions, structure, stresses and treatment. They have been instrumental in educating the public and professionals. Sager et al. (1981) describe the stepfamily, including its historical development and all influences from previous and present family systems (metafamily system). The stage of family life is also given consideration.

The natural life cycle of the family is well described by McGoldrick (1985)–from the beginning of family life to raising and launching children to the family of later life. Discrepancy in the family life cycle between two people who remarry requires additional adjustment.

The specific stages in stepfamily adjustment are well documented by Papernow (1984). The stages imply a gradual awareness of the differences in stepfamilies from the nuclear family, the awareness of the particular conflicts, intense anxiety and confusion about roles and the need to communicate.

That can finally lead to integration of the newly formed family unit. Papernow has been most helpful in "placing difficult and confusing experiences within a normal, chronological, developmental framework."

Some of the following authors focused on *particular issues* in stepfamilies. Regarding the continuous ties with the ex-spouse who also remains a co-parent after divorce and remarriage, Moss (1980) found that "attachment to the previous spouse affects the new marital bond." "Thus for a person who is remarried, a triadic configuration emerges–between the person, the current second spouse and the ex-spouse." (As mentioned before, Sager (1983) also includes all subsystems in his concept of the remarried family.) Messinger (1981) coined the term "permeable boundaries"–implying a need for flexible movement for children between their natural parents' households.

The children are seen as members of both families, where they have different roles, expectations, involvement. Their quality and quantity of contacts between the different homes have a great impact on the remarried family. Several authors *conceptualized* the *parameters* needing to be evaluated in remarried families:

Visher and Visher (1983) in their Workshop Manual provide a list of issues to be considered in stepfamilies.

Sager (1985) further lists nine parameters, including expectations of the partners from each other regarding the relationship with the children, decision making, responsibilities, inclusion or exclusion of members of the remarried family, the degree of autonomy and dependence, differences between the partners' individual histories and their ways of dealing with the previous marital relation.

Ihinger-Tallman and Pasley (1987) summarized the major difficulties in merging two households on the basis of their own study as well as from the available literature. They categorize the main issues both for the children and for the adults: discipline, loyalty conflict, boundaries and resource distribution.

Esther Wald (1981) in her Problem Process Profile organized the issues causing stress in remarried families as due to (1) environment; (2) individual; (3) intrafamilial; (4) interfamilial adjustment problems. Depending on the focus of the main problems, different treatment modalities would need to be implied.

Steinhauer's (1984) and Skinner's (1983) process model conceptualizes family functioning in a most comprehensive, yet easy to follow organization. We have applied this model to the assessment of the remarried family.

DISCUSSION

Conceptual Framework

Any family assessment has to include some information gathering. In a stepfamily situation this need is even more crucial due to its complexity–

the number of people involved, possible interactions, histories. We need to clarify particular aspects of the remarried family. A stepfamily is defined as a family in which at least one of the partners in the couple is biologically related to one of the children, and the other partner is not.

We conceptualize the remarried family as including not only the couple and all their children, but also the non-residential biological partner(s) and the extended family. We define the starting point of the existence of the remarried family as the date when the partners began to reside together.

We refer to present partners as the adult couple, a husband and wife, regardless of their legal status. As least one of the adults is a stepparent. We refer to the ex-spouse(s) as the previous partner(s) of the present couple, we also refer to the ex-spouse(s) as the non-residential parent. The non-residential parent has a biological relationship with the child(ren), regardless of custodial arrangement or frequency of contact.

The children in the remarried family often belong to the two households of their biological families. Their living arrangements vary from no physical contact to occasional visits to 50%-50% custodial arrangements to permanent residence in the remarried family. Residential arrangements are often open to changes. We refer to the child(ren) of the present couple as their mutual child(ren).

We refer to the extended family as parents and close relatives of the couple as well as the ex-spouses. We include the parents and relatives of the stepparent also.

It is known that in remarried families there are no unified ways of identifying family membership. Each person has their own view about who belongs. Having discrepancies in that area likely leads to misunderstandings and hurt feelings. Each individual present at the assessment list who they view as family members.

In assessing a remarried family, particular attention needs to be paid to the life cycle of the new family–What stage the family is at; What child rearing responsibilities exist for the adults towards their own children and towards the family as a result of the union.

Another typical feature of remarried families is the frequent change of residence of the children. Their moves may reflect a healthy desire and flexibility for both parents and children. Often, however, family problems or problems of the parents in one of the homes may lead to expelling a child who then unexpectedly arrives at the other biological parent's home. Children may move back and forth between their natural parents' homes on their own initiative–partly because neither parent is willing to take a full parenting commitment.

Some of the changes regarding the addition or loss of family members in the household are naturally occurring passages in any family's life. For example: children moving away to school, getting married, a family member moving away due to illness, death. The couple may have a child together, or the ex-spouses may remarry–adding new family members.

All of these changes can have a great impact in both households of the children.

The Functioning of the Stepfamily is evaluated by using Steinhauer's Process Model (1984). This is organized according to Steinhauer's six basic categories:

1. Task Accomplishment;
2. Role Performance;
3. Communication;
4. Affective Involvement;
5. Control;
6. Values and Norms.

We discuss each category separately. At the beginning of each category we summarize Steinhauer's definition and describe how we apply each category to stepfamilies in general. The next step is to look at the issues separately as they apply to the new couple, to the stepparent, to the children, to the ex-spouse, and to the extended family.

Finally, each family function is illustrated by case example.

Task Accomplishment

Definition

Task performance refers to the family's ability to accomplish basic development and crisis tasks, as well as allow for the continued individual development of all family members (Steinhauer et al. 1984).

General Issues

It is a great adjustment for all stepfamily members to move from a single parent household to one that incorporates another adult who is not a biological parent and who may bring more children into the household. In a traditional family there are standard models to accomplish tasks, but culturally accepted models do not exist for remarried families. For these families the temptation to fall back on the traditional model is great and almost always self-defeating. A healthy model for stepfamily functioning often has to include the non-residential biological parent in helping to provide for the basic needs of the children.

An ongoing dialogue between the adults in which daily compromises and new approaches have to be made is essential for family functioning. Children are often adversely affected by the divorce and post-divorce adjustment. Accordingly their special needs have to be understood and accommodated by the new family.

Couple

When adults with parental responsibilities become involved with a partner, their responsibility to the children is present from day one. For this reason, the new relationship is often seen by partners as creating demands and stresses that are not experienced by a couple who marries for the first time. Both partners may have to struggle to create the financial and emotional resources for the new relationship and also find the time to develop it.

Stepparent

The temptation to fall into the nuclear family model is often expressed by the tendency of a natural parent to let the stepparent assume parental responsibilities of the same sex biological parent. For example, if the natural father does not pay support for the children, rather than pursuing him to do so, the stepparent may want, and may be expected, to provide financial support for his wife and stepchild. Another example is that of the stepmother who wants to make up for all the losses the children have experienced, and wants to help her husband by assuming a traditional female role replacing or displacing the previous spouse (Morrison et al. 1986). This can create resentment if the affectional bond with the children does not compensate for the increased tasks.

Children

If in a single parent household the children are not expected to share many basic household tasks, they often become quite resentful when a new partner, directly or indirectly, puts expectations on them. If a child has been the oldest child in a single parent household and was actively involved in decision making, that child might find it difficult to be demoted to the child position again, and may, at least in the beginning, refuse to respond to age appropriate expectations.

Children often resent the stepparent doing something for them that they want their natural parent to do for them. For example, the stepmother cannot make up for the meals that the natural mother used to cook, so it would be easier, in the children's perception, if father would continue cooking as he had done before in the single parent household.

Non-Residential Parent and Extended Family

Because of likely emotional conflicts between the ex-spouses and a lack of model of how extended families and ex-spouses can cooperate with the new remarried family, these families frequently experience a lack of the support that could be helpful for all its members.

CASE EXAMPLE: Mary and her two girls had financial support from the girls' father. As soon as they moved in with Tom, Mary decided to reject the support payments for the children so they could be a "real family." Both Mary and Tom wanted to operate on the basis of the nuclear family model.

Role Performance

Definition

Role Performance assesses the family's ability to allocate specific activities to family members, as well as their willingness to assume these roles and follow them up with appropriate action (Steinhauer et al. 1984).

General Issues

At present there are no culturally accepted roles for members of stepfamilies. The culturally defined role of the natural parent in the traditional family cannot be automatically transferred to the stepfamily.

In the new family the most ambivalent and stressful role is of the stepparent. It is ill-defined by society and it must be developed without the benefit of any accepted model. With the formation of the new family the role of the natural parents changes as well.

Couple

The role of men and women in a society depends upon the values that society places on particular family forms and behaviour. Tradition, values and norms are very important when remarried families are formed, because the tendency exists for the stepfamily to fall back on stereotyped male/female roles that have developed in nuclear families. This nuclear family model creates an unattainable position for the stepparent who cannot possibly substitute or usurp the role of the same-sex parent living outside of the household. The development of the role of the second spouse is frequently hindered by his/her partner's inability to free him/herself emotionally from the previous spouse.

The development of the role of the new spouse can also be hindered by the fact that a child, frequently the oldest, has attained a co-partner position in the single parent household. In these families, the child often finds it very difficult to give up this special and privileged position when the new partner joins the family. The biological parent in the home can feel guilty for "demoting" his/her child back to the child position to give room to the new spouse.

Stepparent/Stepchild

This relationship is the most stressful one in the remarried family, particularly because of the need to develop a special role for the stepparent in relation to the stepchild. All members of the new family have to accept that the stepparent has a role to play, and will gradually become more involved in assuming stepparental responsibilities.

Particular difficulties in the stepparent role are related to the ambivalence and to the lack of traditional models for this role (Messinger 1981). Steppartners are often confused, being in a parental role at one time and being in the role of a stranger in the family at other times. The essential task of the stepparent is to build up a relationship gradually with the stepchild before a parental role can be assumed.

Stepchildren react in different ways to the arrival of a stepparent in their families according to their ages and developmental stages. Teenagers particularly do not want to assume the role of a child again and are difficult to integrate in a new blended family. Children who experience loyalty conflict between their natural parents have the most difficulty with the development of the new roles in the stepfamily.

Non-Residential Parent and Extended Family

The role of the non-residential parent has to be accepted by all members of the new family, so that children of this family do not have to cope with unnecessary loyalty conflicts, and so that the natural parent of the child can exercise the right and responsibility to continue the parenting role. The non-residential parent's acceptance and support of the remarried family and the stepparent role are essential.

CASE EXAMPLE: Kim's two stepdaughters spent alternate weekends with their father and her. Kim felt that the girls' mother, Anne, did not prepare the children adequately for the visits because she did not send enough clothes. Rather than discussing the need for more supplies to be sent with her husband or Anne, she took on the responsibility of buying extra clothes, which made Anne quite upset. She felt criticized and did not like the idea of the children coming home after every visit with their father as if it were Christmas twice a month. But Kim did not see that her role was not to substitute the mother's role in regards to the children's clothes. She competed rather than cooperated with her, in conjunction with her husband who basically should have taken on the primary responsibility for the children's care including the discussion about their clothing on their visits every other weekend.

Communication

Definition

Communication is the process of information exchange towards mutual understanding. It includes the expression of affect (Steinhauer et al. 1984).

General Issues

In remarried families, a healthy communication pattern is crucial for the development of new roles for adults and children so that integration into a new family and accomplishment of all tasks can be successful. In contrast to nuclear families, there are no culturally defined norms and standards for communicating between remarried family members. Children often refuse to communicate with a stepparent, stepparents are frequently insecure about how to relate to a stepchild. In many families communication between stepparents and stepchildren, and between divorced natural parents, are particularly strained. Avoidance of communication, as well as indirect and unclear communication, can lead to a great deal of misunderstanding.

Couple

For the new partners, communication regarding values and norms is essential in order to define their expectations of each other and of the new relationship. They bring their tradition, values from their respective parents as well as from previous marital unions.

In a remarried family, the couple frequently does not want to confront differences between themselves because of anxiety about a break-up of the new relationship. Their hostile feelings become suppressed, leading to a distortion of communication. Often this hostility can become displaced onto the stepparent-stepchild relationship.

The couple needs to clarify expectations of themselves and each other as parents, so that their individual philosophies of rearing children become known to the partner. In this way, new approaches of child rearing can be mutually negotiated, or old ways can be tolerated. In the beginning of the remarriage, the natural parent may have a great deal of ambivalence to allow the stepparent to act as a parent. The natural parent frequently communicates ambivalent messages to the stepparent regarding this role. Consequently the stepparent may feel that he/she is not allowed to express any negative feelings in relation to the stepchild's behaviour.

Stepparent

Usually a stepparent approaches this position with uncertainty and insecurity. The stepparent frequently feels that his or her own feelings and needs cannot be brought out openly for fear of rejection by the stepchild. This leads frequently to unclear, non-direct communication, particularly between stepparent and stepchild.

The stepparent tends to bring all complaints about the stepchild to the partner, preventing the development of a relationship between stepparent and stepchild.

Only when the stepparent/stepchild relationship is allowed to develop gradually, with support from both natural parents, will the distortion in communication and the suppression of both negative and positive feelings be ameliorated.

Stepchild/Children

The stepchild initially reacts ambivalently to the stepparent. This is a normal reaction due to the child's anxiety about the new situation as well as to the reawakening of the sense of the loss of the original family. Hostile feelings towards a stepparent are often encouraged by the same-sex biological parent not living in the household. This can coincide with the child's need to protect the relationship with the natural parent. The child may suppress the hostility towards the natural parent and may transfer these negative feelings towards the stepparent. Positive feelings towards the stepparent often create guilt feelings in the child towards the same-sex parent. Consequently, only negative feelings may be communicated, particularly if there is a strained relationship between the natural parents.

Non-Residential Parent and Extended Family

Frequency and type of communication between the natural parent in the home and the parent outside the present relationship have a great impact on the functioning of the remarried family. Communication between them has to be direct so that children do not become caught in the conflict that can exist between the ex-spouses. Hostile and critical communication between the ex-spouses should exclude the child whose need for attachment to both parents is essential, and not be carried out through or with the child.

Communication between natural parents is also important so that the child can make the adjustment of living in both homes with as little confusion as possible. Positive communication between natural parents provides the child with emotional security from both parents and lets the child know that both parents have an interest in his/her well being.

It is important that communication exist between members of the extended family as well. One problem that exists frequently in remarried families is insufficient communication between the natural parents as well as the extended family of the ex-spouses. This problem can be due to excessive feelings of hostility and anxiety about all the changes in the divorced couple's life.

CASE EXAMPLE: Fifteen-year-old Susan was living with her single mother for six years before her mother began living with George. Susan and her mother had become extremely close and the girl did not find it easy to accept George and make room for him in her life. The difficulty particularly resulted from the fact that mother and daughter did not discuss enough about George's role and the girl began to focus on not wanting to call George by any name. This neglect of proper discussion between all three members of the new family made Susan ill at ease, particularly in George's presence. She would not speak to him directly and avoided any contact and the possibility of developing a relationship with her stepfather.

This example points out the importance of discussing with the child what the new stepparent is to be called, and generally discussing the event of remarriage and the change in the child's life.

Affective Involvement

Definition

Affective involvement refers to the emotional interest family members have in each other, providing support as well as autonomy for individual members (Steinhauer 1984).

General Issues

Membership in a remarried family does not start with the union of the two partners only. The two adults can make the decision to remarry or live together on the basis of their emotional involvement with one another, but that does not guarantee the formation of a cohesive family. For feelings of membership among family members to develop, it requires time and many common positive experiences. Stepfamily members generally do not have the same degree of cohesion and affective involvement with one another as in nuclear families at their optimum functioning. This is partly related to the lack of earlier attachment between stepparent and stepchild in the child's life, as well as to the prior attachment of the child to the natural parent of the same sex outside of the home.

Couple

In the couple relationship, the partner's attachment to their previous partners can create conflict in the new relationship. In situations of prior unresolved marital separation, the continuation of the bond with the previous partner can prevent the person from forming a new committed relationship. Jealousy and anger regarding previous partners can also interfere with the trust in the new relationship. Coming to terms with a partner's prior history of attachments is an important task for the new couple, especially where children are involved.

Stepparent/Stepchild

The adult's decision to form a partnership does not automatically imply a positive liking between stepparent and child. It is the natural parent's responsibility to choose a partner who has a capacity for concern for the child. In most instances, the emotional needs of the child are being met by the natural parents, and can only gradually be expected to be additionally fulfilled by the stepparent. The stepparent's primary responsibility in this respect is the development of a relationship that is based on trust, respect and concern for the stepchild. This relationship between stepparent and child develops only gradually, facilitated by time and common experiences. The natural parents of the child in the meantime need to help this kind of a relationship to develop, as a benefit to all the members of the family rather than as a threat to the parents' closeness to the child.

The new family must also allow the stepparent to be his/her own person, to pursue career goals or interests and activities as before, rather than expecting the stepparent to derive all life satisfaction only from the involvement in the new family. This issue is more significant for stepmothers who often want to be (and often are expected to be) supermoms.

In most remarried families, relationships between the members are initially partly negative, sometimes hostile, reflecting often the stepparent's feelings that the care and emotional involvement in the children will take time away from the couple's relationship. Hostility may reflect the children's anger at the new stepparent caused by fear of losing, or betraying, their natural parents.

The integration of the stepfamily, and the development of concern by family members for each other, will take two to five years to develop in most families. To have negative or even hostile feelings expressed by children or adults in these situations is normal and appropriate.

Non-Residential Parent and Extended Family

The non-residential parent's affective involvement in the child's life is frequently underestimated. Fathers used to disappear from children's lives in order to provide room for the "new stepfather" as they perceived it to be their duty for the benefit of the child. Children's attachment to their biological parents and grandparents does not change when the adults make a decision to divorce. Children's concept of family is their biological family. The importance of the continuity of the ties for children who live in a remarried family is essential, and should be allowed, encouraged and facilitated by all adults concerned in their children's lives. The non-residential parent and his/her family have an important role to play in helping children to adjust to the new remarried family. Oftentimes, the non-residential parent feels threatened by a new partner for the ex-spouse. Particularly women are afraid of losing the child's affection to the stepmother and consequently they often put pressure on the child to reject her.

CASE EXAMPLE: Doug and Lynn recently moved in together, pursuing an intense romantic relationship in front of Doug's two children, Karen,

13, and Bob, 15 years old. Karen openly rejected and defied her stepmother and would try to come between the new couple whenever physical closeness was expressed. She felt threatened and betrayed by her father to whom she was very close for years. Doug had been the primary parent to his children. As a single parent, their relationship was more intense than in a two parent family. Both adults had trouble seeing that Karen needed time and continuing closeness to her father in order to accept the new relationship. Bob was not distressed but rather relieved that he could spend more time with his friends rather than worrying that his father was alone on Saturday nights. He enjoyed Lynn's cooking, too.

Control

Definition

Control is defined as the process by which "family members influence each other's behaviour" (Steinhauer et al. 1984).

General Issues

No other aspect of family function creates as many conflicts in remarried families as that of the influence of the family members on each other's behaviour. In order for two single-parent families to join successfully from backgrounds with different moral and cultural values regarding behaviour control, they must succeed at the task of developing a harmonious way to deal with the control function of family life.

Couple

In biological families the adults are confronted from the beginning of this relationship with control functions with respect to their own behaviour as well as their style regarding parenting. Affective involvement between parent and child is not questioned by the other parent even though styles of behaviour control can be diverse in a nuclear family. In contrast, in a remarried family, the biological parent initially resents any challenge to his discipline style towards the children by the new partner. The new partner often mistakenly wants to influence the biological parent's behaviour towards the children as proof of affection and devotion to the new partner/relationship, creating loyalty conflicts.

An important aspect of adjustment for the new couple is their ability to achieve consensus regarding child-rearing values, particularly in the areas of teaching responsible behaviour.

Having suffered prior marital failure, a new partner may shy away from exerting adequate control of his or her new spouse's behaviour for fear of provoking another break-up (e.g., the stepmother who bails out her husband from his agreed responsibilities for his children due to fear of being found not good enough as a wife). Flexibility in behaviour control is most essential for the couple who both have children. The two sets of children involved have different family histories, and the children may be at different developmental stages requiring new routines appropriate for the new family.

Stepparent/Stepchild

Parental control is not a given in a remarried family for the new spouse. The stepparent can only be a delegate for the natural parent, at least initially. Expectation from a child by a stepparent can create confusion and resentment in the child if it is a challenge to either natural parent's expectations. It is already difficult for children of divorce to deal with the two biological parents who are often inconsistent with each other. Rules in one household do not necessarily get reinforced in the other.

Children of divorce are often victims of their biological parents' hostility to one another. As discussed earlier, identification with parents is an important factor in the children's development of a capacity for self-discipline. When there is inter-parental hostility, this capacity can be affected. Children may identify with the parent to whom they feel more emotional attachment even though they are under the care of the other parent. Thus, even though the custodial parent may act responsibly, it is important to appreciate the other parent's influence over the children's development.

Non-Residential Parent and Extended Family

Even though the contact may not be frequent, the non-residential parent can exert a great deal of influence on the children's behaviour, their response to limit setting, and their acceptance of the new family. If the non-residential parent is willing to cooperate, does not put the child into loyalty conflict and allows the child to be involved as part of the new family, this will help the new family to adjust.

CASE EXAMPLE: Tom had been out of town for one week in every month. His two boys were looked after by Mary, their stepmother, and, though Tom expected her to provide stability for the home in his absence, she did not feel that she had any support from him in expecting the boys to be responsible for any aspect of their behaviour. The boys left garbage in their bedroom, their dirty laundry was everywhere in the house. The most distressing problem, however, was that they fought physically and wrecked the new living room furniture. She could not see that the dilemma was primarily between her and her husband to negotiate expectations. Consequently, the boys felt resentment if she asked them to clean their room and did not respond to any expectation from Mary. She was not supported in being able to control the boys by her husband. Tom did not have much control over the boys himself because he felt very guilty about the divorce and wanted to make up to the boys because of the loss they had suffered by having to move and not live with both natural parents.

Norms and Values

Definition

The values of each family are governed by that family's ideals regarding moral and religious values as well as personal social goals (Steinhauer et al. 1984).

General Issues

A number of complex and interrelated processes are involved in a family's value system. This becomes particularly pronounced in stepfamilies. In the stepfamily there are at least two families with their own individual values, norms and group affiliations (extended families) to consider.

The possibility for conflict among these systems multiplies with the number of participants. Children in remarried families move between two households and are expected to deal with two sets of value systems and standards of behaviour. How the two sets of adults deal with discrepancies in values from one another will have a great deal of impact upon the functioning of the remarried family.

Couple

At the beginning when a new family is being formed, it is extremely important that the couple explore each other's values and aspirations. Each partner has to understand the influences of values from their families of origin as well as the previous marital relationship upon the development of their own values. Often the divorce and its aftermath, connected with the emotional pain a person goes through, can provide a great challenge to a person's value system. Adults in stepfamilies tend to have very different values in regard to child rearing. It is of great importance that these values and philosophies of child rearing be clarified at the beginning when a new family is formed, so that future conflict around the children will remain minimal. The new couple will also have to develop their own value system in the new family, incorporating some values from their previous marriages as well as from their families of origin.

Stepparent

Stepparents often feel that they have to make all the adjustments to the values of the biological parents. This frequently creates feelings of resentment. On the other hand, some stepparents would like to take charge and introduce their own value system too abruptly. Consonance regarding values between stepparent and parent cannot be expected to be accomplished immediately. Mutual respect for different values is most helpful, and the adjustment to the new family situation should be made gradually, on the basis of negotiation.

Children

All children who belong to two homes are expected to respect the standards and the explicit and implicit rules, in both households, without having to reject either household. Children are often caught by the dissonance of value systems of the two homes. The expectations of behaviour at times get confused with unresolved hostility between the two parents. Children are often seen by each parent as taking sides with the other parent's values rather than having values of their own.

The Non-Residential Parent and Extended Family

The non-residential parent and his or her own values will also influence the functioning of the remarried family. Undermining of the values of the newly established family will negatively affect the children, whereas tolerance and support will help the children settle in the new household. The values, ideals and norms of the non-residential parent have immense impact upon the development of the children regardless of the frequency of contact with the parent.

CASE EXAMPLE: Karen, a 30-year-old stepmother of two boys, 12 and 15, was very eager to celebrate that first Christmas together, as she did before, going to church on Christmas Eve with her parents. To her astonishment the boys refused to join and wanted to go to their maternal grandparents where they had celebrated Christmas since their birth. The holiday season started with anger and confusion because the traditions of different family members were not taken into account at the planning.

CONCLUSION OF THE ASSESSMENT

Having assessed the new blended family in its various areas of functioning, we suggest summing up the positive factors contributing to the new family's adjustment separately from the problems.

Assessing the *strength of the family* (Knaub et al. 1984; Beavers 1985; Stollman 1983) as a separate focus is particularly important for remarried families. The normal process of adjustment with its anxieties, ambivalence, confusion and loyalty issues may cover the underlying hope, commitment and concern of the family members toward making the new unit successful for everyone.

We consider in determining "strength factor" all facts, function of individuals, subunits and the family as a whole that may contribute toward the healthy functioning and adjustment of the new family. In particular, the support system of the stepfamily as found by Knaub et al. (1984) is a crucial "predictor of perceptions of family strength and success" among the couples studied.

We suggest a way of organizing the "strength factors," as well as the problems, that the family might present in the following way:

1. Environmental factors (resources, money, space);
2. Factors contributing to the functioning of the individual family members (social, emotional, intellectual, health issues);
3. Family function (sum of the assessment of the family according to the 6 categories described).

Though our assessment model does not focus on individual family members in detail, the therapist, through the family assessment, can develop enough understanding of the family members as to decide on the need for further individual assessment and/or treatment. The functioning of the stepfamily can only be understood if the ex-spouses' and extended families' roles are included.

The degree of motivation for making changes and interest in therapy to facilitate those changes is another major factor in the formulation of the intervention plan.

The therapist then concludes the assessment by making recommendations for treatment on the basis of all information and evaluation obtained. The therapeutic contract between the therapist and the family or some of its members will then be formed in order to proceed and agree upon treatment goals.

REFERENCES

Beavers, W. R. (1985). *Successful Marriage*. W. W. Norton and Comp.

Carter, E. A. and McGoldrick, M. (Eds.) (1980). *The Family Life Cycle*. New York: Gardner Press.

Ihinger-Tallman, Marilyn and Pasley, Kay (1987). *Remarriage*. Family Studies Text, Series 7. U.S.A.: Sage Publications, Inc.

Knaub, P. K. et al. (1984). Strength of Remarried Families. *Journal of Divorce, 7* (3).

McGoldrick, M. and Gerson, R. (1985). *Genograms in Family Assessment*. New York: Norton.

Messinger, L. et al. (1981). From Marriage Breakdown to Remarriage: Parental Tasks and Therapeutic Guidelines, *A. J. of Orthopsychiatry, 51*, pp. 429-438.

Morrison, K. and Thompson-Guppy, A. (1986a). Cinderella's Stepmother Syndrome. *Canadian Journal of Psychiatry*, Nov., pp. 521-529.

Morrison, K. and Thompson-Guppy, A. (1986b). *Stepmothers, Exploring the Myth*. Ottawa: Canadian Council on Social Development.

Moss, S. Z. et al. (1980). Remarriage: A Triadic Relationship, *Conciliation Courts Review, 18*, pp. 15-20.

Papernow, P. L. (1984). The Stepfamily Cycle: An Experiential Model of Stepfamily Development. *Family Relations* (Vol. 33, No. 3, July, pp. 355-363).

Sager, C. J. et al. (1981). Improving Functioning of the Remarried Family System, *Journal of Marital and Family Therapy*, Jan., pp. 3-12.

Sager, C. J. et al. (1983). *Treating the Remarried Family*. New York: Brunner/Mazel.

Sager, C. J. (1985). *Second Marriages: New Clinical Concepts in Marital Theory*. Ed. by Oliver J. W. Bjorksten, American Psychiatric Press, Inc.

Skinner, M. A., Steinhauer, P. D. and Santa-Barbara, J. (1983). The Family Assessment Measure, *Canadian Journal of Community Mental Health, 2* (2).

Steinhauer, P. D., Santa-Barbara, J. S., Skinner, H. (March 1984). The Process Model of Family Functioning, Discussion Paper, *Canadian Journal of Psychiatry*, Vol. 29.

Stollman, W. (1983). *Stepfamilies–Making Yours a Success*. Ottawa: Commoner's Publ.

Visher, E. B., and Visher, J. S. (1979). *Stepfamilies–A Guide to Working with Stepparents and Stepchildren*. New York: Brunner/Mazel.

Visher, E. B. and Visher, J. S., (1983). *Stepfamily Workshop Manual*. U.S.A., Maryland: Stepfamily Association.

Wald, Esther (1981). *The Remarried Family: Challenge and Promise*. New York: Service Association of America.

Communication–Family Characteristics: A Comparison Between Stepfamilies (Formed After Death or Divorce) and Biological Families

Shoshana Grinwald

INTRODUCTION

By the year 2000 the stepfamily will be the predominant family structure in the United States and will actually outnumber the nuclear family. In Israel, too, the phenomenon is becoming widespread.

This study deals with three groups of adolescents; two groups from stepfamilies–after the death of the father, and after divorce and subsequent remarriage, and the third group is from biological families–the control group.

One hundred and twenty-four adolescents between the ages of 12-19 have participated in the research program. Forty are from stepfamilies formed after the father's death and the mother's remarriage. Forty-four adolescents are from stepfamilies following the divorce of the parents and remarriage of the mother. Forty adolescents are from biological families.

All studies have been done on the subject of stepfamilies after divorce. As a research study which takes place in Israel, the problems of adolescents in stepfamilies after the father's death are also important. This study therefore draws comparisons between the three groups of adolescents.

Shoshana Grinwald, PhD, is a lecturer in the School of Social Work at Bar-Ilan University, Ramat-Gan, Israel.

[Haworth co-indexing entry note]: "Communication–Family Characteristics: A Comparison Between Stepfamilies (Formed After Death or Divorce) and Biological Families." Grinwald, Shoshana. Co-published simultaneously in *Journal of Divorce & Remarriage* (The Haworth Press, Inc.) Vol. 24, No. 1/2, 1995, pp. 183-196; and: *Understanding Stepfamilies: Their Structure and Dynamics* (ed: Craig A. Everett) The Haworth Press, Inc., 1995, pp. 183-196. Single or multiple copies of this article are available from The Haworth Document Delivery Service [1-800-342-9678, 9:00 a.m. - 5:00 p.m. (EST)].

Another important facet of this study is the fact that the entire research program is based on adolescent response, as only this group has answered the questionnaires. What is "known" of them is actually often the opinion of others (parents, professionals). I think it is important to listen to the adolescents in their particular stepfamily.

The adolescent in the stepfamily created following the death of the father will be referred to as "fatherless adolescent." The adolescent from a family where the parents are divorced will be referred to as "adolescent of divorce." A comparison will be drawn with the adolescent in the biological family. We will study the differences between: (a) groups of adolescents from stepfamilies and biological families in communication, (b) groups of fatherless adolescents and of adolescents of divorce according to family communication.

According to the variable of communication examined, the research produced the same results in two groups of adolescents–those in the biological family, and those in the stepfamily after the death of the father. There are significant differences between those two groups and the third group–the adolescents in stepfamilies after divorce. In this, the third group, communication among family members is the lowest.

A significant difference was found between *genders* in communication, where the poorest is between females, and mother and stepfather in stepfamilies formed after divorce.

Awareness of these differences will aid recognition of the populations at risk.

REVIEW OF THE LITERATURE

The stepfamily is defined as a two-parent family unit created by the legal remarriage of a divorced or widowed person (Coleman and Ganong, 1985; Martin and Martin, 1992). This family is one composed of an adult couple, at least one of whom has a child from a previous relationship (Martin and Martin, 1992; Visher and Visher, 1988). In this unit only one of the couple is the biological parent of the children. This unit is created in two stages: when the nuclear family is disrupted by divorce, or the death of one of the parents; and the surviving parent subsequently remarries. Remarriages require the melding of two systems or two units each with a different history, memories, and value system–a type of assimiliation, not in the accepted sense of the word (Perkins and Kahan, 1979).

The two types of stepfamilies formed after the parent's death, or the parents' divorce, cope with loss. The stepfamilies' members must undergo the mourning process (Granot, 1985; Palgi, 1974; Smilansky, 1978, 1990;

Wallerstein and Blakeslee, 1989; Wallerstein and Kelly, 1984). The children and adolescents of both families face a similar set of problems, at least to some degree.

Transition Theory

This research deals with two transition processes which cause difficulties in the stepfamily.

In professional literature, adolescence is described as a period of transition, where a child is no longer a child, but not yet an adult; this is an internal biological change. The adolescent is often biologically an adult, but from a psychosocial perspective, he is still "straddling the fence" (Decay, 1979; Deutsch, 1973), being at a stage which Erikson (1968) calls "identity versus role diffusion."

The adolescent belongs to a family, which may be going through its own transitions, first to the single parent family, and then to the stepfamily–an external change (Abelson and Saayman, 1991; Carter and McGoldrick, 1980; Golan, 1981; Kimmel and Weiner, 1985; McCubbin and Patterson, 1983; Mikesell and Garbarino, 1986; Terkelsen, 1980).

Adolescents in the Stepfamily

In professional literature, the theoreticians emphasize the difficulty of the adolescent being a member of the stepfamily (Bernard, 1971; Bowerman and Irish, 1962; Einstein, 1982; Kimmel and Weiner, 1985; Knaub and Hanna, 1984; Martin and Martin, 1992; Mikesell and Garbarino, 1986; Sager, 1983; Visher and Visher, 1979). Adolescents reported more conflict than younger children within the stepfamily. Most studies deal with adolescents in stepfamilies as a result of divorce.

Consequently, adolescence brings with it greater difficulties (Schlesinger, 1968). In Wallerstein's research (1984) she found that some problems remain dormant, to emerge five to ten years after the divorce. This indicates that young children, who ostensibly overcome their father's death, may harbor problems that emerge when they reach adolescence in the stepfamily.

Good communication, the primary factor determining the relationship between individuals, and how each deals with his environment, is desirable in every family. Communication skills affect an individual's development of intimate relationships (Satir, 1977). For a stepfamily, communication is often the "make-or-break" factor. Problems are solved, created, or magnified as a result of communication skills. Rewards of affirmation, understanding, and intimacy, are viable products of healthy communication (Hanna, 1992). In a stepfamily, communication will be less clear, with more ambiguous messages.

The gender of the adolescent influences the relationship with his biological and stepparents. Male and female development are dependent on identification with the parent of the same gender as a role model (Santrock, Warshak and Lindbergh, 1982). In a stepfamily following divorce, both parents exist, and they can still serve as role models. In a stepfamily following a father's death, a son may face an identity problem. Females, who develop sexually more rapidly than males, have a better chance for a better relationship with a stepfather as a result of mutual sexual attraction (Canfield, 1983; Kent, 1980). Males, who function as a pseudo-partner, feel competition with the new spouse–the stepfather.

The theoretical section above raises specific hypotheses:

1. There are differences in communication between adolescents in biological families and stepfamilies; communication between members in the biological families will be better.
2. Fatherless adolescents and adolescents of divorce will communicate differently; while communication between members will be better in fatherless adolescent stepfamilies.
3. Male and female adolescents will communicate differently; the poorer communication will be between girls and stepfathers in families formed after divorce.

METHODOLOGY

Subjects

One hundred and twenty-four adolescents participated in the research program (range of ages 12-18; Mean–15.65; SD–1.63), forty-one (33.1%) of them males, and 83 (66.9%) females.

The fatherless adolescents were selected from a list provided by Ministry of Defence, from families in which the father died during army service (war, accident, disease, suicide) and the biological mothers remarried.

The adolescents of divorce were selected from families connected with the Local Agency for Social Affairs and The Marital Counseling Agency.

Adolescents living with two biological parents during the research program represent the control group. This group was selected according to such biographical variables as sex and socioeconomic situation, after the other two groups of adolescents in stepfamilies had been selected. The adolescents in stepfamilies gave a list of good friends who lived in the same environment and studied with them in the same, or parallel, classes.

Instruments

Instruments consist of two questionnaires: (1) Demographic information, and (2) Communication.

1. Demographic Information

Biographical questionnaires for the adolescents consisted of three forms: one for an adolescent in a biological family; a second for an adolescent in a stepfamily formed after a father's death and the mother's remarriage; and a third for an adolescent in a stepfamily formed after the parents had divorced and the mother remarried.

Demographic data such as: age, sex, place in the family, education, religious self-definition and that of his parents, his parents' education, were all collected about the adolescent in this questionnaire. The questionnaire for the adolescent in the stepfamily included questions such as: your age when your father died, or your parents divorced, your age when your mother remarried, and questions about education and religious definition of the stepfather.

2. Parent-Adolescent Communication

This scale was developed by Barnes and Olsen (1982). The intention was to develop a brief scale that would measure both positive and negative aspects of communication as well as aspects of the content and process of the parent-adolescent interactions. The scale consists of two subscales of ten positive items and ten negative items. An example of a positive item is: "My mother/father is always a good listener," while a negative example is: "My mother/father insults me when he/she is angry with me." The adolescent answers the questionnaire separately for the mother and the father so that he answers forty items (positive and negative). He has to answer the item concerning communication with the mother or the father on a scale of five grades: (1) strongly disagree; (2) moderately disagree; (3) neither agree nor disagree; (4) moderately agree; (5) strongly agree.

Procedure

I sent letters to 300 stepfamilies answering the criteria of the research program, seeking their agreement to their adolescent's participation in the research. The adolescent answered the questionnaires in his house, with me, and without the intervention of his parents. The answers were secret. When I met with the adolescent in the stepfamily, I asked him to invite a friend from a biological family, someone of his age, education, and socio-economic status, who would agree to participate in the research program with him (the control group).

I explained questions that were not clear. It takes an hour to fill in the questionnaires together with my explanations regarding the goals of the research program.

RESULTS

The findings will explain the differences between the three research groups in communication.

Communication with Parents

Communication between adolescent and parents was expressed in two measures: communication with the father and communication with the mother. The two measures ranged from 20 to 100, with the higher score representing better communication. Table 1 presents the means and standard deviation of the three research groups in communication with the mother and the father.

In order to examine whether there are differences in the research groups, we did ANOVA (groups × father/mother communication). The ANOVA analysis yielded a significant difference among the three research groups across the two measures of communication ($F(2,120) = 7.01$; $p < .001$).

In CONTRAST analysis there was a significant difference between the adolescents in biological families and the other two groups of adolescents ($t = 3.24$; $df = 120$; $p < .01$). There was also a difference in degree of $p < .10$ between adolescents of divorce and fatherless adolescents ($t = 1.79$; $df = 120$; $p < .10$).

TABLE 1. Means and Standard Deviations of the Three Research Groups in Communication

	Communication with the Mother		Communication with the Father	
	M	SD	M	SD
Death	75.48	11.25	69.07	12.28
Divorced	75.55	14.38	60.61	14.75
Biological	78.24	10.25	75.60	12.27

According to the means presented in Table 1, we can see that the best communication between parents and adolescents is found in biological families, while the most problematic communication is between parents and adolescents of divorce. Communication between parents and fatherless adolescents lies somewhere in between. This finding supports the first hypothesis.

The ANOVA revealed a significant difference between communication with the father and communication with the mother ($F(1,120) = 42.44$; $p < .001$). According to the means presented in Table 1, the communication with the mother is better than that with the father regarding all three groups of adolescents. In the ANOVA there was also a significant interaction effect of groups × father/mother ($F(2,120) = 9.00$; $p < .001$). Figure 1 presents this interaction.

According to the figure, we can see that the biggest difference in communication between adolescents with the father and the mother is with adolescents of divorce. There is less of a difference in communication with fatherless adolescents, and even less in communication with biological adolescents.

FIGURE 1. Mean Scores for Communication with Mother and Father for Adolescents in Different Family Structures.

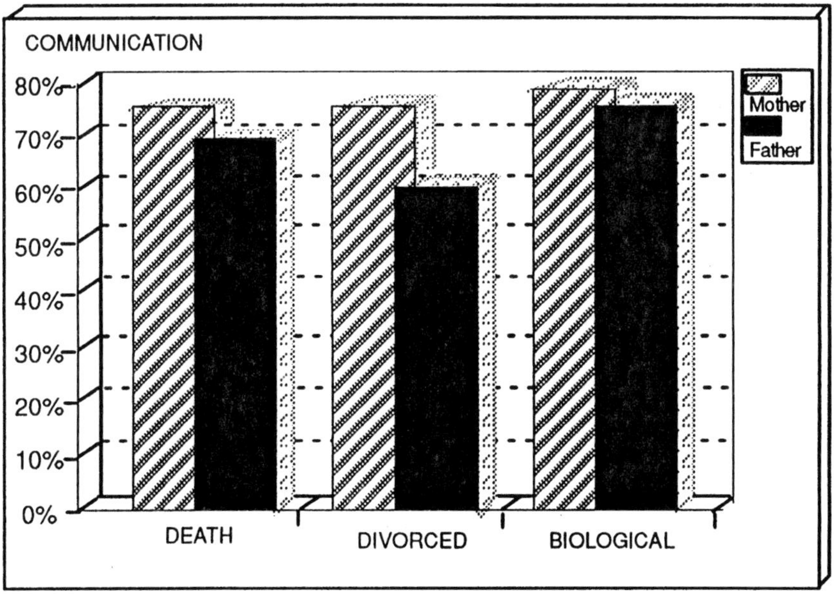

In CONTRAST analysis there was a significant difference in communication between father and mother for adolescents of divorce ($t = 5.59$; $df = 43$; $p < .001$); and for fatherless adolescents ($t = 3.55$; $df = 39$; $p < .001$); while for adolescents in biological families ($t = 1.70$; $df = 38$; $p < .05$). This finding supports the second hypothesis.

In ANOVA analysis there was a significant interaction of groups × gender across the two communication measures ($F(2,117) = 3.23$; $p < .05$). This interaction is presented in Figure 2.

According to the Figure there are small differences between the males in the three research groups ($F(2,38) = .04$; $p < .05$), but there are significant differences between the females in the three research groups, ($F(2,79) = 11.61$; $p < .001$).

In CONTRAST analysis, according to Scheffe, there is a significant difference between the group of adolescents of divorce and the other two groups. This means that the communication of females with the father and the mother in stepfamilies after divorce is less than in the other two groups, while there are no differences in communication between males and parents in all three research groups.

FIGURE 2. Mean Scores for Communication for Adolescents in Different Family Structures According to Gender.

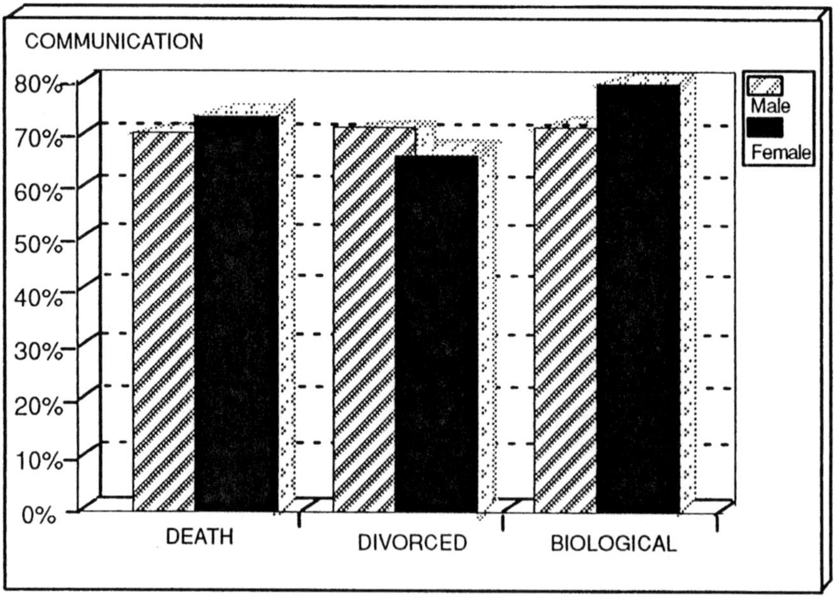

Communication between the *father* and adolescents is best in the biological families; the worst with adolescents of divorce; and somewhere in between with fatherless adolescents.

There are differences in communication between males and females with the father and the mother in the three research groups. There are no differences in communication among the groups between males and parents, while the differences in communication between females and parents are expressed in all three groups of adolescents. In the stepfamilies formed after divorce, communication is less than in the other two groups. This finding supports the third hypothesis.

DISCUSSION

This is the only research that compares two groups of adolescents in stepfamilies–after the death of a parent, and after divorce and subsequent remarriage. All research has been done on the subject of families after divorce. As a study which takes place in Israel, the problems of adolescents in stepfamilies after the death of the father are special. The stepfamilies forming after divorce and remarriage are a widespread group all over the world. In Israel, a country always close to war, there are many widows who remarry and build a stepfamily.

Communication Problems in Stepfamilies

The findings indicate that communication in the stepfamilies after divorce is less than the communication among members in the other two groups. In the biological families, as can be expected, communication is best. We find that communication with the mother is better than with the father in all three groups.

Another important finding is that there is a difference in communication between parents and adolescents according to gender. There are no differences in communication between adolescent boys and their parents, but there are differences between adolescent girls and parents. The result is that the poorest communication among the three groups is between adolescent girls and mother and stepfather in the stepfamily after divorce. These results are consistent with previous studies of stepfather families which indicate that stepdaughters engage in a lower proportion of positive verbal behaviour with their stepfathers than do stepsons (Cligempeel et al., 1984).

In order to understand family relationships, we can evaluate communication between family members which reflects relationships, structure, behavior, rules and norms in the family (Satir, 1977). Communication patterns are stable and rigid rules. But personal communication patterns express a person's characteristics and behavior as a member of a family (Haley, 1982). In a stepfamily after divorce, as opposed to the other two groups, there are two households, one where the adolescent is in a custodial relationship, and the other where he is not. The adolescent who develops his/her relationship with his/her biological parents, tries to communicate in the same manner with his/her biological parent and stepparent. He/she has signals and messages developed over the years while living with biological parents. In using this same pattern of communication, he/she divides his/her stepfamily into two groups, forming a coalition with his/her biological mother, at times to the exclusion of his/her stepfather. We know that using "double bind" is one of the pathological patterns of communication in a family (Haley, 1982). Communication includes affectionate and emotional patterns.

In stepfamilies after divorce, the level of affection between adolescents and the stepfather and biological mother is lower than in other groups, a result of the level of communication (Bowerman and Irish, 1962; Perkins and Kahan, 1979). Perhaps the negative feelings and perceptions with regard to the stepfather are a reflection of the mother's feelings. "Feeding" the child's negative feelings and perceptions with regard to the stepfather may serve to maintain a dysfunctional attachment to the former husband. Or, the mother may be covertly encouraging the child's positive feelings towards her former husband and negative feelings toward her new husband, thereby creating a negative triangle between child, new husband, and herself. At the same time she hangs onto the old, often comfortable triangle with her former spouse. The adolescent is therefore subject to confusion among the members of the family, one that will affect communication.

The poorest communication in stepfamilies after divorce is between adolescent females and their biological mother and stepfather. The adolescent female is in a very complicated situation in this special stepfamily. On the one hand, she lives with her biological mother who is her role figure. On the other, she has a competitive feeling for the stepfather's love and attention (the mother's new husband). This attraction holds some legitimacy as there is no blood tie between them (Canfield, 1983; Kent, 1980). In the second household she has her biological father with whom she has a relationship. Having to maintain so many relationships tends to confuse the situation. Communication is a means to strengthen or weaken these relationships. The adolescent female uses patterns of verbal and non-verbal communication in order to assure her place in the complex family.

Adolescents in a difficult period of transition between childhood and adulthood are asking for emotional-familial help, and they turn to the mother for support. In a stepfamily including a biological mother and stepfather, it is understandable that the mother and adolescents have a good connection. In most cases, the adolescents and mothers (as custodial parents) live for some years as a single-parent unit. In such a structure, special relations form between adolescent and mother. They have special signals, hints, expressions, and body language which only they may understand. Developing communication requires that mothers cooperate with fathers or stepfathers in order to improve the quality of family relations.

In stepfamilies formed after the death of the father, the mother's communication is less effective in relation to the other two groups. Perhaps the fatherless adolescents want to renew their own family. They will try and compare their stepfather to their dead father. Most of the adolescents were between one and two years old when their father died. Because they cannot remember him, they idealize him, and try to create a new father who will be the same.

In order to renew their biological father, they will try to create good communication with their stepfather. Perhaps, in this special structure, it is more important for them to develop communication with the stepfather than with the biological mother. Sometimes the biological mother can interfere with the fantasies of the adolescent concerning the dead father. The mother is aware that memories of the idealized father can interfere with healthy communication with the stepfather, but she sometimes unconsciously furthers this because of her own competition with the adolescent.

CONCLUSION

The hypotheses stemming from the theoretical section are answered in this research as follows:

1. In biological families: communication will be better than in stepfamilies.
2. In stepfamilies formed after the biological father's death, communication will be better than in stepfamilies formed following divorce.
3. Communication with the mother is best in all three groups of adolescents. Communication between female adolescents and parents in stepfamilies after divorce is the lowest of all three groups.

Open and direct verbal and non-verbal communication helps family members relate to each other (Haley, 1982; Minushin, 1982; Satir, 1977). The communication and relationship with the adolescent affect the quality of family relations. The adolescent who is trying to be independent, develops a character of his/her own, and is ambivalent towards his/her parents' relationships. If parents accept the adolescent as a mature adult, and relate to him/her as such, they will develop confidence in their relationships.

CLINICAL IMPLICATIONS

Certain clinical implications derive from this study and, as therapists, we have to relate differently to each group of adolescents.

The most obvious implication is to help both the step-adolescent and stepfather build and cement their relationship. The therapist must assess the degree of positive and negative feeling between stepfather and adolescent, also with regard to the biological father. The feelings and perceptions of the adolescent do not emerge in isolation, but rather from the dynamics of the family system of which he/she is a part.

Thus, negative feelings and perceptions regarding the new father will have to be acknowledged openly, clarified, and dealt with. An aspect of this is often clarification of the old and new rules governing their interactions and expectations. In a stepfather family, there are some triangles in which the adolescent must be encouraged to have a healthy relationship with both his/her stepfather and biological father. In order for this to happen, the adults–father and mother–need to resolve their own separation problems and to construct more functional boundaries between them and the two new families (Halperin and Smith, 1983).

It is very important to examine this population of adolescents from stepfamilies as a group at risk, and therefore to prepare a program of early (preventive) intervention for the children and the parents, and for the family as a whole.

Social workers should explore possibilites of support groups and self-help groups for children, adolescents, and biological and step-couples. They could support family members in the process of remarriage, and help them to adjust to the new family. Therapists help members to reframe their expectations in order to conform to the reality of the stepfamilies. Stepfamily life is different from their life in the first family.

An important function that clinicians and community educators can perform is to inform the public about the realities of stepfamily life. They could also develop and present innovative radio or TV programs targeted to the needs of stepfamilies. Courses for stepfamilies should be added to family life education in agencies, and school administrators should include training programs for teachers in order to raise awareness of the special problems of stepfamilies (Bielenberg, 1991; Pill, 1990).

BIBLIOGRAPHY

Abelson, D. and Saayman, G.S. (1991). Adolescents' adjustment to parental divorce. An investigation from the perspective of basic dimensions of structural family therapy theory. *Family Process, 30,* 177-191.

Bernard, J. (1971). Remarriage. New York: Russel & Russel.

Bielenberg, L.T. (1991). A task-centered preventive group approach to create cohesion in the new stepfamily: A preliminary evaluation. *Research on Social Work Practice, 1,* (4), 416-433.

Bowerman, C.E. and Irish, D.P. (1962). Some relationships of stepchildren to their parents. *Marriage and Family Living, 24,* 113-121.

Canfield, D.G. (1983). Cross-sex parent-child relationship in stepparent families. *Dissertation Abstracts International, 43,* 31-25.

Carter, E.A. and McGoldrick, M. (Eds.) (1980). *The family life cycle. A framework for family therapy.* New York: Gardner Press.

Clingempeel, W.G., Ievoli, R. and Brand, E. (1984). Structural complexity and the quality stepfather-stepchild relationship. *Family Process, 23,* 547-559.

Dautch, H. (1973). *Special problems of adolescence.* Tel-Aviv, Sifriat-Hapoalim (in Hebrew).

Decay, J.S. (1979). *Adolescents Today.* Santa Monica, California: Goodyear Publishing Company.

Einstein, E. (1982). *The stepfamily living, loving and learning.* New York: Macmillan Publishing.

Erikson, E.H. (1968). *Identity: Youth and crisis.* New York: W.W. Norton.

Golan, N. (1981). *Passing through transitions.* New York: The Free Press.

Granot, T. (1985). *Loss.* Tel-Aviv, The Ministry of Defence (in Hebrew).

Haley, J. (1982). *Problem-solving therapy.* Israel, Tel-Aviv, Sifriat Hapoalim (in Hebrew).

Halperin, S. M. and Smith, T. A. (1983). Differences in stepchildren's perceptions of their stepfathers and natural fathers: Implications for family therapy. *Journal of Divorce, 7* (1), 19-30.

Hanna, S. (1992). Communication: The key to successful stepfamily relationships. *Stepfamilies, 12,* (3). Published by The Stepfamily Association of America, U.S.A.

Kent, M.O. (1980). Remarriage: A family systems perspective. *Social Casework, 61* (3), 146-153.

Kimmel, D.C. and Weiner, I.B. (1985). *Adolescence, a developmental transition.* Hillsdale, New Jersey: Laurence Erlbaum Associates, Publishers.

Knaub, P.K. and Hanna, S.L. (1984). Children of remarriage perceptions of family strengths. *Journal of Divorce* 7(4), 73-90.

Martin, D. and Martin, M. with the assistance of Pat Jeffers (1992). *Stepfamilies in Therapy–Understanding Systems, Assessment and Intervention.* San Francisco: Jossey-Bass.

McCubbin, H.I. and Patterson, J. (1983). Family transitions: Adaptation to stress. In McCubbin, H.I. and Figley, C. (Eds.) *Stress and the family.* New York: Brunner/Mazel Inc.

Mikesell J.W. and Garbarino, J. (1986). Adolescents in stepfamilies. In Garbarino, J., Schellenback, C.J. and Sebs, J.M. and Associates. *Troubled Youth, Troubled Families.* New York: Aldine Pub. Com.

Minushin, S. (1982). *Families and family therapy.* Israel, Tel-Aviv Reshfin Pub., (in Hebrew).

Olson, D.H., Partner, J., and Bell, R. (1982). Family adaptability and cohesion evaluation scales. In Olson, D.H., McCubbin, H.I., Barnes, H., Larsen, A. Muxen, M. and Wilson, M. (Eds.). *Family inventories: The family life cycle.* St. Paul, Minnesota: University of Minnesota Press.

Palgy, P. (1974). *Death and mourning in war in Israel society.* Israel: Tel-Aviv, The Ministry of Health (in Hebrew.)

Perkins, T.F. and Kahan, J.P. (1979). An empirical comparison of natural father and stepfather family systems. *Family Process, 18,* 175-184.

Pill, C.J. (1990). Stepfamilies: Redefining the family. *Family Relations, 39,* 186-193.

Sager, C.J., Brown, H.S., Cohen, H.M., Engel, T., Rodstein, E., Walker, L. (1983). *Treating the remarried family.* New York: Brunner/Mazel, Publishers.

Santrock, J.W., Warshak, R., Lindbergh, F. and Meadows, L. (1982). Children's and parent's observed social behavior in stepfather families. *Child Development, 53,* 472-480.

Satir, V. (1977). *Peoplemaking.* (3rd. ed.) Israel, Tel-Aviv, Sifriat Hapoalim (in Hebrew).

Schlesinger, B. (1968). Remarriage–An inventory of findings. *Family Coordination, 17* (4) 248-250.

Smilansky, S. (1990). *Psychology and education of children from divorced families.* Israel: Tel-Aviv, Ach. (in Hebrew).

Smilansky, S. and Dixal, T. (1978). Adjustment of children after the father's death in elementary school. *Megamot,* 23 (2), 143-156 (in Hebrew).

Terkelsen, N.G. (1980). Toward a theory of the family life cycle. In Carter, E.A. and McGoldrick (Eds.) *The family life cycle: A framework for family therapy.* New York: Gardner Press.

Visher, E.B. and Visher, J.S. (1988). *Old loyalties, new ties. Therapeutic strategies with stepfamilies.* New York: Brunner/Mazel.

Wallerstein, J.S. (1984). Children of divorce: Preliminary report of a ten-year follow-up of young children. *American Journal of Orthopsychiatry, 54,* 444-458.

Wallerstein, J.S. and Blakeslee, S. (1989). *Second Chances.* New York: Ticknor and Fields.

COSTS: Please figure your cost to order quality copies of an article.

1. Set-up charge per article: $8.00
   ($8.00 × number of separate articles) __________
2. Photocopying charge for each article:
   1-10 pages: $1.00 __________
   11-19 pages: $3.00 __________
   20-29 pages: $5.00 __________
   30+ pages: $2.00/10 pages __________
3. Flexicover (optional): $2.00/article __________
4. Postage & Handling: US: $1.00 for the first article/
   $.50 each additional article __________
   Federal Express: $25.00 __________
   Outside US: $2.00 for first article/
   $.50 each additional article __________
5. Same-day FAX service: $.35 per page __________

GRAND TOTAL: ______________

METHOD OF PAYMENT: (please check one)

❑ Check enclosed ❑ Please ship and bill. PO # __________________

(sorry we can ship and bill to bookstores only! All others must pre-pay)

❑ Charge to my credit card: ❑ Visa; ❑ MasterCard; ❑ Discover;
❑ American Express;

Account Number: ____________________ Expiration date: __________

Signature: ✗ ______________________________

Name: ____________________ Institution: __________________

Address: ______________________________________

____

City: ____________________ State: ________ Zip: ________

Phone Number: __________________ FAX Number: __________________

MAIL or *FAX* THIS ENTIRE ORDER FORM TO:

Haworth Document Delivery Service The Haworth Press, Inc. 10 Alice Street Binghamton, NY 13904-1580	**or FAX:** 1-800-895-0582 **or CALL:** 1-800-342-9678 9am-5pm EST)